Theatre Lives

Leslie Atkins Durham
Boise State University

Sally H. Shedd
Virginia Wesleyan College

Kendall Hunt
publishing company
4050 Westmark Drive • P O Box 1840 • Dubuque IA 52004-1840

Book Team

Chairman and Chief Executive Officer   Mark C. Falb
President and Chief Operating Officer   Chad M. Chandlee
Vice President, Higher Education   David L. Tart
Director of National Book Program   Paul B. Carty
Editorial Manager   Georgia Botsford
Editor   Melissa Tittle
Vice President, Operations   Timothy J. Beitzel
Assistant Vice President, Production Services   Christine E. O'Brien
Senior Production Editor   Mary Melloy
Permissions Editor   Elizabeth Roberts
Cover Designer   Sandy Beck
Web Project Manager   Alison Parkins

Front Cover
Lee Mark Nelson as Cleon and Kate Eifrig as Dionyza in William Shakespeare's
Pericles, at the Guthrie Lab (February 12 through March 6, 2005), directed by
Joel Sass with set design by John Clark Donahue, costume design by Amelia Busse
Cheever, and lighting design by Marcus Dillard.

All Shutterstock images used under license from Shutterstock, Inc.
Cover image: Photo © Michal Daniel, 2005

www.kendallhunt.com
Send all inquiries to:
4050 Westmark Drive
Dubuque, IA 52004-1840

Brief Contents

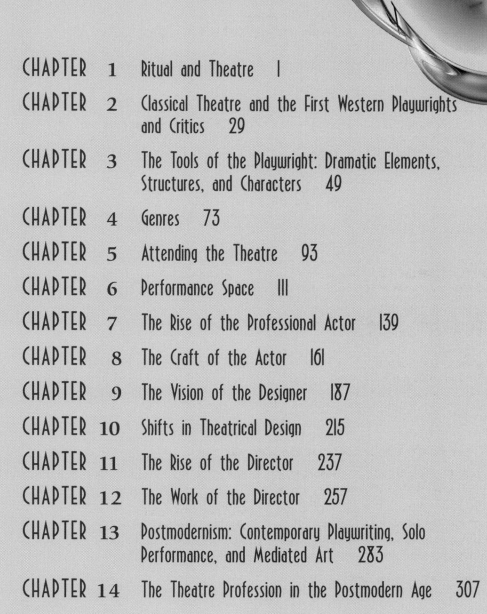

Contents

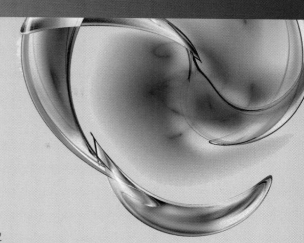

Preface

The dual pronunciation potential of this book's title, *Theatre Lives*, was chosen to evoke mindfulness of the connection between the individuals who create and experience theatre (those who lead "theatre lives"—to include the college student in possession of this text) and the vitality of theatre as an active, living art form. This book is about lives in theatre and theatre as a living art. It is an examination and celebration of the work of theatre artists past and present—their creative process, their training, their unique perspectives on plays, and their influence on the audience's experience in the theatre. It invites students to engage in the theatre event and provides tools for a meaningful experience.

You will find theatre history woven throughout *Theatre Lives*. We hope to facilitate a classroom experience in which theatre practice and theatre history are interwoven and interdependent. For some instructors and students, this approach may seem a radical reconsideration of the relationship between areas often presented as discrete entities. Most introduction text authors, if including history at all, place it in its own section as if it were somehow a compartmentalized area of exploration for theatre students. We believe that such placement fosters a false dichotomy between history and praxis, which is ultimately detrimental to students—both majors and nonmajors alike. For theatre majors, this polarization can impede a fruitful cross-pollination of ideas between the classroom and the rehearsal room. Majors are in danger of seeing themselves as either practitioners *or* scholars, views that disrespect both the artist's creative process and the scholar's ability to fully know and experience that which he or she wishes to investigate academically. The history/praxis divide can be detrimental to nonmajors by further strengthening a suspicion that historical knowledge has little or nothing to do with experiencing the "real world" (of theatre or, by extension, life). At a time when it seems increasingly consequential to convince college students of the vital importance of education and "the life of the mind" for its own sake, as opposed to mere technical training to increase one's salary after graduation, educators should take every opportunity to knock down walls that falsely separate "book knowledge" and "experiential knowledge." It is our hope that this textbook will help to set such course in the introduction to theatre classroom.

FEATURES OF THIS BOOK

Full color photographs are comprehensive and provide visual interest and knowledge to enhance the topics discussed in the chapters.

Spotlights are strategically placed throughout the chapters to focus on people, ideas, opinions, plays, and other topics of interest to theatre students.

A **Glossary of Terms** is provided at the end of the book to provide quick access for students to identify theatre terms.

Activities at the end of each chapter provide a series of practical applications and project suggestions designed to help students explore performance and theatrical possibilities in their own communities and beyond.

INSTRUCTIONAL ONLINE ENHANCEMENTS

Both students and instructors have access to online content that is integrated chapter by chapter with the text to enrich student learning. The web access code is included on the inside front cover of the textbook.

Look for the web icon in the text margins to direct you to various interactive tools.

STUDENT WEB CONTENT

- **Pre-Tests** allow students to check their knowledge of the topic prior to reading the chapter.
- **Chapter Objectives** highlight the central ideas to be gleaned from the chapter.
- **Key Terms** with **interactive flash cards** help students learn language unique to theatre.
- **Interactive Timelines** help students visualize the progress of theatre over the years.
- **Poll Questions** draw students into the subject matter by asking questions relevant to students and the chapter theme.
- **Discussion Questions** help create an active classroom environment.
- **Links to Online Resources** extend theatre knowledge beyond the classroom.

The following chapter descriptions further detail the structure and content of *Theatre Lives*.

CHAPTER I RITUAL AND THEATRE

Many historians see a link between archaic and preliterate ritual performances and the genesis of theatre. This chapter investigates these ideas and enumerates the variants on ritual performance in everyday contemporary life. Though students may come to the course without substantial experience with formal and aesthetic versions of performance, they already possess significant experiential knowledge about the ways humans use performance practices in sacred, secular, and social contexts. Students will learn to "read" the performative elements in the workplace, the school setting, weddings, and homecoming celebrations.

CHAPTER 2 CLASSICAL THEATRE AND THE FIRST WESTERN PLAYWRIGHTS AND CRITICS

The ritual heritage in Western theatre is evident in fifth-century BCE Athens, where the first recorded tragic performances were a part of the annual festival honoring Dionysus. This chapter examines the work of the three extant Greek tragedians, Aeschylus, Sophocles, and Euripides, the context of performance at the City Dionysia, and the evaluation of this early tragic work by the West's first, and still highly influential, dramatic critics, Plato and Aristotle.

CHAPTER 3 THE TOOLS OF THE PLAYWRIGHT: DRAMATIC ELEMENTS, STRUCTURES, AND CHARACTERS

Aristotle's ideas about dramatic structure and the hierarchy of dramatic elements dominated Western thinking about drama for centuries. This chapter explains these ideas, and their common application then examines challenges to this model of reading and writing plays from several practitioner theorists. It also looks at different methods readers can use to analyze the ways in which playwrights construct characters. Finally, the chapter explores the playwright's working process and training.

CHAPTER 4 GENRES

It is important to consider genre, or "type" of play, to fully understand a script or performance. This chapter identifies and analyzes three main genres of dramatic composition—tragedy, comedy, and musical—as well as subcategories such as tragicomedy, melodrama, and farce. Are all serious plays tragedies? Is a comedy simply "a play that makes you laugh?" This chapter will encapsulate over two thousand years in genre development to convey important guideposts for theatregoers.

CHAPTER 5 ATTENDING THE THEATRE

One of the most important facets of any theatrical production is the spectator. This chapter discusses the qualities that make a good spectator and ways of enhancing these particular attributes. It also covers some conventions of theatrical behavior and the impact these "theatre rules" can have on an individual's interpretive choices when viewing a play. Basic etiquette for theatre attendance and tips for writing a paper on the experience will be detailed. Finally, we will discuss "paratheatricals"—the nonartistic elements of a production that affect a spectator's experience—and introduce the theatre workers who work most closely with those elements.

CHAPTER 6 PERFORMANCE SPACE

Even before the play begins, the dynamics of the performance space shape audience experience. This chapter presents the basic styles of theatre architecture and the various ways in which a space can be configured. Our focus will then turn to the type of building in which the performance space is found and its location within the city or town, as well as within the larger backdrop of American theatre. These theatrical patterns will be compared to several key moments in theatre history when the politics of the play-house—who attended, where the theatre was located within the city—had a substantial effect on the audience's theatregoing experience.

CHAPTER 7 THE RISE OF THE PROFESSIONAL ACTOR

In fifth-century Athens, actors were amateurs. In what has long been re-garded as the West's second golden age of drama, the era of Shakespeare's theatrical reign, actors were professionals. This chapter investigates the shift from the amateur, religious performers of the early classical and medieval theatres to the context and conventions of Shakespeare's theatre and the importance of the professional actor during that period. The chapter then moves on to Molière's France and the influence he received from the per-formers of *commedia dell'arte*. The chapter concludes with a trip back to England during the Restoration. During this period, the first English ac-tresses appeared on the professional stage. Their impact on the writing of the era and on theatre history more generally was immense.

CHAPTER 8 THE CRAFT OF THE ACTOR

Though actors in Shakespeare's day learned their craft through apprentice-ship, actors today have a variety of avenues for joining and participating in the theatrical profession. This chapter juxtaposes the dominant approach to training and creating character in the United States, which is psycholog-ically based, to European and Asian models that emphasize physicality. Acting theorists discussed will include Constantin Stanislavski, Uta Hagen, Eugenio Barba, Tadashi Suzuki, and Anne Bogart. The chapter will also ex-amine the actor's work during auditions and the rehearsal process.

CHAPTER 9 THE VISION OF THE DESIGNER

Theatrical designers work with a variety of materials—space, light, fabric, and sound, to name just a few. Despite the unique demands of their me-dia, set, lighting, costume, and sound designers share many aspects of their process and ways of thinking. This chapter explores the four major design areas and proposes ways that students can use this knowledge while watching and interpreting a play. We will discuss the various workers responsible for bringing a design to fruition as well as the technical rehearsal process and the many workers involved in "running a show."

CHAPTER 10 SHIFTS IN THEATRICAL DESIGN

This chapter showcases four important moments in the history of design: the development of perspective painting, nineteenth-century changes in lighting—from gas to electric, realism's impact on costume design, and the advent of digital sound. Artists featured include Inigo Jones, Henry Irving, Aline Bernstein, Irene Sharaff, and Darron L. West.

CHAPTER 11 THE RISE OF THE DIRECTOR

As the nineteenth century unfolded, theatre producers and audiences became increasingly interested in detail, accuracy, and specificity in performance. With this demand, and changes in dramatic writing style, came the need for a single person to coordinate the visual and verbal elements of the theatre and to unify them into a compelling, and sometimes spectacular, whole. Jobs that had, through the history of Western theatre, been distributed to other theatre artists, now were centralized in the hands of the modern director. This chapter looks at the ways Madame Vestris, Richard Wagner, Georg II, Duke of Saxe-Meiningen, Andre Antoine, and Constantin Stanislavsky shaped modern understandings of the work of the director. The chapter also considers playwrights representative of the styles that facilitated that need for the director: Victor Hugo (romanticism), Dion Boucicault (melodrama), and Anton Chekhov (realism).

CHAPTER 12 THE WORK OF THE DIRECTOR

The great wave of early directors studied in the previous chapter sets up a model for the work of the director: a strong visionary who sat at the top of the theatrical hierarchy. This person worked to articulate and enhance the intentions of the playwright and shaped the efforts of the designers and actors with whom he worked to realize this goal. As the twentieth century progressed, however, other models for directorial creation evolved. The chapter juxtaposes conventional understandings of the director's work and process with alternative approaches such as auteur creation and collective guidance and will study the work of Elia Kazan, Bartlett Sherr, Joanne Akalaitis, Richard Foreman, Mary Zimmerman, and Stephen Cosson.

CHAPTER 13 POSTMODERNISM: CONTEMPORARY PLAYWRITING, SOLO PERFORMANCE, AND MEDIATED ART

Questioning master narratives, decentering authority, appropriating existing imagery, blending styles and genres, and fragmenting artistic surface became accepted if not expected by the late twentieth century. This chapter studies the particular theatrical manifestations of these postmodern trends in the work of several contemporary playwrights, writer and performer Anna Deavere Smith, and the United States' most famous alternative theatre company, the Wooster Group.

CHAPTER 14 THE THEATRE PROFESSION IN THE POSTMODERN AGE

This chapter challenges the master narrative of the theatre artist by featuring the unique voices of eight individuals working in theatre today. Occupations represented include playwriting, directing, acting, dramaturgy, design, tech work, and arts management in both Broadway and nonprofit settings. Inspired by these "theatre lives," students are encouraged to chart a path for theatre in their own lives.

Acknowledgments

At Kendall Hunt Publishing, we would particularly like to thank Paul Carty, Georgia Botsford, Melissa Tittle, Elizabeth Roberts, Mary Melloy, Alison Parkins, and Angela Willenbring.

For her gracious assistance with photo selection, thanks to Charla Jenkins, University of Kansas. For additional photo assistance, thanks to Rebecca Desjardins and Bobbie Adams at Virginia Wesleyan College; Marianne Martin and Andy Edwards, Colonial Williamsburg Foundation; Eddie Wallace, Oregon Shakespeare Festival; Hannah Read, Idaho Shakespeare Festival; Jim Bartruff, Emporia State University; Robert Shoquist, Northwestern University; Goeffrey Kent; Andrea Robertson; Mary Burke and Marianne Combs, Minnesota Public Radio; Clay Hapaz, the Wooster Group; Mary Gearhart; Shannon Sidelar, the Ontological-Hysterical Theatre Company; Paula Cort; Stephanie Coen, the Intiman Theatre; Chris Bennion; and Marion Friedman, The Civilians.

We are immensely grateful to the theatre artists interviewed in *Theatre Lives*: Leah C. Gardiner, Martine Kei Green, Terrence D. Jones, Dano Madden, Amy Steinhaus, Zach Stinnett, Lauren Weedman, and Alan Yeong. Thanks also to Lisa Fischer, Colonial Williamsburg Foundation; D. Andrew Gibbs, University of Arkansas; and Mark Reaney, University of Kansas.

In addition, Leslie Atkins Durham would like to thank Boise State University, its Theatre Arts faculty, staff, and students for continuing to expand what she knows and expects of theatre. Special thanks to Richard Klautsch, Jacqueline O'Connor, Tara Penry, Michelle Payne, Daniel Runyan, Bruce Ballenger, and Greg Raymond. Special personal thanks go to Craig and Kate Durham for their love and patience.

Sally Shedd would like to thank Virginia Wesleyan College and Dean Timothy O'Rourke for sabbatical leave support. Special thanks to VWC colleagues Joyce Howell and Travis Malone as well as theatre students past and present. Special personal thanks to David O'Rork for his love and support; and David and Elizabeth Shedd, the latter of whom inspired in her daughter love of the arts and dedication to the intrinsic value of education.

Several readers provided feedback during the development of this text. We are particularly indebted to Jim Bartruff, Emporia State University, and Michael Swanson, Elizabethtown College; our thanks to other readers include the following:

Theresa Abshear
Clark State Community College

Adrianne Adderley
Missouri Valley College

Nancy Andreasen
Inver Hills Community College

Tracy Angle
Florence-Darlington Technical College

Scott Bantum
Mount Union College

Paula Barrett
Gannon University

Jim Bartruff
Emporia State University

Jerry Beal
William Paterson University

Chris Beineman
Texas Southern University

James Bell
Grand Valley State University

George W. Bellah 3rd
Central Washington University

MB Berry
College of Charleston

Ronert Berry
Anne Arundel Community College

Randal Blades
Jacksonville State University

Ro Willenbrink Blair
Edinboro University of PA

Greg Blakey
University of Central Arkansas

Davida Bloom
SUNY Brockport

Zachary Bloomfield
Joliet Junior College

Marnie Brennan
Harrisburg Area Community College

William T. Brewer
Hutchinson Community College

Professor Bruce Brown
University of the Ozarks

Victor Capecce
Harrisburg Area Community College

Jennifer Chapman
Albion College

Richard J. Clifford
BYU–Idaho

Patricia Cohill
Burlington County College

Laura Pulio Colbert
Harper College

Eric Colleary
University of Minnesota

Cheryl Collins
Prince George's Community College

Deena Conley
Drake University

Chris Danowski
ASU

Brook Davis
Wake Forest University

Michelle Douma
Seattle Central Community College

Brad Duffy
Grays Harbor College

Jay Edelnant
U of Northern Iowa

Rebecca Engle
St. Mary's College of CA, Theatre Program

Joseph Fahey
  The Ohio State University

Ross Fleming
  University of Texas–El Paso

Anne Fletcher
  *Southern Illinois University
  Carbondale*

Phillip Franck
  Vanderbilt University

T Gambill
  Concord University

J. Giampaolo
  Joliet Junior College

Ariel Goldberger
  Evergreen State College

Richard Groetzinger
  Heidelberg College

Phoebe Hall
  Fayetteville State University

Katherine Hammond
  ODU

Tim Hanna
  Guilford College

Lani Harris
  University of Central Florida

Mark Harvey
  University of Minnesota Duluth

Terry R. Hayes
  Davis & Elkins College

Clifford Herron
  Okaloosa Walton College

Melanie Hollis
  University of Tennessee, Martin

Helen Housley
  University of Mary Washington

Jennifer Hunter
  Cornerstone University

Walter H. Johnson
  Cumberland County College

Jacob Juntunen
  University of Illinois, Chicago

Lisa Kander
  Wayne State University

Scott Richard Klein
  Cameron University

Daniel Kramer
  Kenyon College

Andrea Lang
  Metropolitan Community College

Ronald N. Lauck
  Muskingum College

Hugh Lester
  Kenyon College

Robert Levy
  Clarion U of PA

Deborah Lotsof
  Mount Union College

Janet Maissen
  Yavapai Community College

Sarah McCarroll
  Indiana University

Maggie McClellan
  Southern Oregon University

Sherry McFadden
  Indiana State University

Charles McNeely III
  McNeese State University

Marcus McQuirter
  Austin Community College

Christy Mendoza
  Clovis Community College

Caroline Mercier
  CSU Stanislaus

Tom Mikotowicz, Ph.D.
University of Maine

Susan Minton
Lindsay Wilson College

Dawson Moore
Prince William Sound Community College

Diorah Nelson
Hillsborough Community College

Ray Newburg
Amarillo College

Connie Oesterle
Lansing Community College

Diana Polsky
Cypress College

Janet Reed
Crowder College

Lee Rose
U Maine Machias

Korey Rothman
University of Maryland

Leah Roy
Wake Forest University

Peggy Sannerud
Winona State University

Peter Savage
Western Carolina University

Carol Schafer
Penn State–Beaver

Juliette Schwab
Sul Ross State University

Eric C. Skiles
Lone Star College–Kingwood

Stephen Smith
Delaware County Community College

Michelle Stephens
Richland College

Aurora L. Strick
Southern Illinois University

Michael Swanson
Elizabethtown College

Kristina Tollefson
University of Central Florida

David Underwood
UNCP

Ronald Wainscott
Indiana University

Dennis Wemm
Glenville State College

Arthur Williams
Olivet College

Cynthia Winstead
Missouri State University

Jeff Wittman
Lynchburg College Theatre

Todd Wronski
Dickinson College

Daniel Yurgaitis
Northern State University

About the Authors

Leslie Atkins Durham

Leslie Atkins Durham is Associate Professor of Theatre Arts at Boise State University. She holds an M.A. and a Ph.D. from the University of Kansas. Dr. Durham has published her work on contemporary theatre in a variety of journals, and her book, *Staging Gertrude Stein: Absence, Culture, and the Landscape of the American Alternative Theatre,* was published by Palgrave Macmillan in 2005. In addition to teaching Introduction to Theatre, she teaches courses in theatre history, dramatic literature, and dramaturgy.

Sally Shedd

Sally Shedd is Professor of Theatre and Humanities Division Chair at Virginia Wesleyan College. She holds a Ph.D. from the University of Kansas and a master's degree from the University of Arkansas. Dr. Shedd has served on the Executive Council of the Association for Theatre in Higher Education's Women and Theatre Program. In addition to Introduction to Theatre, she has taught a wide range of theatre courses including acting, directing, theatre history, theatre of diversity, and feminist criticism.

Ritual and Theatre

Photo by Joan Marcus/Walt Disney Productions/Photofest

The theatrical production for which Julie Taymor is best known is the musical adaptation of the Disney animated film, *The Lion King*.

The lights dim. Bodies shift. An excited hush settles over the gathered group. At last, the curtain is raised, and a whole new world comes to life: the performance begins.

Such a moment, crackling with intensity and bursting with promise—of entertainment, enlightenment, or in many cases both—is one shared by people across great divides of time and culture. In fact, in virtually every society, ancient and modern, rural and urban, Western and Eastern, some form of performance practice has drawn people together. The details of these performances, such as the lines spoken, the costumes worn, the props held, and the music heard, have varied tremendously, but the impulse that draws an audience together is timeless and virtually universal. At our most basic, people are imitative creatures. We love to tell stories and to embody characters. We love to embellish these tales and those who animate them with spectacle and sound. We seek thrills emotional, visceral, and intellectual. Such activities draw us together, in numbers small and large, and make us feel more alive. In turn, the complex, vibrant art form called theatre lives too.

© Michal Daniel, 2001

The ghost of Hamlet's father. The emotional, visceral, and intellectual thrills of *Hamlet* have drawn audiences to the theatre for centuries.

RITUAL: ROOTS AND IDEAS

Before there was organized theatre—before people designated as actors came into the presence of people designated as an audience in a shared place called a theatre—there was ritual. In the West, we date theatre from the first tragic contest at the Greek City Dionysia in 534 BCE. Historians have long assumed that Greek theatre had roots in the ancient rites that predate this great occasion, but it is now impossible to tease apart the details of how this complex process might have worked, not just because many events were not recorded and few tangible artifacts still exist, but also because theatre and ritual are such closely related forms of cultural expression. Today many scholars see theatre and ritual as existing along a continuum of types of performance, and at various points along that line of reference, the characteristics of each form blend together. Ritual can be defined as an action or set of actions executed to gain control—over the environment, over humans' rela-

© Bobby Yip/Reuters/CORBIS

A Chinese opera "Dan" or female role performer emerges from a curtain during a performance as part of a ritual at Sheung Shui Heung in the rural New Territories, Hong Kong. The week-long ritual is a held every 60 years to chase away "ghosts" and maintain peaceful life in the village.

tionships with the divine, or over the transition from one phase of life to another. Rituals have been performed to make it rain, to honor deities, to ensure fertility, and to celebrate life's transitions—among many, many other things. In all these cases, rituals have power. They do and change something. That is their primary purpose—entertainment is incidental, not essential, to ritual performance.

Ritual usually depends on participation. In many contexts there is a leader, who has special skills or powers and who helps guide participants, controlling the event that unfolds in time and space. Repetition is also a powerful force in ritual. Over time ritual structures become solidified. Often, the elements of the ritual—such as place and time of performance, music, movement, gesture, and dress—are highly symbolic. These repeated, specialized patterns, behaviors, and items work to transform the daily into the special and the participant into someone, or part of something, more powerful than he or she was before.

As you begin to think about ritual, you probably hear resonances with the ways you have experienced other kinds of performance—whether in a live theatre, through film or television, at a sporting event, or as part of everyday life.[1]

SPOTLIGHT

Day of the Dead and Carnival

The Day of the Dead, or Dia de los Muertos, is a ritual celebrated in Mexico, Central America, and some parts of the United States on November 1 and 2 each year. This ritual marks the time when, some participants believe, the souls of dead children and adults are reunited with their families. The event now coincides with the end of the yearly growing cycle and with the Christian All Saints' and All Souls' Days, but originally it was celebrated during the ninth month of the Aztec calendar, which corresponds to August.

Children—both those alive and those dead—are honored as part of this folk ritual. They receive sweets, toys and balloons on November 1. Failure to offer gifts to the souls of the dead may be punished by spirits weeping at their graves. November 2 is a national holiday in Mexico often celebrated with skits mocking death and dying and parades containing street bands, music-making dancing skeletons who play tricks on the crowd, and little girls strewing marigolds, all leading to local cemeteries, where graves are embellished with food, drink, and candles. Relatives sit near gravesites on blankets and enjoy the food they

The centuries old tradition of marking the Day of the Dead continues in the main square near the presidential palace in Mexico City, late November 1, 2000.

After an all-night vigil, Cristobal Silva stands amongst graves, which have been decorated with candles and flowers to pay homage to the dead, on the Day of the Dead in Mexico.

© Danny Lehman/CORBIS

brought. Some believe that the souls of the dead are fed by the smell of the food. Chants further honor the dead and bells begin ringing every thirty minutes to summon the departed souls. Some families keep a vigil all through the night. In some communities the culmination of the annual pageantry is the Dance of Death, a festive costume ball. Celebrations differ depending on whether a community is primarily urban or rural. In urban settings, Day of the Dead has become largely secular, but in rural areas, the festivities are still sacred, and in some cases the dead aren't just venerated, they are worshipped.

Beyond entertainment, the Day of the Dead serves the important function of integrating life and death. People in the present celebrate those who are gone as well as those who are here with them. Life and death appear to be part of an ongoing cycle instead of separate phases. The move through that cycle may become less scary when images of death—skeletons, bones, and graves—become playthings, sugary treats, and the objects of humor. This ritual celebration, full of theatrical elements like costumes, masks, and music, empowers people to face the future without fear.

Springtime is another important part of the year for ritual activity. All around the world—from Rio de Janeiro to Trinidad to New Orleans—different forms of Carnival celebrations take place right before the Christian season of Lent. Lent brings a season of restraint and abstinence right before the renewal and rebirth that Christians find in Easter. Carnival (meaning carne vale or farewell to the flesh) is a period of indulgence, which prepares celebrants to undertake the deprivations to the flesh that Lent requires. Its roots may go back as far the pagan rites of the Greek Dionysia, the festival at which tragedy was born, and the Roman Saturnalia. Some scholars argue that the early Christian church co-opted and redefined these pagan celebrations to fit their purposes, much like Spanish colonizers reoriented the Day of the Dead to correspond with their calendar and belief system. A gleeful and sensual chaos rules during Carnival. Normal expectations, order, and mores are abandoned, and hierarchies are overturned. The desires of the

© Lucas Jackson/Reuters/CORBIS

Revelers shout for beads from floats decorated by the Krewe of Hermes as they travel down St. Charles Avenue during Mardi Gras festivities in New Orleans, Louisiana.

Mardi gras Indian. Note the ritualized colors of the costume and the use of black face make up.

© Marc Pagani Photography, 2009, Shutterstock

body can be satisfied with little interference from the conscience. People eat too much, drink too much, show or observe too much skin, and celebrate as much and as publicly as possible.

The most famous American celebration of Carnival is Mardi Gras in New Orleans. Almost as soon as New Orleans was founded in 1718, the French settlers started celebrating Mardi Gras—in the form of costume balls in the homes of the wealthy. Costumed street parading soon followed, but a major date in the evolution of New Orleans' Mardi Gras celebrations is 1857, when the Mistick Krewe of Comus formed. Comus was an elite secret society. Although Comus's lavish costume balls were an invitation-only event, anyone could watch their street processions, which featured music, lights, and elaborate floats. Soon Comus had competition from the Krewes of Rex, Momus, and Proteus, and the parades became more flamboyant and elaborate.

The various krewes exerted tremendous effort each year designing their floats and coordinating the music that accompanied them. As the parades took place at night before the costume balls, some kind of intervention was required to make the pageantry visible. African-American men, called Flambeau carriers, held huge torches to light the way for the floats of the elite whites. Soon "throws" added to the excitement. The masked riders on the float threw a variety of items to the raucous crowd of parade spectators—candy, plastic beaded necklaces, doubloons stamped with the krewe's insignia, and other trinkets were the most common.

With rich whites floating down streets tossing worthless baubles to the masses while black men served to light the way, Mardi Gras showcased and heightened the racial and class differences that dominate this Southern city. Rather than simply playing their part without comment, some groups have chosen to join in the festivities, and in their own spin on Mardi Gras rituals, they offer some critique of the way the world operates throughout the rest of the year. The Zulu Social Aid and Pleasure Club, founded in 1909, played with the racial stereotypes that Mardi Gras traditions reinforced. The black members of the krewe appeared in black face and in exaggerated African costumes. In addition to lampooning racial prejudice, they also play with class prejudice. Invitations to the Rex ball, for example, are still reserved for the top of the social elite, but anyone can buy a ticket to the Zulu ball. Some years upward of 10,000 people attend. And long before gay marriage was a major political issue, gay krewes formed in New Orleans, such as the Krewe of Yuga in the 1950s and the Krewe of Petronius in the early 1960s. The midday drag queen beauty contest continues to play a major part in Mardi Gras festivities. Sexuality of various kinds is ebulliently and publicly celebrated rather than closeted.

Clearly Carnival, its American manifestation in New Orleans called Mardi Gras, and Day of the Dead share several components: parades, masquerade, and costume balls. In addition, Carnival duplicates the Day of the Dead's ability to help people negotiate the cycles of life. It helps them balance delight and deprivation, celebration and contemplation, indulgence and restraint. Meanwhile Mardi Gras adds a variety of social components to the mix. By breaking as many rules as possible within a very limited period of time, it helps some people obey rules as a regular practice, while it helps others recognize social regulations that might demand an overhaul.

INDIVIDUAL RITUALS IN EVERYDAY LIFE

Every day we play multiple roles. The things we regularly do and the ways we often behave reveal the idea. Ritual has the goal of harnessing power and transforming the individual, and consciously or unconsciously, we emulate these structures in our daily life. We use our adapted individual rituals to shape the presentation of ourselves to the world and to get the things we want and need.

At school, you perform the role of student. In the typical college classroom, a variety of ritual behaviors are at work. First, classes begin at a particular time and usually unfold in a set way. From early in the semester, the professor, a kind of leader in this particular ritual, sets up a pattern structuring a typical class. Perhaps she regularly begins the class with announcements, returns graded assignments, asks students to silence cell phones, or maybe plays music relevant to the material you will cover that day. She probably stands or sits in the same part of the room each day, and you do likewise. You and she both dress in prescribed ways as well. You would be surprised if you arrived and found her in exercise clothes, and she would be surprised if you came to class in formal evening wear. There are also prescribed modes of communication in a college classroom. Vocabularies are established specific to the course that a student must learn,

Undergraduate students and professor in an English literature class on Chaucer.

and there are acceptable ways for you to address the professor and for the teacher to address you. It would be unusual, for example, for you to communicate with each other or discuss an assignment primarily through slang or four-letter words.

The structure of this classroom performance, along with the setting, costumes, and forms of dialogue, are all part of this individual ritual. You and your professor both play a role, and through this ritual you establish kinds of power specific to your parts. Your professor enforces her role as leader, as someone who has knowledge to convey—knowledge that is useful to your intellectual development and that the academic community and the world beyond its walls value. The student, meanwhile, demonstrates that she is serious about a class, about learning, and about advancing to another phase of her life, perhaps one designated by the acquisition of a desirable job. There are meaningful consequences to this ritual. Like other forms of ritual, it shapes individuals, betters communities, and marks transitions from one phase of life to the next.

Within hours of leaving the classroom, the same person who performed the role of student may soon perform the role of waitress. If she works in the evenings, she may have to change her persona—the social mask she wears—entirely. When she changes settings, moving from classroom to restaurant, she most likely changes her costume. The restaurant where she works might have a uniform, for example. She will be expected to address the diners in particular ways, offering them drinks and parts of the meal in a set order. If she were to deliver dessert before the main course, this would probably not be appreciated by the patrons, with the exception of the children at the table, who would celebrate this alteration to the ritual pattern. Her conversation with those at the table should be polite, as should the diners' responses to her, but no one is likely to expect to engage in an examination of philosophical or historical issues when she delivers the check that those visiting the restaurant know they must pay.

Although this ritual may seem to have less long-term meaningful consequence than that performed in the college classroom, the proper execution of all its ritualized elements is still essential, and the participants are changed in particular ways. The diners who visit the restaurant

© AVAVA, 2009, Shutterstock.

A waitress performs for the customer.

get to be served. While they were at work during the day, playing different roles of their own at their workplace, they might not have been the leader. Here they get to choose what they want, and they get to have someone else do their bidding. They played their role at work, at least in part, to be paid. Now they see what their labor can buy them—a shift, however brief, in their own power and status. The waitress, meanwhile, gets something from playing this role. If she performs the dining ritual in the way the patrons expect, she will receive a tip. This financial reward gives her power—perhaps the power to help pay for the book she needs to read for tomorrow's assignment at school. The successful completion of this individual ritual allows her to participate in a different one on campus.

GROUP RITUALS IN THE COMMUNITY

Instead of involving a handful of people at a dinner table in a restaurant, some rituals engage a much wider portion of a community. These larger-scale group rituals, may be sacred or secular.

An example of a sacred group ritual is a wedding. Weddings occur in special places—whether it's a church, synagogue, beach, garden, or other spot designated for an event. There are different rituals associated with weddings involving people of different religions, but for purposes of this example, let's consider a conventional Protestant wedding ceremony. These weddings are often held in a church. The church is then decorated with flowers, thus making a special place even more so. The bride, dressed in white and carrying flowers, enters into the space, perhaps on the arm of her father, while familiar music plays. All those in attendance stand up to watch her procession. Bridesmaids, all dressed alike, wait for her at the front of the church, as do the groom and his groomsmen, who are also dressed alike. A minister leads the proceedings, directing a couple when to exchange vows and rings and leading by example when it's time for a reader to recite a special passage of text or when a musician will contribute to the ceremony. Typically the ceremony ends when the minister declares the couple married and invites them to kiss. Then they walk back down the aisle together and wait to greet their friends and family when they exit the church.

The repeated elements of a ritual are often highly symbolic. This is certainly true of those parts of a wedding we just described. The traditional color of the bride's dress usually suggests purity. She may have also selected the particular blooms in her bouquet because of their symbolic value. The practice of having the father of the bride "give her away" is no longer

Lady Diana Spencer arrives at St. Paul's Cathedral on her wedding day, revealing to the world the wedding dress which had been carefully guarded during its design. Ritual elements are present in all weddings, but they are particularly noticeable in royal weddings.

palatable to all women. Ministers used to ask, "Who gives this woman in marriage?" Her father would reply, "I do." Contemporary brides may rewrite this part of the script, asking the minister to say instead, "Who supports this marriage?" The answer might then come from her mother and stepparents as well. Other brides may choose to walk down the aisle on their own, symbolizing the fact that their choice and power alone brings them to this momentous occasion. The still-current practice of having bridesmaids dress in the same outfit comes from an old belief that the bride and bridesmaids should all dress alike, as this would trick evil spirits bent on abducting the bride. The exchange of rings also symbolizes eternal union, and the placement of the ring on the third finger of the left hand reflects an old belief that blood traveled straight from that finger to the heart.

This kind of ritual also has a distinct purpose and conveys power. The primary participants in the wedding ceremony, the bride and groom, undergo a change in status as a result of the ritual. They are "united in holy matrimony" after they make promises to love and care for each other for the rest of their lives. Symbolically and legally they become one. In many cases, this marks a transition into adulthood, though certainly many couples marry much later in life than they used to. As a result of the marriage,

© Philip Gould/CORBIS

Well-wishers hug Jennifer Hale, Louisiana State University's homecoming queen of 1997.

the couple gains status in the community—they gain privileges both legal and social. Those who are only observing the ritual also undergo something important. By witnessing the ceremony, they state their care and affection for the couple. They also affirm the values of the community—of fidelity and monogamy, for example—through their presence at the event.

An example of a secular group ritual is homecoming. Whereas a wedding has religious purpose, a homecoming's purpose is worldly. Nevertheless, it has repeated, symbolic elements and helps to establish a community.

Homecomings usually take place in the fall—a nostalgic time, as leaves are falling, and the year's end approaches. Graduates return to their old haunts, visit classrooms, favorite social spots, and attend sporting events. They probably wear clothing adorned with school colors. Many times a parade is part of the festivities. Students, many from social clubs or fraternities and sororities, build floats bedecked with images celebrating the school and their group's place in it. They may also lampoon the school the football team will play in the homecoming game, doing all kinds of symbolic violence to their rival through humiliation of their mascot. These floats form a procession through important streets in the town, perhaps ending their journey on a football field. Homecoming may also involve the election of a queen and her court as representative of the school and its best qualities. These luminaries may be crowned at a formal dance.

Though these rituals may be less precise and less regularized than those associated with a wedding, they still are repeated over time, mark transitions through and out of studenthood, and help a community celebrate its strengths and promote its values. Entertainment becomes a more prominent factor in this kind of group ritual. If alumni, who have gone out into the world and become successful, come home and rekindle their affection for their alma mater, they may contribute to the institution financially. This becomes an important consequence of this kind of ritual. Beyond good feeling, programs, buildings, and scholarship funds might be enhanced and the experience of those students who built the event improved through these particular participants' responses to the group ritual.

FORMAL AND AESTHETIC PERFORMANCE: THE THEATRE

Rituals sacred and secular, individual and group-oriented, have a great deal in common with formal theatre. But although there are many points of intersection between theatre and ritual, there are also important differences group-oriented, primarily because theatre is considered an art. Its goals, at least in part, are aesthetic. Theatre artists intentionally strive to make something beautiful and/or to heighten people's perceptions—sensual, intellectual, and personal—through the event and experience they create.

A key feature that theatre and ritual share is "live-ness." In theatre, performers and audience meet in the same place and the same time; in ritual, the line between participants and observers may be blurred or completely nonexistent, but all those present for the event exist together in time and space. There are contemporary forms of theatrical performance that complicate this definition—those that incorporate video footage or that employ virtual reality technologies—but throughout history and most regularly today, theatre is understood to be and practiced as a live art. As the title of this book reminds you, theatre lives.

Because both theatre and ritual are live, they are temporally and spatially based forms. These times and spaces are particular and interconnected. Literary arts are often printed on a page, visual art might be captured on a canvas, and music unfolds in time. But theatrical and ritual performance require both time and space. People come together in a shared place for a length of time and experience things that move and change through time and space. And because the theatrical or ritual performance unfolds in time, when it concludes, the work of art is gone. Theatre and ritual are ephemeral forms—like life itself.

The spaces in which theatre and ritual are performed are often marked as special. In the case of theatre, there is often a purpose-built building—a theatre—in which the show is performed. Other times a place originally intended for some other activity, such as a church or a warehouse, might be transformed into a theatre. But whatever the kind of space, theatre happens in it, over time.

Both theatre and ritual observe conventions. A convention is a readily understood practice within a community that communicates ideas. When the lights dim in a theatre, experienced audience members understand that this is a convention letting them know that the show is about start. Audience members who have seen several musicals understand the convention that although people don't generally sing their feelings in real life, this is expected during a musical. In intense emotional moments, characters often break into song. Conventions also become established within a particular play. If all characters on stage are wearing black except for a single character costumed in white, audiences will understand that there is something special or different about this last character. Color can become a convention. Rituals also observe many conventions: Music or sound may indicate the beginning of the ritual, differentiated speech in the form of chanting might be employed, and color often carries particular significance. All these conventions are understood by ritual participants.

Although theatre and ritual do have several important things in common, they also differ because theatre is an art form. It is an "aesthetic" activity. Philosophers, theorists, and critics have argued for centuries about what makes something "art." At its most basic, art is something that is made as opposed to something that occurs naturally or randomly. Art, then, comes into being on purpose. But most people would likely agree that all things that are made on purpose do not qualify as art. Art does something special. In many cases, it helps us make sense of the world, often by organizing our perceptions into patterns, and it gives us pleasure, usually

Actresses Kristin Chenoweth (R) and Idina Menzel (L) perform a number from the popular musical, *Wicked*.

SPOTLIGHT

Peter Brook

In 1968, Peter Brook, a British theatre director and theorist, published a book that stirred the theatrical world to debate: *The Empty Space*. Perhaps one of the most quoted passages from the book is this one from its first pages: "I can take any empty space and call it a bare stage. A man walks across this empty space whilst someone else is watching him, and this is all I need for an act of theatre to be engaged." Here Brook challenges his generation of theatre practitioners to find the most essential elements of the theatre—the empty space, the performer, and the audience—and to strip away all else that might upstage this powerful source.

Brook describes four kinds of theatre. He warns against the deadly—those modern stagings of classic plays that rely on old ideas and methods instead of conjuring a play's sound from it anew so that it might speak to today's audiences. Two other kinds of theatre that of-

British director Peter Brook directs a rehearsal of his play *Mahabharata* on stage at Theatre des Bouoffes du Nord in Paris.

fer alternatives to the deadly theatre are the holy and the rough. The holy theatre, like that created by Polish director Jerzy Grotowski and that theorized by Frenchman Antonin Artaud, forces the audience to see anew, delving below surface perception, to find a higher truth. The rough theatre, like that of German director and theorist Bertolt Brecht, rejuvenates the theatre by reembracing the popular sources of theatre. But the kind of theatre for which Brook most strongly advocates is the immediate (and necessary) theatre. This is the kind of work he tried to stage when directed a famous production of *Marat/Sade* in 1964. Brook was aiming toward a theatre that demanded much of its audience and gave it a great deal in return. He recalled that his best theatre experiences were ones in which an image was burned into his mind—one that outlasted emotion and argument. He also noted that actor and audience must work together to cause such remarkable theatrical magic to happen. Audiences must be active in their attention and concentration, feeding the performance and being fed in turn. This reciprocal act generates something special: a vital truth animated with a spirit of play.

Peter Brook once again inspired debate about the nature of theatre and how it should be made with his *Mahabarata*. It was first staged in 1985 after more than a decade of work; the production then went on a world tour in 1987 to 1988 and was televised and released on video in 1989. Brook and playwright Jean-Claude Carriere adapted the Hindu epic into a nine-hour stage performance in which they attempted to bring together the theatre traditions, music, and visual styles of various cultures. Some scholars regarded the work—which employed a multilingual, multiracial cast and had an enormous budget—as a theatrical triumph, creating a new international community from its artists and audiences; others saw the work as a blatant example of cultural imperialism—that Brook had ripped a sacred text and imagery from its cultural context, slickly repackaged it for Western tastes, and was busy reaping profits from his aesthetic crime. Twenty years later, respected critics are still divided in their opinions about what Brook's ultimate creation entailed and how it defines the nature of intercultural or transcultural theatrical practice.

SPOTLIGHT

What Is Art?

In the following quotations you'll find a sampling of the wide variety of opinions that philosophers and artists have expressed about the nature of art. With whom do you agree?

Art is identical with a state of capacity to make, involving a true course of reasoning. All art is concerned with coming into being . . . for art is concerned neither with things that are, or come into being, by necessity, nor with things that do so in accordance with nature.—Aristotle

I can't tell you what art does and how it does it, but I know that often art has judged the judges, pleaded revenge to the innocent and shown to the future what the past suffered, so that it has never been forgotten. . . . Art, when it functions like this, becomes a meeting-place of the invisible, the irreducible, the enduring, guts, and honor.—John Berger

The person who wants nothing, hopes for nothing, and fears nothing can never be an artist.—Anton Chekhov

Art need no longer be an account of past sensations. It can become the direct organization of more highly evolved sensations.

of an intense, elevated, or serious kind. In the theatre this pleasure also includes entertainment. What art is, or does, is often understood differently by different people at different times. Art is almost always open to some range of interpretation. Standards of beauty and important ideas and the ways they might be most effectively expressed vary widely within and across cultures.

Though art suggests a degree of openness and variation, there are still some recurring features that we can identify within the art of theatre. The first is collaboration. Theatre is most often made by a team of artists working together. Theatre is a complex art that brings many other arts together including acting, music, dance, painting, and writing. When you see a play, you may see the contributions of some combination of a playwright, a director, a composer, a lyricist, a conductor, a choreographer, a scene painter, a set designer, a costume designer, a sound designer, and an actor. It is extremely rare for a single artist to do all these jobs, especially on a single show. A group of artists will divide these many tasks based on their skills,

It is a question of producing ourselves, not things that enslave us.—Guy Debord

Art is either plagiarism or revolution.—Paul Gaugin

True works of art contain their own theory and give us the measurement according to which we should judge them. —Johann Wolfgang von Goethe

Art is so wonderfully irrational, exuberantly pointless, but necessary all the same. Pointless and yet necessary, that's hard for a puritan to understand.—Günter Grass

A great artist is a great man in a great child.—Victor Hugo

Art is the objectification of feeling.—Susanne Langer

Art depends upon the inexactitude of sight.—Friedrich Nietzsche

Through art we express our conception of what nature is not. —Pablo Picasso

Art is too serious to be taken seriously.—Ad Reinhardt

training, and experience. Because art is a purposeful activity, the art of theatre requires a variety of people who can make choices and execute them with a sense of purpose and skill. They have something to express, and they know how to do so effectively. We will explore the work of these artists in detail and at various historical moments in future chapters.

Usually, theatre tells a story; it is primarily a narrative-based form. There are contemporary artists who seek alternatives to the storytelling function of theatre and ways to organize performance around structures that do not depend on plot, or the ordering of incidents in a story, but most plays tell a story and take audiences on a journey of discovery alongside the characters in the play. Characters are the fictive beings in a story who do something. In a play, they are the agents of dramatic action. As they make choices and pursue goals that drive the story forward, we have the opportunity to learn as they do, or as they fail to do so. We understand our world by watching them experience a fictive world on stage. They capture our at-

Lisa Korn and Jayne Houdyshell in *Well* at the Public Theater. Kron functions as both a narrator and a character in her autobiograhical play.

tention and our emotions, sometimes with flair and panache, sometimes with subtlety, which leads to part of the pleasure involved in theatre.

When plays tell a story, the various artists collaborating on the production of the play seek to make their work—in light, costume, set, and acting—help tell that story. Spectacle is an important tool for telling stories in the theatre. Theatre is a visual art form as well as a verbal one. Even though the words of a playwright are most often the starting point for a production, these words are physicalized and embodied in ways that become essential for creating the total art form that is theatre.

The spectacle of *Circus of Tales* at the Theatre de la Jeune Lune dazzled audiences.

RELATIONSHIP TO OTHER PERFORMING ARTS

With a little investigation and effort, it is not hard to distinguish a play from a novel or from a painting. But when we begin to compare theatre to other art forms—popular and elite—that also use performers, include an audience, tell a story, and that require the collaboration of several artists, our task becomes more challenging. To deepen our understanding of what constitutes theatre, we will compare it to film, television, ballet, and opera.

Some performance-based arts are considered popular forms. Studio movies and television are designed to appeal to a mass audience both in terms of storylines and visual conventions. These stories tend to be easy to follow, they build in excitement, and the tensions created in them resolve in ways in keeping with mainstream sentiments and morality. Visually, they tend to aim toward something primarily realistic. It is not hard to identify familiar places, people wear conventional clothing, but the actors do tend be unusually attractive, regardless of their role. Film and television are also visually restrictive forms. The focus and framing of the camera direct the viewer's attention very forcefully. For better and for worse, spectators at the theatre are more independent—they can look at what they want, when they want to. Theatre artists try to lead the eye to particular parts of the

Three collaborators celebrate the author of the play. Tony Kushner (R), George C. Wolfe (L) and Jeanne Tesori (C) arrive for the opening night of Kushner's new Broadway musical, *Caroline, Or Change* at the Eugene O'Neill Theater.

stage through a whole host of conventions, but ultimately the spectator has a much broader range of visual choices while watching a live theatre event than while watching a movie or television program. Two theatre spectators watching the same performance on the same night may see very different things on stage based on their own viewing choices.

At certain moments in its history, theatre has also been considered a popular form. People from a wide variety of backgrounds and classes have, at times, attended and enjoyed the theatre. So it is not a matter of taste or style that absolutely divides theatre from film and television, even in the present moment. But today, a great many more people can view a television episode or a particular movie. Because television and film are broadcast and/or recorded forms, they can be distributed to a very large audience, nationally and internationally. Because theatre is live—actors and audiences come together in a particular place at a particular moment—theatre is very different from television and film despite the fact that they are all frequently narrative-driven forms created through collaboration. Theatre is immediate, it is present, and it is "locally" produced—even when it tours, as we will see in this chapter's spotlight on Julie Taymor. Though a production may be viewed by many people, each individual performance in the "run" of the show is unique. It hasn't been recorded and edited elsewhere.

Within the world of performing arts, there also exist high or elite forms. Many people find that true appreciation of these forms—opera and ballet, for example—require repeat exposure and practiced viewing because the forms of expression they use tend to be heightened and significantly different from those used in everyday life and in popular art forms. Ballet often tells a story, but it does so entirely through patterned and rhythmic movement and music and without dialogue. Opera, meanwhile, uses verbal expression, but it is sung (sometimes in a foreign language) and orchestrated in a complex fashion. Some kinds of theatre, today and at certain moments in history, might also be considered high art. Dramas written in verse sometimes pose challenges to novice viewers, as it can be more difficult to follow dialogue and plot until the ear adjusts to rhyming and metrical patterns, wheras a form like Japanese Noh drama, with visual and story conventions specific to Japanese culture, can also seem difficult to comprehend. So although opera, ballet, and certain kinds of theatre share heightened conventions that might be best appreciated after repeat exposure, each form differs in the characteristic conventions it uses. Because art is consciously made, the types of choices and the tools used to make those choices clear to an audience often mark the boundaries between art forms.

Dancers Mia McSwain and David Martinez perform a pas de deux in David Parson's *Wolfgang* at the Joyce Theater in New York.

Roberto Alagna as 'Doktor Faust' and Angela Gheroghiu as 'Marguerite' perform during the dress rehearsal of Charles Gounod's opera 'Faust' in Vienna.

Noh actor Otoharu Sakai performs "Hagoromo" plumage at a noh stage in tokyo May 17, 2004. Noh, admired as beauty of yugen or restained elegance, is the oldest theatrical art in Japan and combines the essence of dance, theatre, music and lyrics.

SPOTLIGHT

SPOTLIGHT

Julie Taymor (1952–)

Julie Taymor is a director, designer, and puppeteer who has had tremendous success in both theatre and film. She was the first woman to win a Tony Award for her direction of a musical, and her films have received Oscar nominations. Her work combines story and spectacle in ways that appeal across the divide between popular and high art.

Taymor began her theatre training at L'Ecole de Mime Jacques LeCoq in Paris in 1969. LeCoq's approach to theatre is physically based, includes mask work, and draws on popular clown and mime traditions. She also studied at Oberlin College. In the early 1970s Taymor had apprenticeships with Joseph Chaikin's Open Theatre and Peter Schumann's Bread and Puppet Theatre, two major avant-garde American companies, both of which experimented with physical storytelling in provocative, imaginative, and image-driven ways. Then from 1974 to 1978, Taymor traveled abroad, spending the bulk of her time in Indonesia, where she became intimately acquainted with Asian performance and puppet practices and where she became part of the Bengkel Theatre.

Taymor has a varied resume, having directed and designed multiple Shakespearean plays; operas, including *Oedipus Rex* and *Grendel;* the adapted short story *Juan Darien;* and the eighteenth-century comedy by Carlo Gozzi, *The Green Bird*. But the theatrical production for which Taymor is best known is the musical adaptation of the Disney

CHAPTER SUMMARY

Theatre has many points of intersection with ritual and with other performing arts. At the same time, theatre has several unique features, and these features have stretched the imaginations of audiences and artists alike throughout a large portion of human history. Theatre is an aesthetic form—one that should always be considered artistic, regardless of the precise kinds of ways it seeks to create beauty for its viewers. Because of this variety, it has at some points in history appealed to regular people and their tastes, whereas at other times people seeking an elite or "high art" experience have found those desires satisfied at the theatre. Whoever the audience and whatever animated film, *The Lion King*. The musical version of *Beauty and the Beast* preceded Taymor's work, but unlike Taymor's work on *The Lion King*, *Beauty and the Beast* simply translated a cartoon to the stage. Taymor, on the other hand, completely reimagined her source material, filtering it through her experience with theatre of other cultures, avant-garde performance, and puppetry. Taymor's vibrant, visual spectacle combined visual influences from Japan, Indonesia, Africa, and of course Disney while the music ranged from the work of South African performer Lebo M to British pop star Elton John. Thanks to a long run and ten international touring companies, more than 25 million people have seen Taymor's stylistically innovative, theatrically rich, yet crowd-pleasing work.

Taymor also received considerable acclaim as filmmaker—for *Titus* (1999), *Frida* (2002) and *Across the Universe* (2006). Taymor's film work shows the same kind of variety that her theatre work displays. *Titus* is an adaptation of Shakespeare's *Titus Andronicus*; *Frida* is a biopic, telling the story of acclaimed painter Frida Kahlo; and *Across the Universe* is a musical set in the '60s that mixes animation and live action.

Taymor's adventurous, multifaceted work crosses a variety of artistic boundaries: live and recorded, Western and Eastern, classic and modern, mainstream and alternative, popular and elite. She represents the dramatic range of what a theatre artist can be and achieve.

the artistic goals, the inspiration and provocation theatre provides leads to a diverse and fascinating field of study as the following chapters will show.

ACTIVITIES

A Day in the Life

Think about the private and public parts of your day. When do you use elements of ritual to shape your identity for yourself and for others? Make a list of the ritual elements in some aspect of your public performance. Trade lists with another student in the class. Which ritual elements do you have in common? Which elements are unique to you?

Awards Show Analysis

Go to the Web site for the Oscars, the Emmys, the Tonys, the Grammys, or some other celebrity award show. What elements of performance can you observe in these annual events? In what ways are they ritualized? What values are conveyed?

Do You Know Pinocchio?

Puppet theatre has a long, rich tradition around the world. Look at the pictorial examples of Indonesia's Wayang Kulit, Japan's Bunraku, and the stars of *Avenue Q* of the United States. What do these puppets have in common? How are they different? Why do people enjoy seeing puppets instead of or in addition to live human performers? Does puppet theatre challenge your idea of what theatre is, or does it reaffirm your opinions? Research the puppet traditions in either Indonesia or Japan and read an online review of *Avenue Q*. Share your findings with your class.

© Free Agents Limited/CORBIS

An example of Indonesia's Wayang shadow puppets.

An example of Japan's puppet theatre, Bunraku.

The Broadway cast of Avenue Q.

Classical Theatre and the First Western Playwrights and Critics

The Theatre of Dionysus today.

One way to begin to understand Greek theatre and culture, the place where theatre and drama began in the West, is to remember your last trip to the grocery store. As you waited in line to check out, it was probably hard to avoid all the magazine covers and the headlines of the tabloid papers. Unreasonably beautiful people smile from the racks or duck from the camera's view, as the publications promise details of charmed existences or the unsavory exploits of the famous faces. These celebrity images are, in fact, everywhere—on billboards, the sides of buses, printed on T-shirts, inside magazines and even serious newspapers, and dotting many sites on the Internet—and unless you make a conscious effort to avoid them, you are almost sure to have some idea about these figures' publicized triumphs, their carefully cultivated alliances, and their sometimes stinging defeats. When you see these figures perform in a film, act in a television series, or play in concert, it may be hard to separate their fictive personae from the stories of their "real-life" adventures.

Scholars David Wiles and John Herrington, and the famous French poet Baudelaire, have all talked about ancient Greek culture as resembling a "forest of myth."[1] This was a time and place saturated with the iconography of mythology. Images from myth populated public and domestic spaces and decorated household items and jewelry. Not only that, but when the first generation of Western playwrights created plays, inventing both tragedy and comedy and establishing ideas about drama that would remain potent for more than two millennia, they drew from the well-known storylines of mythology, reshaping them and making them their own.

Though there are certainly crucial differences between contemporary celebrity-obsessed popular culture and the stories that fuel its obsessions and the mythological backdrop of playwriting's genesis in fifth-century Athens, there are also clearly some similarities. These parallels make approaching the theatre and the art of playwriting, both of which responded to myth in numerous ways, in Greece's Golden Age of theatre a surprisingly familiar task.

MYTH, STORYTELLING, AND RITUAL

Mythology was a tool the ancient Greeks used to make sense of the world around them. The Greek gods were a family of sorts: Zeus was the head and the king. His wife was Hera, the goddess of marriage, though she was often unhappy as Zeus fathered many children with mortal women and semidivine beings. His children are Aphrodite, the goddess of love, beauty, and fertility; Apollo, the god of poetry, music, prophesy, and healing; Ares, the god of war and vengeance; Artemis, the goddess of the hunt, who helped women in childbirth; Athene, the goddess of wisdom and domestic crafts; Dionysus, the god of wine and theatre; Hephaistos, the god of fire and the forge; and Hermes, the god of travel and commerce. Meanwhile Zeus's siblings also held power. Poseidon ruled the sea, Hestia held sway over the hearth, Demeter governed the fields, and Hades controlled the underworld.

In the description of Zeus's Olympian family, we see several important ideas. First, there are multiple gods. This is a polytheistic system, quite different from the monotheism of the Judeo-Christian contemporary West. Second, we can detect a spatial scheme emerging from the domains of Zeus and his siblings. While Zeus rules the sky, his brothers rule the sea and underworld, and his sisters rule earth and home. David Wiles has argued that the Greeks understood an iconographic shorthand that went with this spatial ordering: Zeus wields a thunderbolt while Poseidon wields a trident, for example. Wiles also sees in the indexing of the gods a categorization of male and female experience. The male gods collectively embody the traits associated with Greek male activity: political leadership, fighting, business, travel, drinking, and artistic creation. The goddesses, meanwhile, represent female traits and experiences: domesticity, marriage, reproduction, and eroticism. Finally, we see in the gods' attributes and in their family lineage that these are not perfect, infallible creatures who exist in a realm entirely separate from the human. The gods have human foibles, become embroiled in human conflicts, and often behave downright badly. They populate fascinating tales. The noble human, seeking to live a good life, does not construct a moral code by modeling the behavior of the gods. He may not even "believe" in the gods in the way contemporary Christians believe in Jesus, for example. Particularly as Athens' defeat at the hands of the Spartans in the Peloponnesian War loomed large, Athenians became increasingly skeptical about their gods. Thus, an Athenian might try to work out what morality should mean to him in relation to, even in distinction from, the exploits of the gods.

Greek playwrights used the body of stories about the gods, as well as legendary tales of war and heroism, when they constructed the plots for their plays. But as they explored this vast, rich store of cultural tradition, they did not reproduce the stories and their characters without some changes. Though most of the tragedies that remain from fifth-century Athens are concerned with three major story lines—the Orestes story, the Oedipus story, and the Trojan War—there is considerable variety in the thirty-one remaining plays. This is because a good portion of the playwright's artistry came from the way he was able to stretch, pull, and emphasize pieces of the old stories, creating something quite new that reflected back on the current social and political concerns of the contemporary audience.

It is also worth noting here that storytelling was not a literary activity for the ancient Greeks—it was a performance activity. When historians make conjectures about the ancient Greek theatre based on the remaining plays (a small fraction of what was actually produced), it is a somewhat suspect activity. Storytelling was part of an oral tradition, often with surprising links to women and the domestic realm, as it was the women who dominated the home and had the opportunity, even the need in the face of repetitive labor and exclusion from the stimulation of the public sphere, to tell and maintain stories. So when we try to make the Greek theatre be about the printed play as an isolated artifact, we do quite an anachronistic disservice. These stories were meant to be told—aloud, in public, and for a particular sociopolitical reason. Men co-opted the power of female storytelling for the public sphere of the theatre. And although our focus is on Athens, it is well worth noting here that theatrical performances occurred in all Greek cities. When Thespis emerged as the first actor and the first winner of a tragic contest in 534 BCE, narration, or the telling of stories, had clearly morphed into the public and civic enacting or performing of stories. As the stories were acted in the theatre, they melded with ritual observance and political practice.

We discussed ritual in some detail in the last chapter, but it is worth recounting a few salient points here. First, ritual is a repeated activity that can be either sacred or secular. Rituals are often performed at the same time of year, in the same place, and with the same fundamental parts. Second, it is a purposeful activity. The time, place, and parts of a ritual have been selected for a reason, and these ritual elements can be read or interpreted as they reveal important information about the culture's values and desires. Finally, ritual is a powerful activity. The participants in a ritual carefully repeat its meaningful elements because they believe the successful completion of the ritual will endow them with some kind of power or will otherwise improve them in an important way.

The performing and viewing of a play was a ritual and political activity for the ancient Greeks. Plays were staged at the City Dionysia beginning in 534 BCE. The City Dionysia was an Athenian festival held in late March or early April each spring to honor the god Dionysus. After a statue of Dionysus was carried into town by a group of young men, thus recreating the god's legendary arrival in Athens, the festival could begin. The next morning all business and legal proceedings ceased, as festival attendance was considered a crucial civic activity. Each of the ten tribes of the city, the

19th Century Antique Vase Illustration of Dionysus and Three Figures

© Stapleton Collection/CORBIS

main political units, brought its sacrificial bull to town. Parades of young men in military training and other political and military displays would follow. The processions moved through the *agora*, or marketplace, the citizens drank wine, and dances honored all the gods. When the processions reached the altar of Dionysus, just below the theatre, the bulls were sacrificed. Some scholars speculate that the honor of sacrificing the first bull went to the tribe that had won the dithyrambic contests, perhaps just preceding the sacrifice. The dithyrambic contests featured choruses of some fifty men, who sang and danced a story from the life of Dionysus or another one of the gods.

The dithyrambic contest was just one of the contests at the festival. Perhaps of greatest importance to the student of theatre are the comic and tragic contests. We will focus on the tragic contests here. Each year three tragic playwrights would compete at the festival. Each of these writers wrote a cycle of three related tragic plays, a trilogy, and a fourth play called a satyr play. The satyr play followed the tragedies and may have lampooned or otherwise comically improvised off what came before.

The tragic contests bring together the three strands we have studied so far: myth, storytelling, and ritual. As an example, we will consider *Medea*, written by Euripides (480–406 BCE) for its first performance in 431 BCE. When Euripides created his famous play, he drew on one of the most well-known stories in the ancient world, the story of the Golden Fleece. In this myth, Jason, the rightful heir to the throne of Iolkos, is sent on a suicide mission by the usurper of the throne, Pelias. If Jason can bring the Golden

Photo © Michal Daniel, 2002

Blood stains the set, costume, and Medea herself, played by Barbra Berlovitz in Theatre de la Jeune Lune's production of *Medea*.

Fleece, which is guarded by a fire-breathing dragon, back from barbarian Colchis, Pelias will give up the throne. Jason builds a magical ship, the Argo, and gathers a crew of heroes to sail with him. When Jason arrives in Colchis, Medea, the local princess, falls in love with him and uses her magical powers to help him get the fleece. Choosing to help Jason means Medea must flee her home. She does, with her younger brother in tow. When Medea's father chases them, Medea dismembers her brother and casts his mutilated body overboard, so her father and his ships will have to stop to collect the pieces of her brother. Jason and Medea sail back to Iolkos and present Pelias with the Golden Fleece. When Pelias refuses to uphold his end of the deal, Medea tricks Pelias's daughters into killing him. She cuts an old ram into pieces and places them in a boiling pot. A young lamb jumps out, convincing the girls to do the same to their father to restore his youth. When Medea's treachery is discovered, she and Jason must again flee, this time to Corinth.

It is here that Euripides begins his tale—with the story of Medea and Jason in Corinth. Two lesser-known sequels covering this same territory already existed. In one, Jason deserts Medea to marry the princess of Corinth. When Medea retaliates by killing the princess and her father, the people of Corinth revenge the death by killing Medea's two children. In the other tale, Medea tries to perform the same magic youth-restoring ritual on her boys that Pelias's daughters performed on him. Something goes wrong, and the boys accidentally die. But Euripides creates suspense, one of the hallmarks of great storytelling, by diverging from his predecessors. In his play, Medea wants revenge for Jason's humiliating abandonment of her, so she kills the princess with a poisoned gown and diadem. When her father tries to help her, he too is consumed by the magical fire Medea created. But this is not enough for Medea. Not wanting to leave her boys to the mercy of the Corinthian citizens or to provide Jason with comfort and heirs, she murders her own sons. At the play's end she tells Jason what she's done and then flies off in the chariot of the sun driven by her grandfather.

Ritual is also in Euripides' play, in the magical, deadly rituals Medea performs, but it is also present in the act of competing at this annual contest—one that Euripides rarely won, perhaps because he was considered quite rebellious and cynical. But we can also see another aspect of ritual in the play. Rituals are performed so precisely because the participants believe some improvement will follow. In *Medea*, the audience has the possibility of being purged and cleansed of the terrible passions that wreak havoc in the lives of Medea and Jason. When some scholars try to make sense of the play, they emphasize the fact that *Medea* was first performed during the first year of the Peloponnesian War (431–404 BCE) between Athens and Sparta. These readers see Jason as representing cold, calculating self-interest, while they see Medea as embodying the kind of consuming passion that demands revenge. These twin forces destroy each other, have the potential to destroy the polis, and are the very factors that motivate war. If audience members allowed themselves to experience the dangerous feelings Euripides' suspenseful, myth-driven storytelling created in the safe environment of the theatre, they could be purged of them—cleansed and clarified—so that they might make better choices when they left the theatre and when regular civic life resumed after the completion of the Dionysian festival's rituals.

THE PLAYWRIGHT AND PERFORMANCE

Theatre Space and Textual Space

The tragic contests at the City Dionysia were performed in an outdoor theatre, or amphitheatre, called the Theatre of Dionysus. This theatre was built into the slope of the hill that featured the Athenian Acropolis at its summit. The theatre's proximity to this important civic site is revealing. As we will see when we explore theatre space later, at some points in history theatres and the districts in which they are housed were often located on the outskirts of a city and/or are connected to a red light district, indicating they are on the fringes of a city's morality. Even on college campuses today, the theatre and arts buildings tend to be on the geographical, if not intellectual, periphery of the institution. But in Athens, the theatre was near important buildings like the Parthenon and its treasury that were vital to the city's stability and security. Theatre was at the heart of what was valuable and crucial for the city. If audience members paused to think about where they were in the city as they watched a play, they would know they were somewhere civically important, and this might color the importance with which they viewed the events transpiring on stage.

© Robbie Jack/CORBIS

Performance of *The Oedipus Plays of Sophocles.* Note the position of the principal actor in relation to the chorus.

Over a period of many years, permanent seating was installed on the hillside. Eventually stone seating, arranged in a semicircle around the *orchestra*, a flat, open space with an altar to Dionysus at its center, accommodated some 14,000 to 17,000 spectators. Because the audience had an elevated vantage on the hill, they could both look down on the actors in orchestra below and over the scene house, which we will discuss in a moment, out to the surrounding landscape. The perspective from above the action provided a literal distance that might have promoted a willingness to judge what was happening, whereas the audience's unobstructed vision of the natural world would have provided a sense of scale. As important as the human struggles taking place in the orchestra and in front of the scene house were, they were dwarfed by the larger geographical setting that was, at least in theory, ordered by the gods. Playwrights had a ready-made visual analogue for their frequent inquiries about the scope of human might, especially as it was juxtaposed with the power of the gods.

The altar at the center of the orchestra also merits analysis. On the one hand, it kept the ritual and religious context of the theatre visible and present for the audience. On the other, it provided the setting for another recurring theme explored by playwrights: the issue of center versus periphery.[2] Because the altar was at the center of the orchestra, the space was carefully mapped. Where an actor stood in relation to this center would have been telling, but that could be made even more stark when the chorus, a communal character enacted by twelve to fifteen men, was also presented. It could become visually clear how the individual related to the community, whether his actions were in keeping with its moral center, of whether he was straying to the edges of the acceptable and desirable. Although no staging records from the period remain, we can use this information to imagine how Sophocles' (496–406 BCE) *Oedipus Rex* (c. 430–425 BCE) might have looked in the theatre. At the play's beginning, Oedipus believes that he is at the very center of the social order. When he declares that he is capable of ridding the city of a devastating plague and of solving the mystery of the old king's murder, he might have been in the midst of the chorus, which represents the citizenship of the city. As the play evolves, however, the audience comes to see that he is truly at the periphery of the society, having killed the old king himself without realizing it. It turns out that the king was actually his birth father and that when he married his queen, he also married his mother. Oedipus punishes himself by gouging out his own eyes and asking the gods for exile. It is possible that the movement of the actors through the space and in relation to the theatre's center made the play's commentary on the place of the individual in society and his relationship to the gods even clearer.

On the side of the orchestra opposite the audience there was a *skene*, or scene house. This too evolved over time. It may have begun as little more than a tent, but like the seating, it eventually became quite elaborate, spanning some 75 to 100 feet and standing two stories high. This architectural unit served as the basic backdrop for the plays, suggesting that the playwright's words were the most essential tool for setting the scene. The scene house did not originally connect to the audience seating. Instead, the spaces at either end provided entrances and exits for the actors. In addition the scene house featured a large door at its center.

Actors could use the door for entrances and exits, but the door also provided a way to show tableaux. It was common for an *ekkyklema*, a wheeled platform, to be rolled through the door, revealing the aftermath of the violence that the Greek writers very purposefully kept offstage. Violence was often an essential part of the play's story, particularly what motivated the violent act

© Robbie Jack/CORBIS

Maia Morgenstern and Adriana Moca in the *Oresteia* reveal the aftermath of violence.

Tara Fitzgerald plays the title role in a production of Sophocles' classic tragedy *Antigone* at the Old Vic Theatre in London.

and what the consequences of that act were. The plays contained vivid speeches by messengers describing what had transpired elsewhere, but enacted violent spectacle was absent. Clearly the Greeks' visual taste and emphasis in storytelling was quite different from that of many twenty-first-century spectators. Classical Greek viewers did, however, see corpses, presented with effigies, on the ekkyklema. At the end of Aeschylus's (523–456 BCE) *Agamemnon* (458 BCE), for example, the audience does not see Clytemnestra murder her husband Agamemnon and his sexual conquest, Cassandra, in the bath inside the palace. But when the deed is done, the audience would see the consequence of the horrible act rolled through the skene's door.

Again we can move from an architectural feature to textual concern. The door on the skene was a threshold between the public and the private, the political and the domestic, and the exterior and the interior. Many of the Greek plays turn on these distinctions, and crises in the plays occur when these distinctions are not maintained. In *Antigone* (441 BCE), by Sophocles, Creon, the king and Antigone's uncle, forbids her to bury her dead brother because he is a traitor against the city. Antigone disobeys and buries her brother anyway. In this conflict, the domestic and interior becomes political and exterior. A Greek audience would have understood that it is a woman's domestic duty to bury the family's dead. The mourning ritual should be an interior act. But through his decree, Creon makes the domestic political. He brings something that should stay inside outside. Gendered roles and duties, also associated with interiority and exteriority, become confused and disrupted, and ultimately tragedy ensues.

PLAYWRIGHTS, ACTORS, AND CHORUSES

The distinction between playwright and actor that exists in the contemporary theatre was not so strictly demarcated for the ancient Greeks. By the time we get to the era of the first of our extant tragic writers, Aeschylus, the writer would be closely involved in the production of the play. When a writer wanted to compete at the City Dionysia, he had to apply to the *archon,* a magistrate, for a chorus. As part of his application, he would present his songs for the archon, performing for this small but very important audience. So at this early phase of production, actor and author were one. If he was granted a chorus, it would then be his job to teach the play to the group—fifteen performers in Aeschylus's day and twelve in Sophocles' and thereafter. Scholars speculate that rehearsal time with the chorus lasted eleven months and would have included training similar to a contemporary athlete's—a controlled diet, physical exercise, dance practice, and in an example unlike the athlete's, careful cultivation of the voice. There was a lottery for principal actors. By Sophocles' day, a rule was established that each author could have three speaking, or nonchorus, actors. After the author learned which actor luck provided for his lead, this lead actor might help select the other two actors.

When you look at a script from the era, you will find that there are many more than three speaking characters. It was a convention of Greek performance that an actor play multiple roles. The use of masks helped tremendously with this practice, and with the practice of having men play all the roles. Though there are many interesting and complex female characters in Greek drama—Clytemnestra, Antigone, and Medea only start the list—none of them would have been played by a woman. Contemporary feminist scholars like Sue-Ellen Case have looked carefully at this practice, exploring the complex performance of gender that an all-male cast for a predominantly or perhaps even exclusively all-male audience, embodies. Actors might also differ widely from character in age or physical type, so once again the mask's ability to conceal would have been of tremendous value.

Masked actors in a 1996 production of the Oedipus Plays in London.

Masks conceal, but they also reveal. In the very large Greek theatre, it helped to summarize a character with simplified visual strokes. Fine detail was not possible in a theatre so large, so it was more helpful to create a single, striking, and memorable image that revealed a key feature of the character. Scholars also suggest that the masks may have helped to reveal the actor's voice. Though the acoustics were quite good in the Greek theatre, the mouth opening on the mask may have had a megaphonelike function, enhancing the actor's vocal production.

In addition to masks, costumes would have helped facilitate the doubling of roles and the cross-gender casting practiced by the ancient Greeks. The basic tragic costume piece was the *chiton*, a long tunic-like garment possibly derived from the robes of the priests of Dionysus. Such a garment would not have revealed great detail about the actor's shape and form. Some items may have been added to the basic tunic to differentiate the different characters an actor played. On his feet the actor would have worn soft, lace-up boots common in the day. As the theatres grew even larger, platforms were added to the soles of the actors' boots, then called *kothurnoe*, to increase their stature and visibility on stage.

The final type of performer we need to discuss is the chorus member. Choruses probably began with fifty members. But as noted earlier, in Aeschylus's day they had fifteen members, whereas Sophocles reduced the number to twelve in his plays. Collectively the chorus formed a very special kind of character—one that served as a bridge between the playwright and the audience. The chorus served several functions. First, they provided music and movement. This added visual and musical interest to the production, providing a counterpoint to the evolving story in the play's episodes with color, movement, and song. Second, their musical interventions into the narrative created a kind of breathing space for the audience. The lyrical shift they provided gave the audience a break from the episode's rhetoric. It also gave them an opportunity to contemplate what had come before. Third, as the chorus members expressed their opinions, discussed what had come before, and sometimes changed their minds about what was happening, they gave the audience a guide to responding to the action. The chorus reacts to the play's events in the way the playwright wants them to because they are his creation. If a spectator follows the chorus,

The chorus is a major part of the production's spectacle.

allowing them to lead him through the production, he can follow the playwright's intentions as well. Finally, the chorus helps cement the play's mood. As they add movement and spectacle, comment on the action, and react to playwright demands, they set the mood and provide emphasis for the key moments in the play.

THE AUDIENCE AND ITS EFFECT ON PLAYS AND PLAYWRITING

If one were to select a single adjective to describe the Greek audience, it would have to be "familiar." Though the audience was very large and they might not have been in close physical proximity to the play's action, they were close to it in a number of other important ways. First, they were regular playgoers. Though theatre was a seasonal activity as part of the City Dionysia, it was a regular part of the life of the citizen. Each spring, he would see twelve plays. He would understand a play's structure, knowing that each play would contain a prologue, the *parados*, or entrance of the chorus, five episodes, a forerunner of the modern act, separated by a choral ode or song, and an *exodus*. He would also know what to expect of each segment of the play, correctly anticipating that the exposition would occur

SPOTLIGHT

Aristophanes, Menander, and Greek Comedy

Aristophanes (448–380 BCE) wrote the eleven surviving comedies from fifth-century Greece. The ideas that contemporary scholars have about the form called "Old Comedy" are based on his works. His plays were satirical treatments of contemporary life, literature, and politics and the Peloponnesian War.

One of his plays that is still regularly produced today is *Lysistrata*. *Lysistrata* contains all the elements typical of Aristophanic, or Old, Comedy. Aristophanes' plays are organized around a far-fetched idea, in this case the idea that a sex strike by the women of Greece could bring an end to the Peloponnesian War. Early in the play, there is a debate over the merits of the sex strike, the idea driving the play. Aristophanes used an absurd situation to point out the absurdity of real life. Then a series of farcical episodes follow—women try to leave the Acropolis that they have occupied by force using a variety of silly ruses to return to their husbands, a husband tries to get his wife to "relieve his suffering," but the wife has an endless string of excuses for denying him, and so on. In the final scene, the men give in, all are reconciled, and the cast leaves for the highly anticipated celebratory "festivities."

Menander (342–291 BCE) wrote the only complete surviving example of Greek New Comedy: *The Grouch*. For many years speculation about New Comedy was based on only fragments of plays, as *The Grouch* was not rediscovered until 1957. New Comedies, which emerged after 336 BCE, were concerned with love, domestic situations (particularly generational conflicts between parents and children), and manners and mores, instead of the political satire that dominated Old Comedy. The most frequent subject of New Comedy involved the desire of a young man to wed a girl, who at the play's start is a socially

in the prologue, so he had better pay attention right from the start. He would also be knowledgeable about the myths and history from which the playwright was drawing his story because they were so prevalent in his culture. Finally, he would know something about the playwrights themselves. Playwrights did not exist on the artistic fringes as they sometimes do today. Instead, the playwrights were actively involved in the life of the city, some-

Photo by Richard Feldman. Image courtesy of American Repertory Theatre.

A scene from the American Repertory Theatre production of *Lysistrata*.

unsuitable match. His father stands in his way until some misunder-standing about the girl's identity or social status is cleared up. The struc-ture of these plays was essentially the same as tragedy: A series of episodes were divided by choral odes.

Though tragedy in Greece declined by the end of the fourth century BCE, comedy continued to be vital for another hundred years. Alexan-der the Great spread both forms throughout Rome and parts of the Mid-dle East, but by the end of the third century, the great period of Greek dramatic writing had come to a close.

times serving in politics and the military, as did Aeschylus and Sophocles. Playwrights in ancient Greece lived long lives. Aeschylus was 69 when he died, Sophocles 89, and Euripides 74. All three men kept writing—art was not a young man's game, as it is in many fields today. Long, famous ca-reers meant audiences would have known the writers and their styles quite intimately over a period of many years.[3]

The Greek Tragedians, Study for the Apotheosis of Homer by Jean-Auguste-Dominique Ingres

ARISTOTLE AND THE BEGINNING OF WESTERN DRAMATIC CRITICISM

When the great philosopher Aristotle wrote *The Poetics* 335–323 BCE, Western dramatic criticism was born. Aristotle was an empiricist, meaning that he thought knowledge should be acquired by studying the phenomena around a person, describing them in great detail, and then drawing conclusions from these details. This was the way he approached dramatic literature. Aristotle looked back on the wonderful examples of dramatic art from the last century and catalogued what he saw. Though future generations of critics would mistake his account for a prescription of what drama had to be, Aristotle was in fact describing the dramatic texts that he encountered, trying to figure out what made them essentially dramatic—as opposed to lyric, epic, or historical—and why these dramas could be useful to the people who saw them, through his famous formulation of catharsis.

We will save most of the details of Aristotle's work for the next two chapters, but for now it is helpful to establish the context for Aristotle's thinking. Perhaps most essentially, Aristotle was a student of another giant of Greek philosophy, Plato. Plato also had some things to say about drama

Detail of Plato and Aristotle from *The School of Athens* by Raphael

© Ted Spiegel/CORBIS

and imitation. In short, he was suspicious of both and thought such things were not beneficial to the ideal state, as he explained in *The Republic*. Plato disliked imitation because it was a way of moving people farther and farther away from the ideal state of things that existed in the realm of ideas. When a craftsman makes an object, Plato argued, he was copying this object from the realm of true forms. But when a painter, poet, or dramatist imitates an object in his work, he is copying the craftsman who is already making a copy. Furthermore, Plato believed that these refracted imitations stirred people up, "feeding and watering the passions," thus making them less manly and rational, two qualities that he held most dear. As far as he could see, imitation, dramatic or otherwise, was far more detrimental than it was helpful.

As the readers of this book are no doubt aware, there is little more pleasing than being able to rebut the arguments of a teacher or authority figure. And that is exactly what Aristotle, himself a future authority figure of the highest magnitude, but never mind that, did. Aristotle believed in teleological progression. This means that all things are naturally driven toward reaching their highest, best, and most complete state. Unlike Plato, this ideal plane was not in some netherworld of ideas. Aristotle's highest place was right here, on earth, among other men. Tragedy had a

SPOTLIGHT

Contemporary Adaptations

Although Greek tragedy continues to hold the stage in its original form, contemporary playwrights often look to the Greek tragedies and other Greek stories as models from which they can draw as they create new plays. Through this process of adaptation and revision, Greek theatre lives on the contemporary stage in new and exciting ways. Following is a brief list of authors and titles you might explore to see the transformations of Greek stories, characters, and themes for contemporary audiences.

Karen Landry and Lester Purry star in Rita Dove's adaptation of *Oedipus, Darker Face of the Earth*, at the Guthrie Theater.

Photo © Michal Daniel, 2000

Bertolt Brecht: *Antigone*
Jean Anouilh: *Antigone*
Lee Breuer: *Gospel at Colonus*
Heiner Muller: *Medeaplay*
Caryl Churchill: *A Mouthful of Birds*
Timberlake Wertenbaker: *Love of the Nightingale*
Rita Dove: *The Darker Face of the Earth*
Charles Mee: *Agamemnon 2.0*
Sarah Ruhl: *Eurydice*

Charles Mee's *Agamemnon 2.0* (as well as the rest of his plays) are available for free online at www.charlesmee.com. Go to his Web site and begin reading *Agamemon 2.0* or one of his other plays. What seems "Greek" to you about the play? What seems contemporary? Why would or wouldn't you want to see this play staged? Do you think this play would inspire catharsis? Does it have some other intention or purpose?

teleological end, according to Aristotle, and one that helped propel man toward his "telos" as well. Tragedy's aim, the place where it should be going and where its purpose was most fully realized, was in catharsis—in that purgation, purification, cleansing, and clarification that could come by play's end. All those emotions, of which Plato was so afraid, had a purpose, in Aristotle's opinion. They could educate people, improve them, and make them better when they left the theatre. Drama had a noble purpose, and it was a tool for helping humans achieve their most noble purpose. In Aristotle, in 335 BCE, theatre found one of the most articulate and persuasive champions it would ever know.

Photo © Michal Daniel, 2005

A scene from Theatre de la Jeune Lune's adaptation of *Antigone*.

CHAPTER SUMMARY

The first generations of playwrights and critics got drama and theatre off to a provocative start. From a dramaturgy that transforms myth and ritual, advances storytelling, and is capable of speaking to the pressing concerns of contemporary culture and possibly helps its spectators to face it more successfully, to a critical work that speaks articulately about the nature and power of drama in the classical world, we see the sparks of inspiration that have fueled creative theatrical exploration for centuries. In the next chapter we will build on the foundation provided by the classical writers, exploring more of the playwright's art and the structure of scripts.

 ACTIVITIES

Tabloid Gods

Look at a tabloid paper, the Web site of a magazine like *People*, or a celebrity blog. Pick a celebrity covered in one of these locations. Where else have you recently seen this person's image? Why is this person famous? What recent adventures has this person had? Why do you think this person fascinates others? What does the cult of celebrity—particularly as it involves your specific example—say about contemporary culture?

Tragedy by Numbers: DIY Orpheus and Eurydice

Writers and musicians adapting Greek myth have long been fascinated by the story of Orpheus and Eurydice. Find the myth online or in the library. How could you adapt this play for a modern setting? Write a brief synopsis of your ideas.

Center and Periphery

With a group of several classmates, try reading a choral ode aloud and on your feet. How is the experience of reading the text out loud different than reading it silently? Read the text two more times. First, gather the entire "chorus" close together in the center of the space in which you are working. Second, spread the group out, clumping small groups of people together around the edges of your space with as much room as you can between the choral clusters. How does spacing further influence your experience of reading the text aloud?

The Tools of the Playwright: Dramatic Elements, Structures, and Characters

Photograph by Brigitte Lacombe/Photofest

A scene from Samuel Beckett's most famous play *Waiting for Godot* provides a strong example of circular plot structure.

One of the great challenges in studying theatre is the nature of theatre itself: It is a temporal and spatial art. Unless a person witnesses a play live, coming together in time and space with the actors in the play and with other audience members, that person has not truly discovered all the theatre event has to offer. But whereas productions of plays and individual performances are fleeting, the scripts that laid the groundwork for these live events endure and are readily available in bookstores, libraries, and online. Scripts cannot offer the complete theatrical experience to a reader, but they are still incredibly valuable as guides to a performance that has been staged or to a performance that might be staged in the future. To see the range of possibility that these guides contain, a reader must be active, imaginative, and knowledgeable. Understanding the parts of a script—the key components of drama—and how playwrights build story, character, and idea is essential to reading a play text (and a fully realized performance) adventurously and well. Learning how the playwright gains skills and refines the craft will further enhance your experience with plays.

ARISTOTLE AND THE ELEMENTS OF DRAMA

Aristotle has probably had a greater influence on how plays have been read than any other thinker in the theatre's history. His theoretical text, *The Poetics* (335–323 BCE), dominated Western thinking about how plays are and should be structured for centuries. Though he was cataloguing and analyzing the great dramatic work of the century prior to the one in which he lived, subsequent readers of his work have sometimes taken his comments to be prescriptive—that is, indicating how things should be done—rather than descriptive—indicative of how things he encountered had been done. In this chapter we will discuss several of Aristotle's ideas applicable to all drama; in the next chapter we will investigate the ways his ideas help shape our understanding of specific types of drama or genres.

Aristotle described tragedy as "an action that is serious and complete and of a certain magnitude." The second word in this definition—*action*—is something that many people regard as being the defining feature of drama in general, not just tragedy. The English word *drama* comes from the Greek word, *dran*, which means "to do" or "to act." Drama, then, is full of doing, acting, and action. But in this context action isn't just physical. In a play one may observe physical action—a sword fight or a dance or a fam-

The Oresteia Tragic action is both physical and psychological.

ily serving and eating a meal—but the theatre's action is also psychological. It can involve characters falling in love, plotting revenge, or coming to a deeper understanding of what it means to be human.

Another important idea in Aristotle's definition of a tragedy that extends beyond that particular form is that the action is complete. This means that stage action has a beginning, middle, and end. Such a structure is so familiar to us in the West that it may seem obvious, but in fact this notion has generated debate. Some theorists have argued that everything necessary for understanding a play and its action are contained within a play. Although this may be partially true, as we saw when studying the play texts of the ancient Greeks, sometimes cultural context is now as lost to us as the masks and costumes the first actors wore. We may understand the basic elements of the story, but without some knowledge of the situation in which the playwright was writing and the ideas to which he was responding, we are likely to miss other layers of what the play means or why the play's action matters. This material is part of the play, but we may require tools external to the play to recognize and process the information. Recent artists have also played with the idea that an action must have an ending. Rather than providing the conclusion for which audiences are psychologically and socially trained to yearn—the happily ever after or the reward of virtue and the punishment of vice—some authors intentionally refuse to conclude the action. They leave audiences without the satisfaction of a tidy conclusion to motivate further thinking on the play's subject.

In addition to his emphasis on tragedy being serious and of a certain magnitude, Aristotle also observed that strong plays have both variety, which helps sustain audience interest, and consistency. Whether or not the action depicted on stage has happened in real life, it must be logical, and a playwright must follow the rules that he set up for this particular dramatic world.

One of Aristotle's most powerful ideas is the notion that tragedies have six major components: plot, character, thought, diction, music, and spectacle. We see these elements in most forms of drama. Aristotle lists his elements in the order of descending importance. At the top of Aristotle's list is plot. The plot is the ordering of the incidents in the play. Important in this definition is not just what story is being told, but how the story is being told. Sequencing is a fundamental component of dramatic structure because dramatic structure often turns on conflict. Conflict involves the eventual collision of opposing forces. How the forces are introduced, how quickly they collide, and what happens as a result of the collision can be just as interesting as the collision itself.

Character is the second most important element on Aristotle's list. The ordering of what happens is fundamental, but nothing happens without someone doing it. That someone is the character: a fictive creation who does something within the world of the play. Because many of Aristotle's other remarks about character—such has his notion of "hammartia," or a tragic flaw—are specific to tragedy, we will return to those in the next chapter.

Thought occupies the third spot for Aristotle, and it might be defined as theme, meaning, or argument. Playwrights have an idea they want to express through drama. This is the play's thought. How playwrights reveal thought to an audience varies widely, but the ordering of the incidents in the play and how the characters respond in these situations bring the thought to life. In ancient Greece, the chorus was often essential to the revelation of thought. In Shakespeare's plays, we might find the thought developing in a major character's soliloquy, a speech given while the character is alone on stage that expresses his or her inner thoughts. Or in one of Samuel Beckett's absurdist plays, which we will discuss later in the chapter, thought might be manifested in a single, repetitive image.

Diction, Aristotle's fourth element, might reasonably be understood as "language." When Aristotle encountered the theatre, and for many centuries after, drama was a very verbal form. Characters communicate with each other through verbal exchanges called "dialogue." The words the

Samuel Beckett conveyed thought through image. In *Happy Days,* Winnie is first buried up to her waist, and later up to her neck, in a mound of scorched earth. The image helps the audience see Winnie's loneliness, the emptyness of life's rituals, and the slow approach of death.

In plays like *Speed the Plow,* David Mamet uses a very recognizable style of diction, both in terms of word choice and line rhythm.

Even straight—non-musical plays—like August Wilson's *Ma Rainey's Black Bottom,* contain many kinds of music.

playwright chooses for a character and what the characters say to each other and about each other shape the play's action, convey a sense of character, and reveal theme and meaning. No matter what the style of the play's diction—whether it rhymes or whether it echoes contemporary urban slang—the writer has selected those words with a purpose that helps to reveal what the play is and can be about.

Music, nearing the bottom of Aristotle's hierarchy of elements, is something over which the playwright lacks complete control. Although the playwright gets to choose the words, sometimes quite consciously playing with vowels and consonants, duration of line lengths, and rhythm, the playwright cannot control precisely how the actor says the words. Actors augment the words of the playwright with resonance, pitch, tone, volume, articulation, and timing. When an actor speaks a playwright's text, choices in vocal characterization complement the written word, leading to something quite unique and remarkable that exceeds what exists on the printed page. Then when the actor's speech meets that of another actor, harmony or dissonance follows. In addition to the musicality of verbal utterance that playwrights facilitate, some writers also include incidental music—playing from a radio, for example—background music or underscoring, and nonmusical and nonverbal sound effects, like the ringing of a telephone that add to the total musical effect of the play.

Notice how different two productions of *Hamlet* can look. Clearly Shakespeare cannot control the spectacle created by contemporary directors.

Spectacle is Aristotle's final element. Like music, spectacle exceeds the playwright's control because though the writer may create the situations, order the incidents and pen the characters, actors come with particular bodies, which are then clothed and lit on sets over which the playwright usually has no say. But about this element, Aristotle was more specific. He says that playwrights who rely on spectacle to create interest or solve problems are making weak choices. Aristotle preferred for words and dramatic action to dominate the play.

Aristotle also believed tragedy had a purpose: catharsis. Reacting against the negative opinions of theatre and imitative art held by his teacher, Plato, Aristotle argued that tragedy could improve people by giving them an opportunity to purify themselves of pity, fear, and other emotions that got in the way of their rationality when they witnessed a tragedy's action. Aristotle's ideas about catharsis might be modified and extended so that they can apply to other forms of drama. When spectators witness an engaging story, taking an emotional and intellectual journey with a play's characters, they have an opportunity to learn as the characters learn. By doing so, they leave the theatre enriched by this multilayered experience. Just as Aristotle's definition of tragedy and his breakdown of the form into particular parts for further analysis all serve to further the noble goal of catharsis, the way later playwrights used dramatic action and the six major dramatic elements helps create a valuable and meaningful experience for today's audiences.

ALTERNATIVES TO CLASSICAL DRAMATIC STRUCTURE

Many artists have experimented with structures other than those proposed by Aristotle. Two of the most famous are Bertolt Brecht and Antonin Artaud. They provide other options for thinking about the elements of drama and dramatic experience.

Bertolt Brecht (1898–1956) worked in a style that he called Epic Theatre. Brecht witnessed the work of the Expressionists in Germany, and this form gave him a foundation on which to build. Expressionism, which flourished in the 1920s, sought to externalize an individual's subjective internal and dream states as a way of promoting social change. Expressionist writing often used short, staccato bursts of dialogue, short scenes, and grotesque imagery, whereas Expressionist production often featured odd angles, distortion, play with shadows, mechanized movement, and extreme coloration. When Brecht discovered Marxism, he found the ideas he needed to give focus to Expressionism's goals. He came to believe that capitalism was to blame for many human problems, and if people could learn how to evaluate the effects of capitalism—first in the theatre and later in the everyday world—they could live better lives.

Furthermore, Brecht came to believe that conventional theatre as it was practiced in his day, conditioned people to ignore the problems in the world around them, making better lives that much harder to forge.

When they became lost in a protagonist's problems, and when those problems were neatly solved in the course of the resolution at the end of the play, an audience member's critical faculties became disarmed. Brecht sought to re-engage the audience's social and political consciousness through what he called "alienation." By making things seem strange to the audience, as he did in his famous plays like *Mother Courage*, *Caucasian Chalk Circle*, and *Good Person of Szechuan*, he hoped to teach the audience to see characters and situations anew and ultimately to demand change. To make the stage picture and the story seem strange, to fire up the audience intellectually, and to shatter the Aristotelian notion of catharsis, Brecht used narrators to comment on the dramatic action; interrupted action with projections or often discordant songs; created stories that ranged freely in time and space—that were epic in scope and related to the techniques of epic poetry; revealed the machinery and technology of the theatre; and encouraged an acting style in which the actor did not disappear into the character.

Photo © Michal Daniel, 2006

Meryl Streep plays the title role in Bertolt Brecht's *Mother Courage*.

Antonin Artaud (1896–1948) wrote in the 1930s, but his theories of the theatre had a great effect on the American avant-garde directors who emerged in the second half of the twentieth century. He is most famous for imagining a "Theatre of Cruelty." He was tired of theatre's reliance on old texts that no longer spoke to contemporary people. He demanded that the theatre abandon such plays and called for "no more masterpieces" in his famous work, *Theatre and Its Double*. Texts were not sacred and could be revised or recreated as needed, he argued. The old texts tended to rely too much on psychological and social problems, thereby missing what truly mattered in people's subconscious. He thought theatre could be like a plague that forced people, against their will, to be purged of what was harmful and destructive. He also wanted to promote the theatre's sensory powers, which he saw as being grounded in its ritual roots, even if currently these powers were mostly subsumed by narrative. He took inspiration from the Balinese theatre instead of his own Western ancestors. He sought to bombard the audience's senses with light, sound, and shocking image surrounding them as they were located in the center of the performance space. Instead of keeping them protected from the performers and the spectacle, he thrust them in the midst of it so that he could circumvent conscious thought and the deadly patterns of rationalization that went with it. His ideas for theatre inverted Aristotle's hierarchy and radically revised almost all aspects of theatre practice.

PLOT STRUCTURES

The most familiar plot structure is called any of three names: linear, causal, or climactic. Each of these terms reveals an important facet of this way of telling a dramatic story. These plots move in a straight line, with one event causing the next, which ultimately leads to a climax in the play's action. This structure is the oldest pattern of storytelling in Western dramatic literature. It was the one used by the Greeks, it reemerged in the seventeenth century, and it has continued to have powerful effect into the twenty-first century.

As this kind of dramatic storytelling moves forward, there are several recognizable stations along the line of the plot. At the beginning of a linear play, one typically finds some degree of exposition, or the recounting of background information about place, character, and prior action. Exposition brings the audience up to speed and prepares them for the point of attack. The point of attack is the place where the story is taken up. In linear structures, the point of attack often occurs relatively late in the story, despite its early position in the play. In the Greek tragedy *Oedipus Rex* by Sophocles, for example, a great deal has already happened—all of which the audience learns through exposition. When Oedipus was born, an ora-

Oedipus provides an excellent example of linear plot structure.

© Photostage

cle predicted that he would kill his father and marry his mother. His frightened birth parents chose to bind the infant's ankles and leave him to die on a hillside. But a kind-hearted shepherd rescued the baby. The king and queen of another land then raised the infant as their own. When the child grew up and learned of the prophecy, he too was frightened. He ran from his home. When he came to a crossroads, he struck and killed an old man who refused to let him pass. He continued on to Thebes, where he solved the riddle of the Sphinx. He was rewarded by becoming king and marrying the queen, Jocasta, whose husband died. All of this happens before the curtain rises.

Many plays built on a linear model feature an inciting incident shortly thereafter. This is the event that puts the main action into motion. In *Oedipus*, a plague is tormenting Thebes. The people of Thebes plead with Oedipus to rid them of the plague. When an oracle says the plague was caused by the murder of the old king, Laius, Oedipus sets out to solve this mystery and punish the offender. Thus the action is set into motion.

In the middle sections of this kind of play, one finds a series of complications. These events are often based on discoveries of new information and sometimes the arrivals of new characters. In *Oedipus*, the shepherd who saved the infant comes to town and tells what he did many years ago and discloses the distinguishing mark that the exposure left. The complications in *Oedipus* and other linear plays keep the action moving forward toward its point of highest intensity, or the climax. The climax may be accompanied by a crisis—or the point at which the outcome of the main action is set. In *Oedipus*, it is increasingly apparent that Oedipus was not the birth child of his adoptive parents, that the old man he met on the road was in fact the king and his birth father, and that he has unknowingly married his mother. Oedipus discovers who he is and what he has done.

The ending of linear plays includes a denouement or resolution. After emotions and actions have peaked, they begin to diminish as the play's end is in sight. Denouement means unraveling. All the complications in the play now become smoothed out. Questions are answered rather than posed, and themes are given a final articulation. At the end of *Oedipus*, Jocasta has hanged herself, and after he blinds himself, Oedipus wants to impose his own exile. Creon forces him to consult the oracle first, reinforcing the important issue in the play that some choices are beyond a human's control. The audience is given final opportunities to consider the blindness that pride imposes and the potential consequences of such arrogance and lack of self-understanding.

A major alternative to the linear form is the episodic play structure. Whereas linear plays proceed with a singular sense of purpose, tend to involve fairly small casts and, if not a single, a very limited number of settings, and operate with a limited time frame, episodic plays evolve through association and juxtaposition, often involve larger casts, and may range widely across both time and place.

One well-known author who used episodic plot structures was William Shakespeare. Though events of his plays such as *Hamlet* do proceed chronologically, and in many cases one event causes subsequent events, Shakespeare's multiple scenes shift across vast geographical distances—scenes in *Hamlet* are set in Denmark, Norway, and England, for example—and cover several months of time. His use of subplots also helps his plots qualify as episodic. In *Oedipus* there was a single story line, but in *Hamlet* there are multiple story lines in which the lesser stories reflect back on the larger one. At the beginning of the play, the audience learns that the king of Denmark died a few months ago. The widowed queen, Gertrude, has just married her late husband's brother, Claudius. Claudius is now king of Denmark. As Hamlet is wrestling with his grief and his anger over the marriage, his friend, Horatio, reports that he and others have seen the ghost of Hamlet's father. When the ghost visits Hamlet, he tells Hamlet that he was murdered and tells him to seek revenge on the perpetrator of the crime, his uncle. Hamlet does not follow this instruction right away. As he justifies his hesitation, he says he is not sure whether the ghost is telling the truth—the ghost might be the devil trying to lure him toward damnation. So Hamlet starts behaving very strangely and asks a travelling band of players to help him stage a play like the crime the ghost described. Hamlet says, "The play's the thing / Wherein I'll catch the conscience of the King." Audiences often ponder whether Hamlet is truly mad or whether this is a role he plays as he tests his uncle's guilt. Shakespeare provides the character of Ophelia, Hamlet's spurned romantic interest, who does truly go mad during the course of the play, as a point of comparison. Another issue in the play is the question of kingship. Not only do we see the recently and wrongfully coronated Claudius deal deviously with the insubordination of Hamlet, but we also see the Norwegian prince, Fortinbras, march across Europe and settle matters at the end of the play, establishing a better order than any we have seen up to that point. To comprehend the thought of the play, audiences must look across plot lines involving multiple characters, times, and places, rather than following a single strand of dramatic action.

Episodic structures are not unique to Elizabethan England. Contemporary authors also use episodic structures. One such writer is the feminist playwright Caryl Churchill (1938–). In *Top Girls*, Churchill begins her play by assembling women from across time and space—Pope Joan from ninth-century Europe; Isabella Bird, an explorer from the nineteenth century; Lady Nijo, a courtesan from Japan; Dull Gret from a Breughel painting; Pa-

Photo © Michal Daniel, 2003

In her episodic play, *Top Girls*, Caryl Churchill invites the audience to question its assumptions about the construction of gender.

tient Griselda from Chaucer; and Marlene, a businesswoman from London in the 1980s—for a dinner party to celebrate Marlene's promotion to head of the Top Girls Employment Agency. During the course of the dinner, the women reveal what they had to sacrifice to become "top girls" in their own time. The short scenes that follow the long opening move in reverse chronological order, showing the effect of Marlene's choices on her daughter Angie, who is being raised by Marlene's sister, Joyce. The actresses who played the historical women in the first scene reappear in subsequent scenes cast as women seeking employment from Marlene and as those who work in the agency, and Angie is played by the same performer who played Dull Gret. Churchill's scenes that play with chronology and multiple casting help reveal thought in the play. She used these techniques to make performers visible beneath their roles so that audiences might see that social roles are no more natural and inevitable than theatrical ones, and that people inside and outside the theatre have the potential for radical transformation.

Another alternative to the linear plot structure is the circular plot structure. Perhaps the most famous example of this method of ordering the incidents of a play comes from Samuel Beckett's (1906–1989) absurdist masterpiece, *Waiting for Godot*. Beckett is one of the most famous and highly regarded of the absurdist playwrights, an international group of writers whose viewpoint emerged following World War II. These writers, reacting to the mass destruction of the war and embracing existentialist philosophy, changed the ways plays were written in their own time and continue to influence artists writing today.

The existentialist playwrights—Jean-Paul Sartre and Albert Camus most notable among them—staged philosophy in conventional terms. They explored what it might mean for people to be alone in the universe, absent a god to tell them what is right and how to live, but they did so using conventional characters and dialogue and linear plot structures. The absurdist playwrights, on the other hand, had the radical idea of matching form and content. They too envisioned an irrational universe where humans had the sole responsibility of finding meaning and purpose, but they distrusted language and how those in power had used it to sell their corrupt ideas. They thought a logical plot made no sense for exploring the illogical human condition. They created dramatic worlds where audience members had to make their own dramatic sense. Plots were circular, characters were archetypal, places were general, language was darkly playful and sometimes nonsensical, and a single or repeated stark stage image—like the slow rise of the moon in the night sky near the end of both acts of *Waiting for Godot*—was capable of crystallizing the most complex of philosophical thought.

Act 1 opens with a character named Estragon trying to take off his boot. Vladamir enters. The dialogue establishes that both have spent the night in the area. They can't leave, as they are waiting for someone named Godot. They aren't sure they are waiting in the right place. They aren't sure Godot is coming. They aren't sure how long they have been waiting. A character named Pozzo arrives. He is leading a man named Lucky by the neck with a very long rope. Pozzo visits with Vladimir and Estragon, both of whom, we get the impression, he has not met before. Lucky says nothing until his hat is removed. At that point, he gives a very long and seemingly nonsensical speech. Pozzo and Lucky exit. Estragon and Vladamir once again consider leaving. But they can't. They are waiting for Godot. At the end of the act, a Boy enters and tells them that Mr. Godot won't come this evening but will come tomorrow. When asked if he came the day before to deliver a similar message, the Boy replies that he did not. The Boy exits. Vladimir and Estragon indicate that they will go. But they do not move. This marks the end of Act 1.

Act 2 begins, once again, with Vladimir and Estragon. They have spent the night in the area. While Vladimir remembers the visit with Pozzo and Lucky the day before, Estragon seems to have only a vague recollection. They establish that they must wait for Godot. They discuss how to pass the time. Eventually, Pozzo and Lucky enter. Pozzo is now blind. He doesn't remember meeting Vladimir and Estragon the day before. Lucky says nothing. Pozzo and Lucky exit. The Boy enters. When asked, he denies having come the day before. He has a message from Godot: Godot will not come this evening but will come tomorrow. The Boy exits. Vladimir and Estragon indicate that they will go. But they do not move. And this is how the play ends.

The structure of *Waiting for Godot* is called circular because many of the same "occurrences" happen in both acts. Act 2 even ends with the same lines that end Act 1 under the light of the same moon. Beckett's events, dialogue, and imagery that irrationally circle back on each other, confounding the ways dramatic action and character are typically regarded, reveal the existentialist thought on which is play is based.

CHARACTER

As we survey the history of dramatic character, looking from ancient Greece to the present, we find a continuum of kinds of characters. At one end of the spectrum, we have characters representative of general categories of people; at the other end, we have characters so specifically drawn that they seem highly individual. An anonymous medieval author named his central character Everyman, and Samuel Beckett named characters things like Woman and Voice in *Rockaby*. Down at the other end of the line we have Henrik Ibsen creating the title character, Hedda Gabler, and Tracy Letts's Violet Weston from *August: Osage County*. Somewhere in the middle reside characters like Tennessee Williams's Blanche du Bois in *A Streetcar Named Desire* and August Wilson's Troy Maxson from *Fences*. This continuum of characterization shows us that specificity and individuation do not follow a strict chronological order. Whereas Everyman appeared in the sixteenth century, Beckett was writing at the end of the twentieth. And though Hedda did not grace the stage until the end of the nineteenth century, characters with whom she would have much in common continue to tread the boards and delight audiences in the early twenty-first century.

As you read a script or watch a performance, there are several ways to analyze character. First,

James Earl Jones plays Troy in *Fences*.

Marlon Brando plays Stanley and Jessica Tandy plays Blanche in *A Streetcar Named Desire,* 1947.

you might consider some of the dramatic categories of character. The protagonist is the central figure in the main action. This character's choices and behaviors are the play's central focus, and his or her actions tend to affect the rest of the characters. It is possible to have a group of characters or even something abstract like an idea as the protagonist, but most often, the protagonist is an individual character. Oedipus from Sophocles' *Oedipus Rex* provides a fine example.

The antagonist opposes the central figure in the main action. Sometimes this character is a kind of "bad guy," but not always. It is also possible for a social force or a group of characters to serve the function of antagonist. Perhaps the most memorable and complex plays involve protagonists and antagonists who are well matched—who both have compelling desires and who voice them persuasively. Stanley Kowalski is a fierce antagonist for Blanche DuBois in *A Streetcar Named Desire*, battling for the heart and loyalty of Stella, his wife and Blanche's sister. Furthermore, Stanley is often read as representing the New South—a place of industrialization, newcomers, and progress—whereas Blanche is read as representing the Old South—a place of manners, refinement, and fading cultural capital. Stanley and Blanche demonstrate that characters can be both highly individuated and representative of abstract concepts at the same time.

The foil offsets another character. The foil may be the "straight man" to the comic lead, thus providing a kind of complement or opposite. The golden age of Hollywood film provides numerous prime examples. But a foil can also echo qualities of a central character. Shakespeare provides many fine examples of this dramatic strategy. In *Hamlet*, Laertes is a foil to Hamlet. Both characters seek revenge for the deaths of their fathers, but the different way each approaches his grief and displays his anger is revealing of character and the play's thought or theme.

The raisonneur is the character who most clearly voices the author's opinion and helps reveal the play's thought. Many times this is not the protagonist. Instead, the raisonneur may be a less central figure—one with enough distance from the heart of the action to provide commentary. In

Photograph by Joan Marcus/Photofest

The main character, Catherine, and her confidante, Claire in *Proof* by David Auburn. Shown from left: Johanna Day, Mary-Louise Parker.

Tartuffe, Molière gives his audience Cleante. Although Orgon is the protagonist, the head of the family who falls under the sway of the religious hypocrite and con man Tartuffe, it is Cleante who states Molière's ideas about truth and faith.

The confidante is often a secondary character, sometimes a friend to the lead, who provides the playwright an opportunity to reveal the inner thoughts and desires of the main character through the conversations with the confidante. As the name suggests, this is a character in whom another character confides. In *Proof*, by David Auburn, conventional, stable Claire is confidante to her sister Catherine, for whom the threat of madness will recede as she emerges as a mathematical genius capable of matching her father's brilliant achievements by play's end.

Although these character types can be very helpful, they are not the only way to analyze character. One might also analyze characters based on their traits: physical, social, and temperamental.[1] Some playwrights provide very little information on how a character looks—height, weight, age, sex, race, and degree of attractiveness—but others are quite detailed, providing a substantial description alongside the cast of characters and/or embedding this information in dialogue. In many cases, the physical traits of a character not only influence who the character is, but also behavior and interactions with other characters. In *Moon for the Misbegotten*, Eugene

The character, Sister Aloysius, played by Cherry Jones from *Doubt* by Patrick Shanley.

Eve Davies plays Josie, with Kevin Spacey playing Jim, in the Old Vic's 2006 of *Moon for the Misbegotten.*

O'Neill describes Josie, who believes she isn't worthy of love, in considerable detail in the stage directions beginning Act 1: "Josie is twenty-eight. She is so oversized for a woman that she is almost a freak—five feet eleven in her stockings and weighs around one hundred and eighty. Her sloping shoulders are broad, her chest deep with large, firm breasts, her waist wide but slender by contrast with her hips and thighs. She has long smooth arms, immensely strong, although no muscles show. The same is true of her legs. She is more powerful than any but an exceptionally strong man, able to do the manual labor of two ordinary men. But there is no mannish quality about her. She is all woman." Physical traits can have a direct effect on the play's action (how Josie reacts to Jim Tyrone), but also on its thought (the nature of love and the possibility of grasping it) and spectacle (how Josie looks when the curtain rises on Act 4, with the sun rising as she holds the sleeping Jim to her ample breast, like a child).

Playwrights also vary on how clearly they spell out a character's social traits. These might include things like what familial relationships a character has (is she a daughter, sister, wife, mother), her class status (is she a chamber maid, a student, or a CEO), and her religious practice. These details help construct the play's time, place, and sociological environment.

In *Fences*, by August Wilson, Rose is a wife and mother; in *Tartuffe*, by Molière, Dorine is a maid; in *Doubt*, by John Patrick Shanely, Sister Aloysius is a nun and a teacher right at the time that Vatican II is reshaping the doctrine and practice of the Catholic Church. Again, these features may be laid out clearly next to the list of characters, or they may be revealed gradually through dialogue and action, but in each case, the character's social traits have a direct effect on what happens in the play.

In addition to the physical and social traits of character, playwrights usually imbue their creations with particular temperamental traits. Among the things to consider when studying a character are what kinds of thing a character wants—does she yearn for fame, stability, true love, justice, revenge—and what she's willing to do to get what she wants. How does she react when she encounters an obstacle to her goals and desires? Does she play by social and moral rules? Does she formulate her own moral code? Will she stop at nothing to succeed? The temperament of a character—revealed through plot events, diction, music, and spectacle—often provides a direct line of access to the thought of a playwright.

Harper, a character in Tony Kushner's *Angels in America*, presents a strong example. Harper is married to Joe, who admits to himself he is gay. This would likely be a challenging situation for many women, but Harper is a Mormon, and her church does not recognize homosexuality or condone divorce. Harper escapes her pain over the disintegration of her marriage by taking pills. Her drug-induced hallucinations free her imagination (her monologues include soaring passages that are among the most moving in the play), and she travels beyond the confines of reality to a psychic place more to her liking. Through Kushner's construction of Harper's temperament, he reveals key facets of his thought—about the nature and types of illness, the power of the imagination, and versions of the American journey.

In plays that employ imagistic, abstract structures, it may be more helpful to regard the personages in the play as figures instead of characters. In Anne Washburn's play, *The Apparition*, for example, she labels the figures, A, B, C, D, and E. Characters may be drawn with physical and social traits, but a playwright who is eschewing psychological narrative in favor of image and pattern may give little if any attention to temperamental issues or may intentionally give a single figure multiple and conflicting temperamental issues to suggest that people create themselves from a set of sometimes incoherent ideas and that they experience a range of emotions that isn't neat and tidy.

No set of criteria will work for every play or every reader. Learning about as many ways of reading as you can is the best preparation for appreciating and enjoying the variety that today's theatre has to offer.

THE WORK OF THE PLAYWRIGHT

The word *playwright* has an interesting spelling. When you hear the word, you might assume that its final syllable would read *write* because playwrights write plays. But the final syllable is *wright*. Though the ear might be tricked, the eye comes to recognize the importance of craft in the making of a dramatic text. In many important ways, the playwright is a craftsperson, much like the maker of a boat—a boatwright—is a craftsperson too.

Playwrights don't come to practice their in craft in a single way. Some go to school, earning first bachelor's degrees and later a masters of fine arts in playwriting. Others, rather than completing such a comprehensive and organized study involving seven years in higher education, take classes or workshops with practicing artists. Still others learn through observation, either while working other jobs in the theatre or just by noticing what pleases and moves them onstage or on the page. Some others train themselves by seeing the world around them and recording their thoughts and experiences in dramatic form.

The playwright's process varies just as widely as his or her training. Some begin by outlining the entire plot. Others write a single important scene and craft the other scenes around it. Still others take an image, situation, or single character as a starting point. But as playwrights move forward, they are almost sure to consider some of the ideas discussed earlier in the chapter. They will decide what kind of plot structure works for the story they want to tell and what kind of characters with what kinds of traits they want to emphasize. They will have an idea that they want to express and feelings or thoughts they want to invoke in the audience. They will also make choices about the way their characters talk and other ways that they might include music in the script. Spectacle will also figure into the script, perhaps in ostentatious ways or maybe in small naturalistic ways. Playwrights may have composed the script at the computer, written it out longhand, or even spoken words into a recorder.

After creating a draft for the script, playwrights are likely to revise. They may do this simply through a process of private reading and rewriting, but they may be lucky enough to have a way to share the new script with others. They may have the opportunity to "workshop" it in a class or with friends and colleagues. These people may read a typed script and then offer feedback, or there might be a reading of the play so that the writer and those responding can hear the dialogue. Sometimes such readings take the form of "staged readings." Staged readings—the term is loosely used— sometimes involve lightly rehearsed and directed actors reading the scripts

Photo © Michal Daniel, 2006

Writer Suzan-Lori Parks and director Michael Greif at work on a production of Parks' play, *365 DAYS/365 PLAYS*

placed on music stands. Other times staged readings feature more extensively rehearsed actors who move through blocking and stage action.

A fully mounted production is the best way for a playwright to assess the progress of the script. Some organizations around the country, such as the Actors Theatre of Louisville, are committed to producing new work and giving writers a chance to develop their plays. After such a production, and in many cases after any production of a play, writers will keep working on a script, having learned a great deal about their own writing through their interactions with directors, actors, and designers. They may also gain insight into their own work through critical reaction and public response to the play.

Sometimes writers send their scripts to a theatre directly, hoping their work will be produced in the company's season. Theatres accepting unsolicited scripts often request a brief summary of the play and an excerpt before devoting the literary staff and dramaturgical team's energies (we will discuss the dramaturg's job in more detail in Chapter 12) to a full script. Some theatres receive many hundreds of submissions each year. Many writers find it useful to gain the representation of an agent. Though they typically pay agents 10 percent of their earnings, agents have important contacts that gain their clients visibility, and agents understand contracts and the business side of producing a play. They can help match writers to theatres well suited to the style and subject of their work.

SPOTLIGHT
Playwrights on Playwriting

Contemporary playwriting features a wealth of variety in terms of voices and techniques. Here are some comments by major writers about their craft to help stimulate your thinking. If you've never heard of these writers or read their work, consider finding one of their scripts.

Adam Rapp: I tend to not write for a long period of time until I can't not write, and then I write first drafts in gallops. I won't eat. I forget to do my laundry. I have a dog now, and I have to remember to walk him. When I write, that takes over and I can't do anything else.[2]

Suzan-Lori Parks: A lot of times I don't know what I'm doing. I'm wandering through the wilderness of my imagination, so I have no road map. I have very few clues. I'm just wandering, seeing what I can find, what I can hear, what's there.[3]

Harold Pinter: The author's position is an odd one. The characters resist him; they are not easy to live with; they are impossible to define. You certainly can't dictate to them. To a certain extent, you play a never-ending game with them, cat and mouse, blind-man's bluff, hide-and-seek.[4]

Maria Irene Fornes: I never imagined that I would be a playwright. I never imagined that I would be dedicating my life to this. I started as a painter. So when I started writing, a play just came, . . . without any intention of being my future or my profession or my career. I started doing it out of some sort of inspiration that came to me. But once you have that kind of experience, you have to be crazy to give it up. And it happened almost accidentally, almost like you're walking along and then there is an electric wire and you touch it and you get almost electrocuted. And there it is.[5]

Edward Albee: I like to think that my plays will not only heal me but also possibly others, that they have enough universality, that the writing of them is not a private act. All art must be useful. If it's merely decorative, that's not enough. It must tell about our society, about realities we pretend to face.[6]

Naomi Wallace: If writers can reimagine language, with an effort that aspires to fluency in history and its myriad forces, then we can reimagine ourselves and our communities—and that, for me as a writer, is the highest aspiration.[7]

For many years, most writers saw a New York production, and more specifically a Broadway production, as the ultimate playwriting goal. When this was the case, the "out-of-town tryout" was typical. Before exposing a new play to the high demands of New York City critics and audiences, producers and playwrights would try out the script and its production in a smaller city. This provided the artistic team with an opportunity to fine-tune various aspects of story, character, and staging before opening on Broadway.

The Broadway production is not always the primary objective of contemporary playwrights. First, it is not a very realistic ambition. Very few "straight" plays—nonmusicals—play on Broadway in a given theatre season. The costs of producing on Broadway are stratospheric, so unless a play has the potential to bring in huge box office numbers (a hard task for any straight play, much less a new title from an unfamiliar writer), it is unlikely to appear on the "Great White Way." Second, productions in professional theatres around the country can be of very high qual-

Pulitzer Prize-winning playwright Nilo Cruz poses in front of the Broadway marquee for his show, *Anna in the Tropics*, on the afternoon of the show's opening.

© David Bergman/CORBIS

ity. Regional theatre artists and audiences are quite sophisticated, and a mounting in any number of theatres around the country is a high achievement. In 2003, Nilo Cruz won the Pulitzer Prize in Drama, generally considered the highest award a new American play can earn, for *Anna in the Tropics*, which played only at the New Theater in Coral Gables, Florida, prior to winning that year's top dramatic honors. It was the first time in Pulitzer history that none of the judges or the ruling board had seen a production of the play that won the prize. Only after winning the Pulitzer was *Anna* produced at the McCarter Theatre in Princeton, New Jersey, and then on Broadway.

CHAPTER SUMMARY

The playwright is the artist who crafts the dramatic text or script. Among the playwright's tools are story and how the story is structured; character—created from among an array of historical types and including some combination of physical description, social status, and temperament; thought, theme, or idea—an issue or concept that can be explored in dramatic form; words themselves in all their musical variety; and image—sometimes grand and sweeping, other times small and poignant. As we will discuss in the next chapter, which explores the dramatic genres, the work of the playwright can be analyzed further according to type of play—tragedy, comedy, musical, and more. But however we choose to break down a script, we see that the playwright creates the foundation on which other artists will build as they produce a play and a point from which we can further our study of this complex and vital art form.

ACTIVITIES

High Fashion Characters

Select an advertisement from a fashion magazine, picking a model about whom you know as little as possible. How does the image create a character for the model? Which attributes of character seem to be emphasized? Which attributes of character can you imagine to make the image more interesting?

Nursery Rhyme Plots

Take the plot of a nursery rhyme or a folk tale and rewrite it first in episodic form and then in circular form. Feel free to create your own subplots or weave together multiple tales as needed. Which version of the tale do you find most engaging? How does form affect meaning?

Eavesdropping

Go to a public place and listen to the conversations around you. Instead of focusing on what people are saying to each other, listen to how they are talking to teach other. How much variety do they have in their vocabulary? How long are their sentences? How quickly are they able to reveal their thoughts and intentions?

Now compare your observations to the speech of a character from a play you've read or seen in class. In what ways are the overheard conversations and stage dialogue similar? How are they different? Compare your findings with those of a classmate.

Genres

Tragedy is a genre or type of play. Here Hamlet (played by David Tennant) contemplates revenge upon Claudius (played by Patrick Stewart) in a production of the Shakespearean tragedy *Hamlet*.

Dramatic literature—more commonly called "plays"—can be divided into several basic genres or types. Familiarity with various genres is helpful in the interpretation of plays and performances by allowing you to generally categorize a script and, according to that categorization, refer to an associated set of guidelines or expectations. As an introduction to the concept of genre, this chapter will provide a brief history of three main genres: tragedy, comedy, and musicals. Distinguishing characteristics of these genres will be identified, as well as ways in which those characteristics have evolved over time to include the development of several subcategories. Throughout, we will discuss utilizing knowledge about the basic genres and subcategories to more aptly interpret a theatrical performance.

TRAGEDY

Today, the word "tragedy" or "tragic" is often used in popular culture to describe an event causing great sorrow or sadness. Within the context of dramatic literature, the definition of tragedy is much more specific. The dramatic form called tragedy originated at the City Dionysia in Athens. The first tragic contest was held in 534 BCE. Many of the ideas established at the form's inception continue to dominate thinking about tragedy. As discussed in the previous chapter, the ancient Greek philosopher Aristotle analyzed tragedy in detail. Hundreds of years later, during a period called the Renaissance, writings from the ancient civilizations of Greece and Rome became quite influential in European intellectual life. European critics based new, strict rules for playwriting on the writings of Aristotle. These "neoclassical rules" were articulated in the sixteenth century and would dominate playwriting and dramatic criticism for 200 years. In this chapter, the neoclassical rules are particularly relevant due to the dictate that serious and comic elements not be mixed. This demand for "purity of genre" would greatly affect the evolution of both tragedy and comedy.

You will remember that Aristotle describes tragedy as "an action that is serious and complete and of a certain magnitude." Based on this description, the neoclassicists decreed that tragedy must depict characters of high status, such as royalty, and end unhappily. Tragedy involves important people caught up in serious situations that have significant consequences for a larger community. Usually tragedies involve crises that culminate in violence or death. Most simultaneously celebrate the potential of humans and recognize the limitations—physical, psychological, social, and moral—that challenge that potential.

Aristotle suggested that a tragic hero suffers due to a tragic flaw in his or her character. He called this flaw *hammartia*. Sophocles' *Oedipus Rex*, discussed at length in Chapter 3, is arguably the best sample of Greek tragedy and the one most discussed by Aristotle. The title character is typically considered the quintessential tragic hero. Oedipus's tragic flaw is one common in Greek tragedy: *hubris*, or excessive pride. Oedipus thinks that, by leaving Corinth, he can outsmart the prophecy that he will kill his father and marry his mother. By the end of the play, he realizes that the actions he had taken years previously to avoid fulfilling the prophecy (running away from home and the people he believed to be his parents) were the very actions that brought him to the place where the prophecy would indeed come to pass. In addition to depicting a royal figure with a tragic flaw, *Oedipus Rex* fulfills the classical definition of tragedy by ending unhappily in a climax marked by violence and death: Oedipus blinds himself, and Jocasta, his wife and mother, commits suicide.

Aside from the plays of ancient Greece, some of the finest examples of tragedy were penned by William Shakespeare (1564–1616). Though he wrote at a time when the neoclassical rules were heavily affecting European playwriting, Shakespeare, writing in Elizabethan England, rarely adhered to the rules. (Indeed, his relative "freedom" from these rules greatly inspired a later movement called Romanticism.) Nonetheless, he created many masterful tragedies and is known for creating heroes dominated by

© Robbie Jack/CORBIS

Vanessa Redgrave as the title character in the Greek tragedy *Hecuba*.

tragic flaws: Macbeth's flaw is ambition, Othello's is jealousy, and Hamlet's is inaction. Many critics consider *Hamlet* (1601), described at length in Chapter 3, to be the finest tragedy ever written. Its protagonist is royal: Prince Hamlet of Denmark. Prior to the opening scene, Hamlet's father has died, and his mother, Gertrude, has married Claudius, Hamlet's uncle. In the first act of the play, Hamlet is visited by his father's ghost. The ghost asks Hamlet to "Revenge his foul and most unnatural murder" at the hand of Claudius. As the play progresses, Hamlet cannot move himself to action. In the following speech, he laments his own inability to act and compares it to a moving, theatrical scene just enacted by a traveling player:

> O, what a rogue and peasant slave am I!
> Is it not monstrous that this player here,
> But in a fiction, in a dream of passion,
> Could force his soul so to his own conceit
> That from her working all his visage wanned,
> Tears in his eyes, distraction in his aspect,
> A broken voice, and his whole function suiting
> With forms to his conceit; and all for nothing!
> For Hecuba!
> What's Hecuba to him, or he to Hecuba,
> That he should weep for her? What would he do,
> Had he the motive and the cue for passion
> That I have? He would drown the stage with tears
> And cleave the general ear with horrid speech,
> Make mad the guilty and appal the free,
> Confound the ignorant, and amaze indeed
> The very faculties of eyes and ears. Yet I,
> A dull and muddy-mettled rascal, peak,
> Like John-a-dreams, unpregnant of my cause,
> And can say nothing; no, not for a king,
> Upon whose property and most dear life
> A damn'd defeat was made. Am I a coward?

Hamlet recognizes that his flaw is inaction—and he does so in a speech thought to be among the most beautiful, moving poetry written by William Shakespeare (in addition to royal characters and unhappy endings, elevated or "lofty" language is also associated with tragedy). Aristotle particularly lauded "complex tragedies"—tragedies in which the protagonist recognizes what leads to his downfall. *Hamlet* is a complex tragedy. In the course of the play, the title character discovers his true nature.

Evolutions in the composition, structure, and ideologies of society eventually broadened the scope of tragedy: Changing economic and political conditions brought about the emergence of a middle or merchant class in Europe in the eighteenth century. Philosophers began to question the ideology that rulers governed by "divine right." Given this climate, it would seem to follow that perhaps plays, even serious ones, could focus on characters of lower political and social status. French philosopher Denis Diderot (1713–1784) began to argue for "middle genres"—plays that varied from the strict dictates of tragedy and comedy as narrowly prescribed by the neoclassicists. One of these middle or mixed genres was called bourgeois or middle-class tragedy. As the name indicates, the primary distinction of this new form is that it features middle-class protagonists. For example, *The London Merchant*, by George Lillo (1693–1739), focuses on the fall of George Barnwell, an apprentice led astray by his love for a woman and ultimately executed for his crimes.

Some scholars argue that tragedy is impossible in the contemporary era because of our beliefs about what it means to be human and what role religion plays in many people's lives today. First, the greatness of humans perceived in the classical age of Greece and in the Renaissance has been tempered today. Whether or not people attribute their common assumptions to Sigmund Freud, Charles Darwin, or Karl Marx, since the late nineteenth century, most people recognize limitations on human choice and potential imposed by psychology, biology, and class. Tragedy, as it was originally conceived, depends on a hero making a choice and taking responsibility for that choice. Today we see the ways a person's choices are constrained because of the ways a person's agency is not independent of many complicated forces beyond the individual's control. In many regards, people are not, as Joseph Wood Krutch argued in his twentieth-century essay, "The Tragic Fallacy," noble any longer. In addition, for fate and the gods, we've substituted ideas like repressed subconscious desires, evolution, and class exploitation. Playwrights continue to ask complex and difficult questions, but the philosophical and scientific backdrop against which they pose these

SPOTLIGHT

Arthur Miller, *Death of a Salesman*, and the "Tragedy of the Common Man"

Playwright Arthur Miller

© Deborah Feingold/CORBIS

Controversies about dramatic criticism and the importance of Aristotelian ideas did not end with the neoclassical age or even the development of middle-class tragedy in the eighteenth century. When Arthur Miller (1916–2005) wrote *Death of a Salesman* in 1949, he earned a Drama Critics Circle Award, the Tony Award, and the Pulitzer Prize, but he also generated intense debate with his essay, "Tragedy and the Common Man," which was published in the *New York Times*.

Death of a Salesman tells the story of Willy Loman, a family man and struggling salesman, who has unrealizable dreams for himself and his two sons. When he finally becomes overwhelmed with financial pressures and a realization of the part he played in his favorite son, Biff's, failures, he commits suicide.

Though it was hard for most contemporary critics to deny the power of Miller's script, not all felt that Willy Loman's plight qualified as tragic. He did not, after all, tumble from a high place. As his name makes clear, he is a "low man." Miller argued passionately against this reading of Lo-

queries has changed considerably. Due to these "advances," classic tragedy might be considered a dated genre. Yet plays such as *Hamlet* and *Oedipus Rex* still occupy our stages and seemingly continue to resonate with audiences today. Perhaps an element of human nature has remained unchanged in the thousands of years since tragedy was first performed in Athens.

As you read or view serious plays, place them in the context of tragedy: Are you seeing a classical tragedy unfold? Or does the playwright seem to

Willie Loman is a middle-class tragic figure in *Death of a Salesman*

man and its implicit restatement of Aristotelian values. Miller wrote, "I believe that the common man is as apt a subject for tragedy in its highest sense as kings were. . . . If the exaltation of tragic action were truly a property of the high-bred character alone, it is inconceivable that the mass of mankind should cherish tragedy above all other forms, let alone be capable of understanding it."

Miller helps to rearticulate what tragedy can mean in the contemporary era, and the situation that forced him to do so speaks to the enduring influence of Aristotle on playwriting and dramatic criticism.

be playing off the traditional tragic form with variances such as a middle- or lower-class protagonist or a liberal number of comic scenes interspersed throughout? If a serious play does not meet the expectations of a classical tragedy, is it necessarily ineffective? Or does it, instead, reflect a new course for drama? You can use your knowledge regarding evolving definitions of tragedy to help determine what a script or production has set out to accomplish—information that provides major clues as to how the playwright wishes the play to be interpreted or "read."

SPOTLIGHT
Sanskrit Drama and Genre

The plays of Sanskrit drama, an Indian form over a thousand years old, are not categorized as comedies or tragedies. Instead, Sanskrit plays aim to establish an appropriate *rasa* or fundamental mood. The eight *rasas* are erotic, comic, pathetic, furious, heroic, terrible, odious, and marvelous. A play may contain elements relating to several *rasas*, but one must dominate. Reflective of the Hindu faith on which Indian culture is grounded, the final goal of a Sanskrit play is to create a sense of harmony. For that reason, though laughter and tears may be mixed throughout the play, the conclusion must be a happy one. All Sanskrit plays have happy endings.

COMEDY

Tragedy and comedy, like the masks sometimes used to represent them, are often paired as opposites: The tragedy mask is frowning, and the comedy mask is smiling. This simplistic representation reflects the most basic difference between these genres. As with tragedy, however, the classical definition of comedy is more specific than a generalized assumption that a comedy is "a play that makes me laugh." Like tragedy, comedy dates back to ancient Greece. Early Greek comedy, called "Old Comedy," was political and satirical in nature, but with the advent of New Comedy in 336 BCE, its focus became more "domestic." New Comedy focused on the everyday lives of Greek citizens. Having read about their rules for tragedy, it should come as no surprise that the neoclassicists used this classic model of comedy to establish strict rules for the genre. They decreed that comedy must deal with "common people" (as opposed to tragedy, which dealt with the royal and powerful) and must end happily.

In general, comedy involves regular people caught up in humorous situations that affect a relatively small group of people—most often a family. Mishaps abound, but the comic world is a safe one—mortal threats are

A scene from the Shakespearean comedy *A Midsummer Night's Dream*.

© Will Burgess/Reuters/CORBIS

out of place here. Comedies tend to celebrate rebirth and renewal and traditionally ends in a dance, feast, engagement, or wedding. Like tragedies they can explore serious ideas, but they provoke laughter rather than pity and fear as they teach their lessons. As an example of a classical comedy, let's consider *The Brothers Menaechmi*, an ancient Roman comedy by Plautus. The play takes place on a street in Epidamus in front of several houses. In contrast, *Oedipus Rex* takes place in front of the palace in Thebes. Right away, the setting of *The Brothers Menaechmi* emphasizes the domestic and everyday versus the political and royal class. At the beginning of the comedy, a chorus tells us that, years ago, young identical twins were separated. One was found and raised by a man in Epidamus, who named the young man Manaechmus. The action of the play takes place in front of Manaechmus's house. Unbeknownst to Manaechmus and everyone else in town, his long-lost twin, also named Manaechmus, is coming to town in hopes of finding his brother. This situation creates numerous instances of mistaken identity—all creating the type of "low-stakes" results typical of classical comedy. In other words, there is no threat that the ensuing confusion will lead to "life or death" consequences. Instead it leads to a jealous wife, an angry courtesan, and, at the end of the play, happily reunited twins.

SPOTLIGHT

"-isms"

Like art and music, styles of dramatic literature are sometimes reflective of particular philosophical theories. You are already familiar with neoclassicism, a European movement based on the desire to revive the classical theories of the Greeks and Romans. Following are summaries of several other theatrical "-isms." We discussed some of these famous "-isms" in the previous chapter and will continue to explore others in the coming chapters.

Romanticism: Revolt against the strict rules of neoclassicism. The artist is a genius not to be forced to conform to precepts or rules set by others. Idealized feeling and instinct over rational order. In Heinrich von Kleist's *The Prince of Homburg* (1811) the main character is ultimately rewarded for making his own decisions instead of following the commands of his military superiors.

Realism: Developed in the late nineteenth century. Greatly influenced by the theories of Charles Darwin (natural selection) and Sigmund Freud (founder of psychoanalysis). The plays of Henrik Ibsen (1828–1906) helped establish realism in the theatre. He abandoned verse, did away with soliloquy and asides, and introduced such unsavory topics as venereal disease (*Ghosts*) and wives leaving their husbands (*A Doll's House*).

Naturalism: An extreme form of realism. Aimed to mirror life. Most closely associated with the work of writer Emile Zola (1840–1902). Its emphasis on reproducing an environment in complete detail (such as a production of *The Butchers* (1888) for which real beef carcasses were hung onstage) greatly influenced scene design.

Surrealism: Based on the belief that the subconscious is the highest plane of reality. Like a dream, surrealist plays mix fantastical and

Clearly, *The Brothers Menaechmi* deals with a domestic situation concerning everyday citizens and ends happily. As opposed to the situations depicted in *Oedipus Rex*, which affected the entire community by bringing blight and death to Thebes, the situations depicted in *The Brothers Menaechmi* affect only the family concerned and are not life or death in terms of consequences. Whereas the action of *Oedipus Rex* is driven by a everyday elements in ways free from everyday logic. One of the earliest representative plays, *The Breasts of Tiresias*, by Guillaume Apollinaire, was first performed in 1917. In one of the play's many surrealistic moments, a woman's breasts are turned into balloons and float away.

Expressionism: Based on belief that truth is subjective. Example from the visual arts: The famous painting *The Scream* by Edvard Munch (1863–1944). Presents reality through the eyes of the individual. Uses distorted lines, abnormal coloring, and mechanized movement. Expressionist plays such as Georg Kaiser's *From Morn to Midnight* (1917) often depict a symbolic journey undergone by the main character.

Existentialism: Opposed to the idea of a rational and ordered universe. Individuals must choose their own paths and take responsibility for their own actions. Most closely associated with philosopher and writer Jean-Paul Sartre (1905–1980). In plays such as *No Exit* (1944), Sartre explored his revolutionary ideas within the context of traditional, linear plot structure.

Absurdism: Took the existentialist belief in an irrational universe and explored it through nonlinear plots and nonsensical language. Representative playwrights are Samuel Beckett (1906–1989) (most famous for *Waiting for Godot* [1952]) and Eugene Ionesco (1909–1994). In *The Bald Soprano* (1950), Ionesco used a circular plot: The final lines of the play are a repetition of the opening lines of the play.

This is only a sampling of the immense variety of dramatic literature to be experienced. Even the most conservative theatergoers must learn to cultivate an appreciation of theatre's endless ability to question and evolve through nontraditional, avant-garde works in order to fully grasp the power of this art form.

hero with a tragic flaw, the action of *The Brothers Menaechmi* is plot driven. Tragedy emphasizes the decision making of a central character. Comedy is more likely to emphasize the situations and circumstances surrounding the characters.

There are numerous subcategories of comedy: Farce is an extreme form of comedy, often involving visual and physical humor, where authority and pretense are challenged and the ridiculous and anarchy often ensue. Disorder is celebrated in farce, at least for a moment. Stage versions of farce date back to the Middle Ages but farce also succeeds on film—from the Marx Brothers to Jim Carrey. "Slapstick" is used to describe a play that features over-the-top, even violent, physical comedy. This subcategory gets its name from a device featuring two long pieces of wood, which, when slapped again each other, make an exaggerated slapping sound.

Diderot's appeal for middle genres, which brought about middle-class tragedy, also allowed for a mixing of serious and comic elements that made new forms of comedy possible. With tragicomedy, a form that as the name suggests mixes elements of the comic and tragic, audiences have the opportunity to see aspects of the two major dramatic genres undercut each other. Tragicomedy often contains small or archetypal characters caught in situations that, although darkly humorous, are lonely and alienating. Many times they are isolated, not just from meaningful human contact, but also from any kind of value system or social structure that would make sense of the world. Writers labeled tragicomic include Anton Chekhov, Samuel Beckett, Edward Albee, and Sam Shepard. *Waiting for Godot* has been called a tragicomedy.

Whereas tragicomedy reflects the world as it is, melodrama creates a world that we might sometimes wish existed. This genre features very easily identifiable good and evil characters who generally get what they deserve. Problems aren't created by heroes; they are external to heroes and usually surmountable. The form also tends to rely heavily on spectacle. Melodrama has a distinct structure associated with it: Suspense builds throughout the play with a climactic event happening at the end of each act. Melodrama started in France, but was very popular in America in the nineteenth century. Today we can see melodrama in many varieties of film like Westerns and action-adventure blockbusters. On television, melodrama has greatly influenced daytime drama—commonly called "soap operas." Soaps feature good and evil characters and rely very heavily on suspense: How many Fridays have you watched *The Young and the Restless* and, in the final moments, witnessed an event for which you had to tune in on Monday to see the resolution?

Even serious plays such as *Hamlet* can have comic elements (consider the gravedigger scene). After Diderot's appeal for middle genres, comedy and tragedy were mixed with increasing frequency. When

Photo courtesy of the University of Kansas Theatre.

In a "Comedy of Manners," such as Noel Coward's *Hay Fever*, the conventions of social class are mocked.

watching a play with comic elements, consider whether these seem to function as "comic relief" within a play you would otherwise categorize as a tragedy or to tie directly into the classical definition of comedy or one of its subcategories. Do not base your assessment of whether or not a play is a comedy solely on the subject matter. Comedies can be written about very serious subjects (Paula Vogel won the 1998 Pulitzer Prize for *How I Learned to Drive*, a comedy dealing with pedophilia). It's how a playwright chooses to treat the subject matter that is most significant in the distinction between tragedy and comedy.

"Slapstick" features broad over-the-top physical comedy.

MUSICAL THEATRE

The musical has been called an indigenous American genre. To be indigenous is to originate from or occur naturally in a particular place. Although it is true that America is generally acknowledged as the birthplace of the musical, it would be incorrect to assume that the development of this popular genre wasn't influenced by earlier forms. To more fully understand the evolution of the musical, we will discuss opera, ballad opera, vaudeville, and revue.

The first opera was written at the end of the sixteenth century. Opera combines instrumental and vocal music with the storytelling and visual aspects of theatre. Unlike in a musical, however, music is played continuously throughout an opera, and very little or no spoken text is included. Dialogue is uniquely spoken/chanted/sung to music in a manner called recitative.

The most famous operas are by Wolfgang Amadeus Mozart (1756–1791) (*The Magic Flute, The Marriage of Figaro*), Richard Wagner (1813–1883) (*The Ring Cycle, The Flying Dutchman*), Giuseppe Verdi (1813–1901) (*La Traviata, Aida*), and Giacomo Puccini (1858–1924) (*Tosca, Madame Butterfly*). Though many of the operas that today comprise the canon of classics most revered by music lovers were written almost 100 years ago, new operas continue to be written and performed. *Nixon in China*, a work based on the 1972 visit of President Richard Nixon to China, written by American composer John Adams (1947–), was premiered by the

Houston Grand Opera in 1987. André Previn composed an opera based on the Tennessee Williams play *A Streetcar Named Desire*, which premiered at the San Francisco Opera in 1998. *The Fly*, an opera by Howard Shore, based on the 1950s and 1980s horror movies of the same name, premiered in Paris in 2008.

Opera and musical are so closely related in form that some musicals, such as *Jesus Christ Superstar*, have been called "rock operas." There is also a significant amount of plots and stories shared between the genres: The aforementioned opera based on *Streetcar* is one example, but there are many others. *Faust*, an opera by Charles Gounod (1818–1893), was based on a French play, which was based on an earlier play by Johann Wolfgang von Goethe (1749–1832). Goethe did not create the Faust story—he had, in turn, been influenced by earlier versions of the Faust legend, including Christopher Marlowe's *The Tragical History of Doctor Faustus*, which had been published in 1604. Verdi wrote several operas based on Shakespearean plays: *Macbeth*, *Falstaff*, and *Otello*. One of the most popular musicals in recent years, Jonathan Larson's *Rent* (1996), is based on the Puccini opera *La Boheme* (1896). The Tim Rice/Elton John musical *Aida*, which premiered in 1999, is based on Verdi's opera by the same name.

As previously mentioned, one of the main distinctions between traditional opera and what we now call the musical is the continuous use of music and lack of spoken dialogue in the former. The development of the ballad opera in eighteenth-century England is therefore a milestone in the history of the musical. Ballad opera parodied the traditional form of opera and, most important to this discussion, eliminated recitative or sung dialogue. Instead, ballad opera utilized spoken dialogue interspersed between songs set to melodies that were popular at the time. The first (and most famous) ballad opera was *The Beggar's Opera* by John Gay. *The Beggar's Opera* was first performed in London in 1728. It has been called the single most popular theatrical work of the eighteenth century. This popularity led to it being staged frequently in colonial America.

Vaudeville and revue, entertainments popular in late nineteenth- and early twentieth-century America, were the immediate antecedents of musical theatre. Vaudeville featured numerous unrelated and diverse acts presented as part of a single evening's entertainment. The wide variety of acts that a single bill might include—trained dogs, comedians, acrobats, dancers, a "legitimate" actor performing monologues by Shakespeare—led to the development of the phrase "variety show," which is still used today. Vaudeville was a fertile training ground for entertainers of all kinds, but particularly the dancers, singers, and actors that would be utilized in musical theatre. In addition, by providing reasonably priced entertainment suitable for the whole family, it helped to build audience demand that would eventually be met by the development of the musical. Revue was quite similar to vaudeville—with more emphasis on spectacle. The most famous revue was the *Ziegfeld Follies*, produced annually by Florenz Ziegfeld from 1907 to 1931. Part of his emphasis on spectacle focused on the glorification of the "American girl." Each revue featured a chorus of beautiful, elaborately costumed showgirls called the "Ziegfeld girls." Revues often featured original songs. The list of composers who wrote for the *Ziegfeld Follies* includes names significant to the early development of musical theatre, such as Jerome Kern and Irving Berlin.

While continuing to produce his *Follies*, in 1927 Ziegfeld produced a show critical to the evolution of musical theatre as distinct from vaudeville and revue: *Showboat*. Previous musical comedies had featured light, frothy plots (some with arguably little or no plot at all) and stereotypical characters. With *Showboat*'s premiere, the musical began to be considered a serious art form. *Showboat*, with music by Jerome Kern and lyrics and book by Oscar Hammerstein II, features a serious and cohesive story peopled by fully drawn, three-dimensional characters. Set on the Mississippi River, the musical includes both black and white characters, as well as a main character of mixed race. The show deals with topics ranging from bigotry to gambling to alcoholism. Numerous songs from the show are now classics in musical theatre: "Ol' Man River," "Can't Help Lovin' Dat Man," and "Life Upon the Wicked Stage." In contrast to the variety show approach, in which an evening's entertainment was assembled from a wide variety of acts, songs and dialogue work together throughout *Showboat* to convey depth of character development and nuance of story. *Showboat* was immensely popular and proved to producers that a musical could work in a cohesive way to present a story of weight and significance.

The integration of music and dialogue that distinguished *Showboat* as a milestone in early musical theatre culminated with the premiere of *Oklahoma!* in 1943, an event considered the beginning of "the golden age" of musicals. *Oklahoma!* was the first collaboration of a team to become synonymous

The original 1943 cast of *Oklahoma!*

A contemporary production of *Oklahoma!*

with musical theatre: Richard Rogers and Oscar Hammerstein II. They would go on to write such classics as *The King and I, South Pacific,* and *The Sound of Music.* Songs featured in *Oklahoma!* include "Oh, What a Beautiful Mornin'," "The Surrey with the Fringe on Top," "I Cain't Say No," "Kansas City," and the title song.

Each song in *Oklahoma!* has a dramatic purpose—some further the dramatic action, others illuminate the relationship between characters. Through her revolutionary choreography, Agnes de Mille made dance a vital communicative element in the show. Nowhere is this more evident than in the "dream ballet" that closes the first act: Laurey falls asleep and sees a "dream self" move through a psychologically complex and metaphoric dance with her two potential suitors, Jud and Curly. Until *Oklahoma!,* the potential of dance as indicative of plot and character development had gone unrealized.

Oklahoma! is the quintessential "book musical." A book musical is one in which the emphasis is on story. Plot and character development are given heavy focus. Book musicals often include as much spoken dialogue as sung dialogue. Book musicals dominated throughout the golden age of musicals. The 1968 premiere of *Hair* (book and lyrics by James Rado and Gerome Ragni and music by Galt MacDermot) is thought by many to have marked the end of this golden age and heralded the rise of the concept musical. Whereas a book musical emphasizes linear narrative or storytelling, a concept musical is typically organized around a central idea. The characters depicted in *Hair* are representatives of the counterculture movement of the 1960s. Songs titles include, in addition to the title song, "Aquarius," "Hashish," "Sodomy," "Easy to Be Hard," and "Good Morning, Starshine." There is little story or narrative. The glue that holds the play together is the strong sense of protest so characteristic of the 1960s.

A Chorus Line (1975), conceived and directed by Michael Bennett, is another example of a concept musical. Developed from recordings of 24 dancers discussing their careers and lives, it pays homage to career chorus members called gypsies. Gypsy is a term used to describe performers who play chorus roles in show after show. They typically go unappreciated—usually a show's star performers get all the attention—but without them the show could not go on. The setting of *A Chorus Line* is a Broadway audition

A 2008 production of *Hair* at the Public Theatre in New York.

for chorus parts. As the audition progresses, individual characters perform numbers that share humorous and moving aspects of their lives. In "Dance: Ten, Looks: Three," a young woman shares with us her reasons for getting breast enhancement surgery. "Nothing" tells the story of a performer struggling with acting classes that ask her to "be" an ice cream cone. "At the Ballet" and "Hello Twelve, Hello Thirteen, Hello Love" are ensemble numbers dealing with adolescent angst and its ramifications on later life. These numbers are juxtaposed with numbers that are actually part of the audition, such as "The Tap Combination" and "One." At the end of the musical, the show is "cast" from those that auditioned but all of those involved—even those not cast—do a production number in glittery chorus costumes.

Concept musicals such as *A Chorus Line* do not present a story in the traditional sense. The show's concept—in this case a chorus audition—provides a context or a central theme that brings the various characters together. Today, musical theatre as a genre is relatively eclectic. Both book musicals and concept musicals are written and staged. In addition to new musicals, old favorites are remounted on Broadway. This restaging is called a "revival." A revival of Rogers and Hammerstein's 1949 musical *South Pacific* at Lincoln Center dominated the 2008 Tony Awards, garnering eleven nominations and taking home seven prizes. The Antoinette Perry Awards (nicknamed the Tony Awards) are given annually to recognize excellence on Broadway. Broadway musicals and nonmusicals (also called "straight plays") are eligible for Tony Award nominations. (Incidentally, Best Musical and Best Revival of a Musical are separate Tony categories, as are Best Play and Best Revival of a Play.) Similar awards for

SPOTLIGHT
Major Names in Musical Theatre

Aside from Rogers and Hammerstein, there are other "big names" in the world of musical theatre. Following are a few with which you should be familiar.

Irving Berlin (1888–1989)—Composer and lyricist. Much of his work was done for revues. His most famous musical is *Annie Get Your Gun* (includes the song "There's No Business Like Show Business"). He also wrote "God Bless America," "White Christmas," and "Blue Skies."

The Gershwins—George (1898–1937) and Ira Gershwin (1896–1983) were songwriting brothers who teamed up for the opera *Porgy and Bess* (1935) and numerous musicals, including *Strike Up the Band* (1927), and the Pulitzer Prize–winning *Of Thee I Sing* (1931).

Cole Porter (1891-1964)—His best works are thought to be *Anything Goes* (1934) and *Kiss Me, Kate* (1948).

Lerner and Lowe—Alan Jay Lerner (1918–1986) wrote lyrics/libretto, and Frederick Lowe (1901–1988) wrote music for such Broadway classics as *Brigadoon* (1947), *My Fair Lady* (1956), and *Camelot* (1960).

Stephen Sondheim (1930–)—Mentored by Hammerstein, Sondheim's breakthrough came when he wrote lyrics for *West Side Story* (1957). He typically writes both music and lyrics, and his work includes *A Funny Thing Happened on the Way to the Forum* (1962), *Sweeney Todd* (1979), *Into the Woods* (1987), and *Assassins* (1990).

Andrew Lloyd Webber (1948–)—British composer whose musical theatre contributions include *Jesus Christ Superstar* (1970), *Evita* (1976), *Cats* (1981), and *Phantom of the Opera* (1986).

Image courtesy of the Office of College Communications, Virginia Weslyan College. Used with permission.

Students at Virginia Wesleyan College rehearse the musical *A Funny Thing Happened on the Way to the Forum.*

Off-Broadway shows are called "Obie Awards." Other areas of the country also have theatre awards, such as the Jeff Awards in Chicago, the Kevin Kline Awards in the St. Louis area, and the LA Stage Alliance Ovation Awards in Los Angeles.

When attending a musical, consider whether the piece is a book musical or a concept musical. Does the focus seem to be on linear "cause-and-effect" story progression, or does the show seem centered around a particular concept or idea? Making this distinction is crucial in the interpretation of the musical. If you expect every musical to tell a story in the traditional sense, then you will be utterly confused—perhaps even annoyed—by your first experience with a concept musical. Even if you think you prefer one type of musical over the other, you should be able to understand both. Keeping an open mind is important for audience members seeking to honestly engage with each production encountered.

CHAPTER SUMMARY

When reading or viewing plays, it is helpful to consider genre as part of the interpretive process. The genres of comedy and tragedy date back to ancient Greece. In classical terms, tragedy focuses on a noble hero with a tragic flaw and ends unhappily. As the genre evolved, tragedies began to be written about middle-class or "common man" figures. Classical comedy depicts ordinary characters in domestic conflict and ends happily. Subcategories of comedy include farce, slapstick, tragicomedy, and melodrama. The genre known as musical theatre came to full realization in twentieth-century America. In the early years, the genre was dominated by the book musical but more recently, concept musicals have become common. Familiarity with the various types of theatre and the expectations such knowledge fosters can provide valuable context against which to place a particular script or production.

ACTIVITIES

It's Sad . . . but Is It Tragic?

Select a favorite serious or sad movie or play. Compare your chosen play or movie to neoclassical rules for tragedies: Does it mix tragic and comic elements? Does it depict a royal protagonist with a tragic flaw? Does it end unhappily? Does it culminate in violence or death? Although the movie may be sad, would it be considered a tragedy in the classical sense?

Developing Musicals

Choose a partner. Together, take a story from a recent newspaper and, from it, develop a musical: First, decide whether the play will be a book or concept musical. Identify the main character or characters. Select titles for a few musical numbers. Will the score be accompanied by a small group of musicians, an onstage piano, or a large orchestra? What style or styles of music will be included? What kind of dancing will be featured? Tap? Ballet? Modern? In what location (or locations) is the musical set? On a ship? In a living room? At a high school? In a convent?

Once you have made your selections, trade newspaper stories with another pair of students in the class. Repeat the preceding exercise with their chosen story. Once you have finished, compare your team's ideas with the other team's ideas for the same story. Discuss the similarities and differences. Try to avoid the trap of judging ideas in terms of which is "better." Instead, seek to understand and identify different ways in which any particular story can be treated onstage.

Attending the Theatre

The audience is an integral element of any theatre performance.

The introduction of the audience to a production is greatly anticipated by performers, directors, stagehands, and designers. It is the culmination of a rehearsal period lasting several weeks or even months. The initial performance is called "opening night." To mark this occasion, the individuals involved in the show often give each other gifts and cards called "break a legs" (a reference to the practice of wishing actors "break a leg" instead of "good luck"). Actors typically experience a surge of energy on this occasion, sometimes called "opening night jitters." The director usually gives a special preshow speech to the actors. Some theatre artists have special customs or superstitions that they follow to ensure a good performance. These customs can range from the merely eccentric to the downright strange: For example, a director might give each actor in the play a teabag so that no one (such as a critic or audience member) will "bag" (or disparage) that actor's performance. Another director might ask all the actors to form a circle backstage and clasp pinkie fingers with each other while she says: "Twinkle, dammit." Anyone who has ever been backstage on opening night knows that it brings an energy that is palpable. This reverence and excitement for the introduction of the audience to the theatrical event is based on the certainty that without the audience, theatre is not theatre. When the audience finally arrives, the circle is complete.

As evidenced by these anecdotes, actors and other theatre artists know that audience members play an important role in the theatre event. But how does the average theatergoer view his own participation in this artistic interaction? After all, he just enters the theatre and sits there, right? What lies at the heart of his experience at the theatre? What, if anything, is within his power to control in terms of the quality of his experience with theatre? What does an audience member "do" at a play?

This chapter will detail qualities that make a good spectator and ways of enhancing these attributes. It will cover some conventions of theatrical behavior—and ways in which theatre-going is different from movie-going. We will present tips on how to view a performance in order to write a paper on the experience. Last, we will consider how "nonartistic" aspects surrounding the theatre event—such as interactions with front of house staff and other spectators and aspects of the space itself, such as the lobby—affect our experience as audience members.

KEEPING AN OPEN MIND

Throughout history, the types of plays written, produced, and deemed aesthetically pleasing have varied greatly. On today's stages, one can find a wide variety of presentations, and the savvy audience member can understand and appreciate a range of options. One play might emphasize spectacle, such as the popular Andrew Lloyd-Webber musical *Phantom of the Opera*, whereas another, such as Lorraine Hansberry's *A Raisin in the Sun*, might instead highlight character, plot, or theme. A naïve spectator with enthusiasm for pyrotechnics might assume that *Phantom of the Opera* (1988) is a more praiseworthy production due to the "eye candy" available in it, which is lacking in *Raisin*. "If only *Raisin* had a simulated chandelier crashing down into the audience and candelabra floating magically up from the floor as the main characters go on a boat ride, THEN it might be a top-of-the-line theatre experience." For individuals more knowledgeable about theatre, this is a ridiculous comparison. Hansberry's *A Raisin in the Sun* (1959) was the first play written by a black woman to be produced on Broadway. It focuses on a black fam-

Original cast members Sarah Brightman and Michael Crawford in *The Phantom of the Opera*.

ily dealing with racism and poverty while living in Chicago's Southside. Special effects such as those presented in *Phantom* would distract from characters and issues on which Hansberry wished to focus attention. On the other hand, *Phantom*, a Tony Award–winning musical, showcases the visuals of its fictive world in a truly breathtaking way. In-depth character development is simply not what *Phantom* is about. And that doesn't necessarily diminish its value as a theatre experience. Both *Raisin* and *Phantom* are worthwhile theatre endeavors. The savvy spectator knows that not all plays are out to do the same thing in the same way and welcomes the variety that makes each performance a unique experience.

Just as plays vary in terms of which dramatic elements are emphasized, they also vary in terms of style. You might remember from the previous chapter's section on theatrical "-isms" that plays are sometimes reflective of particular philosophical theories. Especially if you have limited previous experience with theatre, it is likely that the plays you have seen were realistic in style. *A Raisin in the Sun* is an example of a realistic play. The action unfolds in a very traditional, linear way: Three generations of a working-class black family living together in a cramped apartment await an insurance check that will provide them with the opportunity to change their lives. Walter Lee Younger (a recent Broadway revival of the production starred Sean "P. Diddy" Combs in this role) has plans to spend the money on a business venture: He wants to open a liquor store with some "business partners." Lena

© Bettmann/CORBIS.

Original cast members Ruby Dee, Sidney Poitier and Diana Sands in *A Raisin in the Sun.*

Younger, the matriarch of the family, decides to put the money into a new house— small but affordable because it is in an all-white subdivision. However, when the check arrives, she decides to entrust Walter Lee with a portion of the money with the stipulation that he is to put the remainder of it away for his sister's education. Walter Lee is duped out of the money— his share and his sister's—by his "business partners." Desperate to regain the financial loss, he considers taking a payoff from residents of the white subdivision in return for the family's agreement not to take up residency of their new home. In a climactic final scene, Walter Lee stands with his son and proudly tells the subdivision representative that the family intends to move into the home. In the last moments of the play, the family is seen rushing about the house on moving day. Lena makes a big deal of coming back into the house to get a scraggly potted plant that has been referred to several times throughout the play. The plant barely gets any light and is not in good shape, but she is determined to take it to the family's new home. The curtain falls as she walks out the door of the apartment with the potted plant.

Whereas some playwrights craft realistic plays like *Raisin*, others rely on our expectations of realism to thwart them in significant and creative ways: Samuel Beckett's *Waiting for Godot* forces the spectator to confront the lack of traditional, realistic action present in the play. It is a play about waiting. There is little to no "story" being told. To fully appreciate *Waiting for Godot*, an audience member must reassess the definition of action or throw out the idea that plots must be action driven or "tell a story." Why would Beckett create such a nontraditional play? The plays of Samuel Beckett are typically classified as "Theatre of the Absurd." Absurdists explore an existential belief in an irrational universe through nonlinear plots and nonsensical language. The circular structure of *Godot* and the lack of conventional "action" are intended to comment on the irrationality of the universe. These are purposeful, symbolic choices made by the playwright to align the structure of the play with a philosophy regarding the meaning of life (or lack thereof). It's not like Samuel Beckett set out to write a traditional play and failed. He purposefully created something different.

You may not have come into this class with much exposure to theatre, but most college students today are skilled at appreciating a wide range of

This production of *Waiting for Godot* was part of a Beckett Festival at New York's Lincoln Center in 1996.

© Robert Maass/CORBIS

artists in music. If you listen to popular music, chances are that you have been exposed to a wide range of musical artists. Though you may prefer hip-hop, you recognize country music when you hear it. Perhaps your iPod contains both—along with a variety of other popular genres. Just as there are many different kinds of music, there are many different kinds of plays. Being frustrated that *Waiting for Godot* isn't written in the same style as *A Raisin in the Sun* or that *A Raisin in the Sun* isn't as visually spectacular as *Phantom of the Opera* would be like getting upset that Beyoncé does not sound like Kenny Chesney. It's a waste of energy and a misunderstanding of what the artists are trying to create. You may ultimately end up with a favorite style of theatre, but this class presents an opportunity to investigate a range of theatrical art with an open mind.

TAKING PLEASURE IN SOLVING THE PUZZLE

Though knowing more about theatre will certainly enhance your viewing experience and provide a framework and terminology helpful to you in expressing feedback on the experience, the single most key element to enjoying theatre isn't grounded on any particular aspect of theatre knowledge. It may be a quality you were born with. If not, it is a quality you can cultivate.

SPOTLIGHT

Assessing Acting

Acting is usually the aspect of theatre that spectators feel most comfortable "judging." In actuality, many spectators overestimate their ability to discern nuances in an acting performance. Like a talented ice skater or basketball player, good actors make acting look effortless. If you've ever tried acting or taken an acting class, you might have been surprised by the skill required (at semester's end, "It's so much more than memorizing lines!" is often said with a certain amount of disbelief) and the amount of rehearsal time and creative choices involved in staging even a three-minute scene in a workshop setting. Here are some basics to remember as you assess an actor's work.

Keep in mind that an actor works within certain parameters given by the playwright, the director, and other theatre artists involved in the production. In most performances, the actor doesn't choose what happens in the play or create the words said (those are provided by the playwright) nor is the actor responsible for the overall production concept (this is the realm of the director) or clothing worn (the creative work of a costume designer). The actor is, however, responsible for developing—with the guidance of the director—physical and vocal choices specific to the character being played, as well as making various interpretive choices particular to that character. An example: Listen for the "line readings" of particular sentences that seem significant in the production. A line reading is how a particular actor says a given line (Which words are emphasized? Does the character seem sarcastic or sincere?), and it can significantly affect the impression of what is actually meant by the line. The playwright may have a character say, "I love you" but the actor playing the character may purposefully say the line in such a way as to create doubt in the audience's minds about the character's sincerity. We may instead think that the character is lying to manipulate the other

It requires no college degree or any particular intellectual background. It is difficult to capture this quality in a single word: It can be described as "willingness to make meaning." Audience members who take joy in "deciphering the code," who are confident in their skills of interpreting the symbols and signs of theatre, make the best and happiest audience members. Although some plays, such as *Waiting for Godot*, might seemingly make no sense at all until the audience member "cracks the code," even the simplest character and achieve an objective. Selecting line readings is a major way in which an actor affects our experience of the character.

The ability to accurately assess acting is a skill that can be cultivated. For example, from further exploration (on your own, in this course, or by taking an acting course), you can become familiar with major approaches to acting. Working from that knowledge base, you can assess acting performances in even more detail: Does the production you are watching seem to emphasize a psychological approach to acting or a physical approach? The psychological approach to acting is typically utilized by actors in realistic plays, whereas a physical approach is often more useful in nonrealistic plays. This is one of the basic distinctions in acting theory and practice, and it creates a distinguishable difference in how roles are finally staged. Does the work of the particular actor in question seem to emphasize physicality over psychology? Psychology over physicality? If so, does this emphasis seem to carry through to the work of other actors in the production? Does the approach chosen seem to be part of the production concept for the show as a whole or an interpretive choice made by the particular actor? Once acquainted with acting terms such as "objective" and "tactic," you can incorporate that knowledge into your assessment: Did the character seem to have a clear objective or goal that he or she was trying to accomplish? How did they attempt to reach that goal? What means or tactics did the actor use?

Don't fall into the trap of assessing another actor's performance solely in terms of "how I would have played it." Placing an actor's performance within the larger context of choices determined for the actor by the playwright, the director, and the designers; weighing interpretive choices attributable to the actor; and using as context a knowledge of predominant acting theories and terminology will provide a more accurate assessment and a more enlightened experience for you as an audience member.

of plays usually has interpretive layers—deeper meanings—to be mined by an audience member ready and willing to plumb its depths.

As previously stated, the action of *A Raisin in the Sun* is presented in a realistic, traditional way. Provided that audience members are awake and giving the production a reasonable amount of attention, it is unlikely that they would leave *A Raisin in the Sun* confused about the play's theme or the plot events that communicate the story. However, an audience member ready to mine the production for deeper meaning will know to give additional thought to the recurring symbol of the potted plant. Why does the plant get such focus in the play? Why does Lena seem so connected to it? Why is it important to take that scrawny plant to the new house? The plant could represent the Younger family: In this cramped apartment, they have done their best to survive. Lena has done her best to nurture them. They have fought for light and growth. The new house brings the promise of light and space and fresh air. They are, perhaps, on their way to a place where they will thrive and grow. Consider the title of the play: "A raisin in the sun" is a line from a Langston Hughes poem. Hughes is a famous black author, and the poem in question talks about dreams that are delayed or put off. The plant can be linked to this idea as well. The dreams that have struggled to stay alive in this small, overcrowded space are moving with promise and hope.

Savvy audience members don't get frustrated by having to work for the meaning. They enjoy it. They actually seek out plays that give them the opportunity to flex their interpretive muscles. It's the joy of solving a puzzle. Many college students today are highly trained in skills of interpretation in other aspects of life but don't think to use those skills in the theatre. When you think about it, with symbolism so common in music videos and films, it seems strange that many college students are confused and distanced by symbolism in the theatre. It might, perhaps, have to do with lack of familiarity with theatre or the driving expectation that meaning in plays should be evident and straightforward. Sitcoms have likely cultivated in you the expectation that the basis of dramatic conflict should be easily grasped and neatly resolved within 30 minutes (even less when you factor in commercials). Predigested meanings are highly overrated. Some of the most rewarding audience experiences are built around the audience member's ability and confidence in interpretation. Learn to enjoy and embrace being part of the theatrical event! Expect to leave the theatre discussing the play with your friends. Argue about the significance of the ending. Debate the main character's real motivation for a deadly deed in the final scene of the play. You are an active participant in the theatrical event, and your engagement is vital to its success.

THEATRE-GOING BASICS

It is likely that you have spent more time in a movie theater than in a playhouse. Your movie-going experience can assist you as you begin to attend live theatre more regularly—provided that you are skilled in the ways of a courteous, thoughtful audience member for the former. Here are some audience basics and ways that they "translate" to theatre attendance.

Which audience is watching a movie and which attending a play? On what evidence are you basing your response? What stereotypes about movie audiences and theatre audiences might these photos perpetuate?

Do not talk during a performance, even if you are talking about the performance you are watching. Talking of any kind is rude once the play has started.

Do not talk, text, or utilize your cellular phone or MP3 player in any way during a performance. Such devices should be turned off before the performance begins and placed in your pocket or purse until after the final bows. Even if the use is silent, the light emanated from the device is distracting to the performers, technicians, and audience members. In addition, an audience member engaged with an electronic device is not fully engaged with the unfolding performance. To appreciate and understand a play, or any other art form, you have to give it concentration and focus.

Do not enter the theatre after the performance has started, and once there, do not leave your seat during the performance unless it is an emergency. The seating of latecomers is distracting to performers and other audience members and should be avoided if at all possible. At the very least, wait for the house manager to assist you. He will know how to minimize the distraction as much as possible.

Make every effort to reach the theatre in ample time to find your seat and look the program over before the performance begins. Unlike at the movies, audience members at a play are provided with "programs" or guides to the performance. The program typically includes information about the play, the performers, the designers, and the technical crew. Some of this information, such as the time period in which the play is set and/or the time elapsed between scenes, can be vital to understanding the stage action. Audience members who forgo perusing the program prior to the performance do so at their own risk.

A theatre audience shows appreciation for the efforts of the actors, crew members, and other theatre craftsmen responsible for the production by

Actors Audra McDonald, Sean Combs and Phylicia Rashad at curtain call for a 2004 Broadway performance of *A Raisin in the Sun*.

applauding at the end of the performance. To facilitate this applause, a "curtain call" is staged that typically includes bows for each actor (or sometimes small groups of actors) as well as a group bow for the full company. If the playwright is in attendance, it is common for that person to stand at some point during curtain call or even join the actors onstage, particularly if this is the premiere performance of the play. When the audience is particularly appreciative of the performance, they will rise and give what is called a "standing ovation."

Appreciation may be sprinkled throughout a comedic performance in the form of laughter. Sometimes, when a comedic moment is played particularly well, it is met with spontaneous applause. However, a tragic moment played well is most appropriately met with stillness and silence from the audience. At musicals, it is common for the audience to applaud at the end of each musical number. In addition, the audience applauds as the conductor approaches the podium from which to conduct the orchestra or "pit band" (slang term for the musicians typically seated in a sunken area called the orchestra pit). If you attend a play in which a well-known actor is cast (most likely to happen on Broadway or in a large regional theatre), you will likely hear the audience applaud when the star performer first comes onstage—even before he or she says a line!

Unlike movie theatres, most playhouses do not allow food or drink in the auditorium. Check the policies of the theatre in which you are viewing the play. Upscale theatres typically have refreshments available in the lobby prior to the play and at intermission. Many college theatres sell food only at intermission and maybe not even then.

Image courtesy of the Idaho Shakespeare Festival. Used with permission.

Here are some practices specific to theatre attendance: If the lights in the lobby appear to be flashing on and off (or if you hear a "chime" or other audible signal), go find your seat in the auditorium. The play is about to begin (or to resume following intermission). If your seat number is K5 and your friend's is K7, you may still be sitting next to each other. Many times, seats on the right side of the house utilize even numbers, whereas the stage left side uses odd numbers or vice versa. If you want to know for sure, ask the box office staff member, house manager, or usher.

Audience members enjoy dinner whille attending a performance at the Idaho Shakespeare Festival.

If the play is being performed in an amphitheatre or outdoor space, some audience "rules" are a bit different than for an indoor playhouse. Often, audience members bring a picnic or buy dinners onsite and eat them during the performance. Expectations regarding audience movement are also loosened. Coming and going during the show is a bit more tolerated, though you should always be courteous to your fellow patrons and limit any behavior that could distract from activities onstage. It's a good idea to check the amphitheatre's Web site or call the box office prior to show attendance to ask about policies particular to the venue.

PARATHEATRICALS

It's pouring rain. You drive to the theatre and can't find a place to park. After driving around for ten minutes, you finally locate a parking space four blocks away. As you get out of the car, you step into a puddle. You begin to walk to the theatre, and the wind blows your umbrella inside out. On reaching the theatre, you lose your footing on the slippery marble of the entrance foyer. You head to the box office window, only to find that the tickets you had purchased and requested be held under "will call" for you to pick up on your way into the performance were mailed to you at an old address. After straightening the matter out with the box office staff, you are

SPOTLIGHT

How to Write About Theatre

Most students taking a class in theatre appreciation or introduction to the-atre are required to attend one or more plays and write a "critique" or re-sponse about the experience. Viewing plays to discuss the play in the context of a college class and, ultimately, write a paper requires skills that you might not have utilized in your previous experience as a spectator. Many students find that developing these critical skills "opens their eyes" in a positive way and forever affects how they view plays, films, and other media interactions.

There are many different ideas about how theatre could or should be viewed and assessed. Plato and Aristotle were debating dramatic the-ory and criticism back in Ancient Greece. And the debate has continued for over two thousand years. . . . Some individuals spend their lives study-ing dramatic theory and criticism. Entire college classes are built around the topic. Though you might eventually take a course solely devoted to theory and criticism, here are some basic tips to get you started as you begin to view plays with an eye toward writing about the experience.

Resist the urge to focus on whether or not you liked the play or performance. Often when we slap the label of "like" or "dislike" on an object or event, we cease to note the details necessary for an in-depth analysis. In essence, we stop processing the work at all. Most writing assignments do not ask whether or not you liked the play. Read your assignment carefully. Chances are that whether or not you en-joyed the play is irrelevant. You can hate the production and still write a compelling and articulate paper—provided you don't let your feelings distract you. As a matter of fact, depending on the assigned topic, it might be a better paper if the reader were left with no clear indication as to whether or not you enjoyed attending the play.

Read the program—and take a copy home with you! Important information is often contained in the playbill or program. The date, time, and location(s) in which they play is set is usually included, as well as any gaps in time (such as "Act II takes place a year after the action de-picted in Act I"). The list of character and actor names will come in handy if you decide to mention any by name in your paper (all names should be spelled correctly in your paper). Pay special attention to any program notes from the director, designers, or dramaturg.

Take notes during or immediately after the performance. To uti-lize adequate detail in your paper, you will need to refer to specific moments in the production. Take a small notebook or blank piece of paper with you to the theatre. Jot down notes at intermission and immediately following the production. Write down particular lines, lighting effects, costume details, and acting choices that seem significant. You might not utilize all of these in your paper, but you will have a range of specific moments to choose from as you write. Don't assume that you will be able to recall particular lines or moments in sufficient detail without making notes. Often students write the required paper days after attending the performance. You will be glad that you can refer to the notes to sharpen your articulation of the observations you want to use in your paper.

Consider viewing the assigned play more than once if time and budget allow. The second viewing will allow you to listen closely for particular lines and watch certain moments more carefully.

Work from an outline. Most paper assignments require the writer to focus on a particular thesis or argument. Your paper shouldn't simply list various things you observed as you watched the play. It should include only observations related to your argument. Every interesting thought you have about the performance doesn't belong in the same paper. Working from an outline will help you to identify what is appropriate to include and what is a digression from your purpose.

Don't watch the movie! Movies based on plays are often very different from the original source material. Unless your instructor suggests watching the film, it's best to avoid it.

Use the script only as a resource. Reading a play is no substitute for seeing the performance. Although the script will provide some familiarity with the events in the play and assistance in quoting specific lines in your paper, use scripts with caution. Many a student has optimistically submitted a paper crafted almost solely from direct quotes from the script and been sorely disappointed on receiving an unsatisfactory grade. A script is merely a blueprint for a performance. On stage, "theatre languages" (costumes, lighting, sound effects, scene design, properties, and acting choices) are utilized to bring to life a unique interpretation of the script. Those choices come together to create the "performance text" of that particular production. Differences in performance text make it possible to see ten different productions of *Hamlet* and, in effect, not see the same show twice. A production is based on a script but, ultimately, through the necessary addition of theatre languages, presents much more!

shown to your seat by a rather surly, gum-popping usher. After squeezing down the row toward an empty seat in the middle, you realize that the man seated on your left evidently has issues with bathing regularly. Apparently, he doesn't. The woman seated next to him proceeds to verbalize a running commentary regarding the clothing and behavior of every individual in nearby proximity. The curtain hasn't even gone up yet, and already, you're convinced that the performance will be a dismal failure.

The preceding paragraph illustrates the power of nontheatrical aspects of theatre attendance on our experience of the theatre event itself. These nonartistic elements, ranging from the temperature of the venue to the choice and volume of lobby music, can be called "paratheatricals" or "paraesthetics." The prefix "para-" is used to mean "beyond." Example: Paranormal means beyond the normal. Paratheatrical is used to denote elements beyond those of the artistic or aesthetic that nonetheless affect our interactions with a theatre event. Paratheatricals affect the expectations we have of the theatre event. For example: What impact could the lobby of the facility possibly have on your expectations regarding the play you are about to see? Let's consider two lobbies of contrasting styles:

Lobby #1 is a large, open space comprised of several spacious rooms linked together. The ceiling could be described as "soaring." The floor is covered with a mosaic made of marble. Your feet echo a bit as you move through the space. Several large crystal chandeliers hanging from the ceiling provide a gentle, warm light. The temperature is pleasant with no discernable drafts. No backstage noise is audible. The restroom area is rather large and contains an outer lounge area in addition to the stall area. A bathroom attendant, with tip jar nearby, is on duty.

Take a few moments to reflect on how this lobby experience might affect your expectations: Would it make you more aware of how you are dressed? Do you think there would be many other college students in the audience? Would you feel out of place? Would you, perhaps, speak more quietly and act more reserved? Do you think your fellow audience members would do the same? What kind of play would you expect to see at such a venue? How much would you expect to pay?

Lobby #2 is a small space that could most accurately be described as a hallway outside the performance space. The floor is covered in a shabby carpet with numerous worn spots. It needs vacuuming. The temperature is a bit warm until the outer door opens to let in

SPOTLIGHT
Careers in Theatre Management

House management, public relations, and box office management fall under the umbrella term "theatre management" or, more generally, "arts management." These positions blend business skills with the creative aspects of theatre. Many individuals working in this field have a major in business and a minor in theatre (or vice versa) or a specialized degree in arts management. Coursework for this degree typically includes marketing, fundraising, strategic planning, media relations, and arts and the law, in addition to general management courses such as organizational behavior and accounting.

Following completion of a degree program, individuals pursuing careers in arts management might complete an internship or fellowship with an organization such as Wolf Trap Foundation for the Performing Arts or the Kennedy Center for the Performing Arts. Information regarding these internship programs and others like them is available online. Every arts center across the country employs individuals in the field of arts management. In terms of employment after college, this line of work is perhaps the most reliable among careers in the arts and, to many individuals, immensely rewarding.

the cold outside air along with the next patrons. The space begins to feel rather cramped as additional audience members arrive. The restroom area consists of one stall and is in need of cleaning. There is no toilet paper, and the soap dispenser falls off the wall as you attempt to use it.

Would you expect to encounter more college students in the second lobby than the first? Do your fellow patrons speak louder and act less reserved? Would you expect to pay less than the play produced in the theatre with Lobby #1? Do you expect to "like" the play better?

Lobbies, ticket prices, and the attitudes of box office staff, house managers, and ushers affect our experience as spectators. Paratheatricals are an important part of the theatre experience and for some theatre professionals are the primary focus of their work. One example is a house manager. The house manager schedules and trains ushers, greets the public, deals with seating mix-ups, and seats latecomers. In case of emergency, she is the individual responsible for the evacuation of the theatre. House manager is one of several careers in the field of theatre management. Other positions emphasize aspects of theatre management such as public relations (cultivating relationships with press organizations, organizing and distributing press releases and photos, creating newsletters), audience development (working with area schools and civic groups, creating educational materials for each production), and box office management (hiring, training, and scheduling box office staff, overseeing box office computer systems). In Chapter 14, we will hear from two professionals working in arts management.

Though not a part of the play itself, paratheatricals undoubtedly affect our experience at the theatre. By acknowledging and understanding these periphery influences, we can perhaps learn to separate our responses to what happens onstage from our responses to what happens in the lobby or the parking lot. Isolating these responses can give us the ability to thoroughly appreciate a performance despite any negative experiences that might surround our attendance.

CHAPTER SUMMARY

Audience members are a vital element of theatre. Basic qualities of a good spectator include the ability to appreciate a wide range of plays and willingness to engage in the process of making meaning or "solving the puzzle." Although film attendance and play attendance have some things in common, several aspects of theatre-going are unique. Some basic tips can better prepare you for attending plays and writing papers on that experience. Nonartistic elements of the theatre event, called paraesthetics or paratheatricals, can affect audience expectations. Some theatre professionals make a living overseeing these nonartistic elements.

ACTIVITIES

Lobby Match Game

Look at the lobby photos that follow and match each to the sentences expressing expectations about the theatre event one might attend there. After you have finished, write down any additional thoughts or impulses each lobby brings to your mind. Be prepared to support your decisions. Compare your

© Dan Forer/Beateworks/CORBIS

© Stuart Westmoreland/CORBIS

Photo courtesy of Sally Shedd.

responses with a fellow student. Discuss the reasons for your pairings. Which event/lobby is most like the theatre events that you have attended? Which seems most foreign to your previous audience experience? How might you better prepare yourself for attendance in that kind of venue?

1. Most of the audience is in jeans and other casual clothes.
2. I won't be able to understand the play.
3. The ticket to this event was quite expensive.
4. A wide range of ages is represented in the audience—even small children.
5. Some audience members are wearing diamonds and fur.
6. The ticket to this event was moderately priced.
7. I expect lots of "eye candy" in terms of set pieces and special effects.
8. The ticket to this event was equivalent to the price of a movie admission.
9. I expect to see something modern and "edgy" in terms of content.

But I HATED that play!

Read the following sample writing assignments from an introduction to theatre class and discuss with a partner or small group whether or not your enjoyment level at the play (whether or not you "liked" it) would be relevant if you were required to write a paper on that particular topic. If not, what area does the question seem to focus on?

Sample A. The director chose for each actor in *Everyman* to play multiple characters (a practice called "doubling"). What are some challenges this presents for audience members? Choose an actor in the production and identify physical and vocal ways in which she or he created distinct, unique characters. Describe a few instances when it wasn't easy for you to distinguish between the characters and identify why you might have been confused.

Sample B. In the Downtown Theatre, audience seating can be arranged in many different configurations. Describe the configuration utilized for *Our Town*. Why do you think the director and designers chose this particular configuration? How did it highlight thematic elements of *Our Town*? Identify how the seating configuration affected your experience of the play.

Sample C. Choose a genre in which to place *Picnic* (such as comedy or drama). Give specific examples from the performance text of the university theatre production to defend your choice.

Performance Space

© Steve Raymer/CORBIS

Performance space can significantly impact the theatre experience. Here are audience members sitting in the "nosebleed section" in a proscenium theatre.

Theatre requires a shared space where people designated as actors come into the presence of people designated as spectators. Yet performance space is likely the most underestimated aspect of the theatre experience for audience members and performers alike. This chapter will encourage you to think about how the dynamics of the space affect your viewing experience. The main styles of theatre architecture will be identified, as well as pros and cons of each. Toward the end of the chapter, we will move outside the space itself to consider the type of building in which the performance space is found, as well as the geographical location of the building. Along the way, we will consider a few key moments in theatre history to provide context against which to place contemporary performance spaces.

THEATRE ARCHITECTURE

The basic styles of theatre architecture are proscenium, thrust, arena, outdoor amphitheatre, and black box. You may never have considered how style of architecture, particularly the location of the acting space in relation to the placement of the audience, can affect your experience with a play. Because audience members encounter the dynamics of the space before the performance even begins, impressions and impulses inspired by the architectural style can begin to shape the theatre experience long before the lights dim and the first words of the play are spoken.

PROSCENIUM

The most prevalent form of theatre architecture today is the proscenium theatre. Even though the term *proscenium* might be new to you, you have likely encountered proscenium theatres so exclusively that it is difficult for you to imagine seeing a performance in another kind of theatre. The proscenium theatre gets its name from a significant architectural detail: the proscenium arch. As you sit in the audience and look toward the stage, the proscenium arch forms a visual frame around the performance space. Indeed, the development of the proscenium arch is linked by many theatre scholars to the need for a "picture frame" around the perspective scenery of the Italian Renaissance. The advent of theatrical realism in the late nineteenth and early twentieth centuries and its continuing popularity have

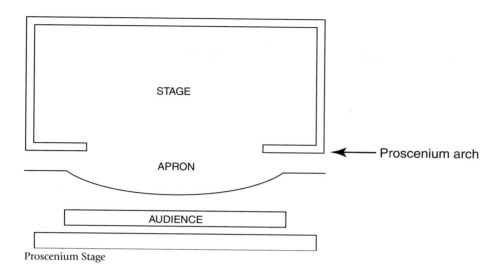

Proscenium Stage

contributed to the dominance of the proscenium stage. In historical theatres, you can find distinctive, very noticeable proscenium arches. Often
these arches are gilded and feature ornate carvings. Today, most proscenium arches are simple, black "frames." This more neutral version of the
arch gives contemporary designers a blank slate on which to create the visual elements of each individual production.

In a proscenium theatre, the audience sits in rows of seats all facing the
same direction (looking through the same "picture frame"). If the rows are
raked (meaning the rows in the back are higher than the ones in the front),
then even audience members seated in the back rows can see the stage fairly
well despite feeling a bit distanced from the action on stage. Many large
proscenium theatres have one or more balcony seating areas. Whereas seats
near the front of a balcony are often highly valued and provide audience
members with a unique and interesting vantage point of the stage, seats
near the back of a balcony can make one feel a bit too distanced (the phrase
"nosebleed section" might have been coined to speak particularly to this
experience!).

Whether seated in a balcony or on the floor, many audience members
have to sit a considerable distance from the action in a proscenium theatre due to the fact that the audience is seated on only one side of the stage.
This physical distance can be emotionally distancing as well. Some audience members experience this physical distance as a negative aspect of
proscenium theatres, but other audience members are more comfortable
feeling distanced from the onstage action. Indeed, some spectators take
great pains to select seats far enough away from the stage that they can be

The proscenium arch in these theatres ranges from ornate to plain.

SPOTLIGHT
Wagner's "Mystic Chasm"

The space between the audience and the stage in a proscenium-style theatre has significance for some theatre artists that goes beyond mere architecture. One such artist was director and composer Richard Wagner (1813–1883). Wagner wrote numerous operas, such as his famous series called *Der Ring des Nibelungen* (*The Ring Cycle*). His works include tunes you are familiar with, even if you aren't aware that they were written by Wagner (the bridal march from his opera *Lohengrin* is commonly known as "Here Comes the Bride," and his "Ride of the Valkyries" from *Die Walküre* is the tune to which Elmer Fudd sings, "Kill the Wabbit, Kill the Wabbit" in a famous Looney Tunes cartoon parody).

In addition to his work as a composer, Wagner's performance theories have had a significant impact on theatre. His *Festspielhaus*, or Festival Theatre, which opened in 1876 in Bayreuth, Germany, was revolutionary for its time. In addition to changes in audience seating, which prompted the innovation of a uniform ticket price (as opposed to a tiered seating scenario with a range of prices), Wagner's theatre hid the orchestra pit from view by extending much of it beneath the apron of the stage. This change created a "mystic chasm" or gulf between the world of the audience and the onstage world. This actual distance became an aesthetic distance, which is to say that it began to have artistic meaning. Wagner also began the practice of darkening the auditorium during performances, an innovation that further distinguished the fictive world of the stage from the "real world" of the audience.

Wagner's Festival Theatre

© Vo Trung Dung/CORBIS SYGMA

unconcerned with actors who might leave the stage in search of audience interaction and, perhaps, bring audience members onstage.

Proscenium theatres can utilize a wide range of scenic capabilities. Because audience seating is confined to one side, the other sides can conceal mechanics necessary for a great number of theatre illusions. Large scenic pieces can be utilized. If the theatre has a "fly loft" (and many proscenium theatres do), then these large scenic pieces can be "flown" up and completely out of audience sight when not needed. The front curtain can be lowered so that scenic changes are hidden from the view of audience members. Of the different styles of theatre architecture, proscenium-style stages have maximum potential to hide the mechanical aspects of theatre. As a result, spectators can be dazzled by special effects such as the famous chandelier-crashing moment in Broadway's *Phantom of the Opera*.

THRUST

The thrust stage gets its name from the positioning of the acting space in relation to the audience space: the former juts out into the latter. Because the playing space projects into the viewing space in this way, spectators surround the action on three sides. Today's thrust stage can be linked to the stages of ancient Greece, medieval Europe, and Elizabethan England. Theatres in ancient Greece, outdoor structures with audience seating typically built into hillsides, included a circular area at the foot of the hill in which,

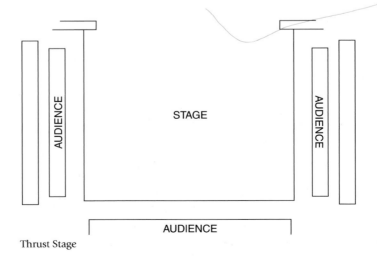

Thrust Stage

The Oregon Shakespeare Festival's Elizabethan Theatre is a replica of an Elizabethan theatre complete with a thrust stage.

Image © T. Charles Erickson, courtesy of the Oregon Shakespeare Festival. Used by permission of the photographer.

it is believed, the chorus performed. This circular area, located in front of a building called a *skene*, was surrounded by audience seating. In medieval Europe, actors sometimes performed outdoors in front of wagons containing necessary props and costumes with audience members surrounding the playing space on three sides. In Elizabethan England, public theatres were open-air structures with actors performing in front of a "tiring house" (similar to the positioning of the Greek *skene* and the medieval pageant wagon) on a platform stage extending into the audience space. Once again, audience members surrounded the action on three sides.

As we discussed earlier, proscenium theatres, because they position all audience members on one side, sometimes place audience members at a considerable distance from the acting space. As a result, some directors and companies have consciously chosen to build thrust stages in an effort to place audience members in closer proximity to the actors. Contemporary theatres with thrust stages include the Vivian Beaumont Theatre at Lincoln Center, the Guthrie Theatre in Minneapolis, and the Mark Taper Forum in Los Angeles. Another reason to build contemporary stages in the thrust configuration is the effort to replicate theatres of the Elizabethan period. The Festival Theatre, home of the Stratford Shakespeare Festival in Ontario, Canada; the Elizabethan Theatre at Oregon Shakespeare Festival in

SPOTLIGHT

World Theatre Spaces

Although this chapter focuses on performance spaces found in the United States, it is worthwhile to note that in other cultures different types of performance spaces are sometimes utilized. Here are some examples.

The *Natyasastra* (The Art of Theatre), dating from the second century CE, chronicles the practices of Indian Sanskrit drama. It details a rectangular theatre of 96 feet long by 48 feet wide and divided into two

This interior view of a Kabuki Theatre dates back to the mid-eighteenth century. On the left, an actor can be seen making his way towards the stage on the *hanamichi*.

Ashland; and the new Globe Theatre, opened in London in 1997, are examples of contemporary thrust stages falling into this category.

A benefit to the thrust stage is that it accommodates both the desire for closer actor/spectator proximity and the utilization of large scenic devices. The upstage wall (related to the historical *skene*, pageant wagon, or tiring house) can still feature a "fly loft" or, even if it doesn't, allows for equal parts: auditorium and stage. The auditorium had four pillars (white, red, yellow, and blue) thought to symbolize the four castes (rigid class divisions in Hindu society) as well as geographical regions and compass points.

Noh is a traditional Japanese theatre form dating back to the late fourteenth century and still performed today. Standardized since about 1615, the Noh stage consists of two principal areas: the *butai* and the *hashigakari*. The *butai* is an 18-foot × 18-foot acting area. The *hashigakari* is a bridge, usually about 20 feet long, that leads from the actor's dressing room, called the *gakuya*, to the stage. The audience sits on two sides of the stage: directly in front of the *butai* and on the side in front of the *hashigakari*. Both the *butai* and the *hashigakari* are roofed. The stage roof is supported by four columns—each with its own name and significance. Noh theatres today usually seat 300 to 500 people.

Kabuki, also a Japanese theatre form, is usually traced back to 1603 and was originally performed on temporary stages modeled on the Noh stage. By the mid-eighteenth century, it would develop one of its most distinctive features: a raised narrow platform, called the *hanamichi*, connecting the stage with a small room at the rear of the audience seating area. Actors often make entrances and exits—and even perform short scenes—on the *hanamichi*. This feature was so popular that a second *hanamichi* was added by the 1770s. Eventually, Kabuki would abandon the roofed stage of Noh and extend the stage the full length of the auditorium. Spectators sat on mats in front of the stage between the two *hanamichi*. In the twentieth century, use of a proscenium arch became standard and the second *hanamichi* was eliminated (although it is sometimes installed when required for a particular play).

the use of drops or flats without jeopardizing audience views of the stage. Of course, large scenic pieces or drops cannot be utilized on the portion of the stage extending into the audience without affecting sightlines. Stage curtains, typical of a proscenium theatre, are not utilized in a thrust setting unless masking only the upstage area. Therefore, scene changes are made in full view of the audience.

ARENA

If you have been to a professional sporting event, you are likely familiar with arena staging. In an arena theatre (also called theatre-in-the-round), the stage is in the middle of the space with the audience completely surrounding the action. One of the most famous arena theatre companies, Arena Stage, in Washington, D.C., takes its name from its history of utilizing performance spaces in this style.

Arena spaces can be challenging for many different kinds of theatre artists: Difficulty in blocking is one of the drawbacks of the arena stage. When creating stage movements, directors must limit each actor's time in any one position to avoid obscuring any particular audience member's view for an extended period of time. The director must also avoid extended periods of time in which any given audience member views only an actor's back. Scenery options are limited when staging a play in an arena space. Stage designers cannot utilize tall pieces of scenery. Curtains cannot be utilized to mask offstage areas.

One of the assets of arena-style performance space is that, on average, audience members sit much closer to the action than in a proscenium theatre. Greater intimacy with the actors makes the theatre experience more "personal," yet having audience members surround the action, and therefore in full sight of each other at all times, makes the theatre experience,

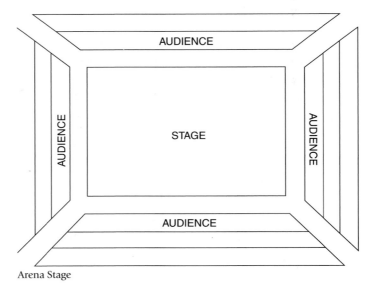

Arena Stage

Image courtesy of the Idaho Shakespeare Festival. Used with permission.

The amphitheatre in which the Idaho Shakespeare Festival performs is nestled in the beautiful mountains surrounding Boise.

ironically, more "public." The balance of public and personal can be quite engaging. For these reasons, some theatre artists are devoted to arena staging. They find that the benefits outweigh the drawbacks.

OUTDOOR AMPHITHEATRE

Another type of performance space, also closely related to the sports arena, is the outdoor amphitheatre. Ancient Greeks staged theatre performances in outdoor amphitheatres, utilizing hillsides to create a raked audience seating area. The outdoor amphitheatre remains in use today. Examples range from the ancient Greek theatre at Epidaurus (where productions are still staged) to the Delacorte Theatre in New York's Central Park. The Idaho Shakespeare Festival presents numerous productions each summer in an outdoor amphitheatre in Boise. Audience members bring a picnic (and a jacket!), come early to socialize, and enjoy an evening with the bard under the stars.

BLACK BOX

Many performance facilities include a space called a "black box" theatre. Usually this space is a one-level square-shaped room with a black floor, black walls, black ceiling, and black drapes. Whereas audience seating in arena or proscenium spaces is usually built into the space—meaning chairs are bolted to the floor in rows that are fixed—audience seating in a true black box theatre is flexible. Any risers utilized are moveable. Chairs are not bolted down. A lighting grid covers the ceiling of the space so that light can be focused anywhere needed in the room. The intention is to create a blank slate on which the designers, director, and other theatre artists can have full freedom to create a customized theatre experience unique to each particular production. A black box theatre has no permanent architectural features and is usually much smaller than the proscenium theatre housed in the same performance facility. Though a black box theatre is less ornate than many proscenium houses, its utilitarian looks enhance its potential for a unique viewing experience. Performances in black box theatres are typically more innovative and experimental than those given in larger more traditional spaces. One might think that, due to the wide range of staging possibilities inherent to the black box theatre, it would be the most common type of performance space. It is ironic, then, that the most common style of theatre is a proscenium theatre, and black box theatres are almost solely found in performance facilities with multiple spaces. In short, facilities with only one performance space tend to house a proscenium theatre.

FOUND SPACE

Theatre can also be performed in "found spaces." This phrase indicates that the performance space was originally constructed to serve another purpose. Performing in found spaces has a long history: In seventeenth-century France, it was common for plays to be performed in converted indoor tennis courts. Some theatre scholars believe that the architecture of Elizabethan theatres such as the Globe was influenced by theatrical performances given in inn yards before the advent of buildings dedicated solely to theatrical performance. In the 1960s, an interest in found space as a performance venue was revived with the "environmental theatre" concept popularized by Richard Schechner. Although some groups perform in found spaces out of necessity or happenstance, Schechner viewed the use of found space as part of a concerted effort to break down what he considered to be

Arena

Image © by David Cooper, courtesy of the Oregon Shakespeare Festival. Used by permission of the photographer.

Thrust

Image by Jenny Graham. Courtesy of Oregon Shakespeare Festival. Used by permission.

Alley

Image by Jenny Graham. Courtesy of Oregon Shakespeare Festival. Used by permission.

The New Theatre at Oregon Shakespeare Festival is a black box theatre. Here we see it in different seating configurations.

An audience watches an opera performance in the ruins of a Swedish church destroyed in 1525.

an artificial division between performer and audience. In 1968, Schechner founded The Performance Group. The group performed in a converted garage with various added towers and platforms utilized by both performers and audience members.

CUSTOM CONFIGURATIONS

One of the major assets of a black box theatre is its potential as a "shape-shifter." As we mentioned earlier, a black box typically has moveable audience seating and a metal grid on the ceiling so that lighting instruments can be focused in various directions. It can be configured as an arena space, a thrust space, or a proscenium space. Other alternate staging possibilities for a black box theatre include alley staging (dividing audience seating into two sections facing each other and separated by a long, narrow space for performers), corner staging (placing the performers in a corner of the space with seating for audience members fanned out accordingly), and end staging (placing the performers at one end of the room).

Photo courtesy of the University of Kansas Theatre.

Architecturally, the Crafton-Preyer at the University of Kansas is a proscenium theatre seating 1,188.

Photo courtesy of the University of Kansas Theatre.

In its Stage Too! configuration, instead of utilizing the theatre's permanent seating, audience members are seated in risers placed on the stage alongside the set—such as for the world premiere of *The Girl, the Grouch and the Goat: A Modern Fable* in 2008.

However, potential for adaptability isn't solely limited to the black box. Despite its permanent architectural features, almost any performance space can be adapted into a different style. Even theatres with traditional (non-moveable) audience seating can be creatively reenvisioned. For example, one way to bring actors closer to the audience in a proscenium-style theatre is to utilize a thrust. In this scenario, a section of stage that goes beyond the proscenium arch and reaches further (or "thrusts") into the auditorium space is created. Thrusts are sometimes built over the orchestra pit or over the first few rows of seats (leaving the seats in question unusable by audience members for that particular production).

Sometimes a creative configuration solves a recurring architectural need without the expense of building a new facility. For example, Murphy Hall, at the University of Kansas, houses numerous performance spaces utilized by KU's University Theatre. The largest space, the Crafton-Preyer Theatre, is a traditional proscenium theatre originally seating 1,188. The black box theatre, called the Inge Theatre, seats about 85 (depending on its configuration). Several years ago, the University Theatre recognized a need for a medium-sized performance space. With innovative thinking, the dilemma was solved by creating a new performance area utilizing the stage space of the Crafton-Preyor Theatre. The audience was placed onstage with the actors. The new space, called Stage Too!, seats about 250 to 300 people using a moveable seating system that is stored away when the Crafton-Preyer Theatre "regular" auditorium is being utilized. Without building a new facility, Stage Too! adds the option of a medium-sized performance venue to Murphy Hall.

The configuration of the performance space is often chosen to enhance the content of the particular play or to suit the needs of the performance group. For example, David Mamet's play, *Oleanna*, deals with the alleged sexual harassment of a female student by a male faculty member. The play, featuring a cast of only two characters—the professor and the student, is set in the faculty member's office. For a production of *Oleanna* at Virginia Wesleyan College in 2001, the small, black box theatre was configured into an arena-type space seating about 40 audience members. Most of the audience were either faculty, staff, or students. Sitting in that very small space, surrounded by individuals engaged in the same basic daily activities as the characters depicted in the play, watching them watch the action of the play, watching them watching you, was meant to heighten the conflict of the situations depicted onstage. In this case, the choice of space was directly connected to desired audience outcome. The production would have played quite differently in a 300-seat proscenium space.

Sometimes, however, the choice of configuration is determined by practical needs. If a space is being used for several different kinds of performance within a relatively short span of time, it may have to remain in the configuration most suitable for all performances. To change the audience seating, risers and chairs have to be moved. To alter the direction of the lighting instruments, technical staff must have sufficient time to refocus the lighting plot. So, although the choice of configuration can be related to the artistic intent, sometimes it is a matter of production schedule.

Whether architectural feature or custom configuration, the interior attributes of the performance space can significantly affect audience interaction with a play. When entering a performance space, take time to note what appear to be permanent architectural features as well as configurations seemingly created for the particular production you will be viewing. How do the permanent features of the space affect your experience as a viewer? If the space has been adapted into a configuration created specifically for the show at hand, try to imagine what the theatre artists associated with the production hoped to communicate with that choice. How does performance space—via permanent architectural features as well as particular choices in terms of configuration for that show—affect your experience of the production? Does your opinion change as the show progresses?

WHERE IS THE PERFORMANCE SPACE?

Now that you have given thought to the permanent architecture features of the interior of the theatre as well as ways in which it might be customized to suit a particular production, consider the building in which the performance space is housed: Some theatres are isolated spaces with one auditorium housed in a single structure. Others are multiuse facilities with several venues clustered together. Many performance facilities, particularly those on college campuses, are found within a larger complex called a fine arts center or a performing arts center. These centers usually contain multiple performance spaces to meet the needs of a variety of theatre, music, and visual art events. Spaces contained within an arts center typically include a large proscenium space, a black box or studio theatre, and a recital or concert hall.

The Krannert Center for the Performing Arts is a premiere example of an arts center. Located on the campus of the University of Illinois at Urbana-Champaign, this facility contains four indoor theatres, including the Foellinger Great Hall, a concert hall known for its acoustics. It seats over two thousand people. The Tryon Festival Theater seats about half as many people and is used for operas, plays, musicals, dance companies, and

SPOTLIGHT

Architect Edward D. Stone

Architect Edward D. Stone (1902–1978) is most known for his designs of the Museum of Modern Art in New York City and the Kennedy Center for the Performing Arts in Washington, D.C.

In 1958, Stone was chosen to design what was then called the National Cultural Center, a multitheatre complex hoped to become the heart of America's performing arts scene. Stone developed several

Aerial view of the Kennedy Center for the Performing Arts

© Charles E. Rotkin/CORBIS

concerts by soloists and small ensembles. Colwell Playhouse seats just under seven hundred people and serves as the main stage for college theatre productions as well as hosting some touring companies. The Studio Theatre is a small, flexible black box space that, depending on how the seating is configured, can seat up to 200 people. In addition to these indoor spaces, the Krannert Center also includes an outdoor amphitheatre.

ideas for the design, including one sketched in 1961 on which he placed a high pointed rotunda on a rather rounded complex with two points sticking out from the sides and labeled: "soup tureen with handles," before settling on a rather elaborate, many-sided pavilion with several auditoriums and a design that implied that it would be best approached from the river. Two fountains, illuminated at night, would spout from the river in front of the terrace. Stone, however, was sent "back to the drawing board" to create a more cost-effective design. His new design for the building put the three major performance spaces—the opera house, the concert hall, and the playhouse—side-by-side in a rectangular building. In this form, the John F. Kennedy Center for the Performing Arts opened to the public in 1971. In addition to housing many other theatre and arts events, each spring the Kennedy Center hosts the culmination of the Kennedy Center American College Theatre Festival, a theatre program involving thousands of students from over 600 academic institutions across the country.

Prior to designing the Kennedy Center, Stone designed the Fine Arts Center at his alma mater, the University of Arkansas. Opened to the public in 1951, his design reflected what was then an innovative approach to arts education by housing training facilities for multiple artistic disciplines under one roof. Dr. Lewis Webster Jones, university president at the time of the opening, described the facility as: "A workshop, a place where painting, sculpture, architecture, drama, music, and dance live and grow, and from which their civilizing influence spreads into our daily lives." Still in use today, the facility includes a proscenium theatre, a concert hall, an exhibition gallery, a library, a three-story classroom block, and offices and studios for arts faculty.

Arts centers usually house not only multiple performance spaces but spaces for supporting activities as well. Due to complex and full production schedules, rehearsals can't always take place in the performance space itself and are often held in large rooms or halls (to accommodate stage movements that will be usable in the performance space, these rooms have to be as large as the stage on which the play will be performed). Arts centers

typically contain technical theatre spaces to accommodate scenery, properties, and costume construction and storage; lighting and sound booths and
storage areas; dressing rooms; one or more "green room" spaces (the name
for the area in which actors wait to go onstage); box office and management space; reception and meeting rooms; lobby, bathroom, and refresh-
ment facilities for spectators; and offices for technical personnel. When
located on a college campus, an arts center is typically a teaching facility as
well and contains classrooms and faculty offices.

WHERE CAN *YOU* SEE THEATRE?

Theatre is assumed by many to be most often associated with New York
City—specifically with a particular area in Manhattan called "Broadway."
Today, although the New York theatre scene remains vibrant and significant, professional and nonprofessional theatres can be found across the
United States. Many theatre workers—such as directors, actors, designers,
and support personnel among others—make a living in theatre without
living in New York. This decentralization of theatre, which can be linked to
the concentrated efforts of several individuals in the past century, also
makes regular theatre attendance possible for individuals who live outside
the confines of Manhattan. Regional theatres, educational theatres, and
community theatres coast to coast position theatre as a popular art form to
be produced and enjoyed by people of all backgrounds in diverse geographical locations.

The branches of non-professional theatre with which you are likely
most familiar are educational theatre and community theatre. Assignments
for your introduction to theatre course probably include attendance at a
college or university production. Community theatres are found in many
towns and cities and provide amateurs with opportunities to perform outside an educational setting. Community theatres sometimes have the
phrase "little theatre" in their title, such as Little Theatre of Norfolk (located in Norfolk, Virginia, population 234,403) and Foothills Little Theatre
(located in Ozark, Arkansas, population 3,525). The term "Little Theatre"
can be traced back to a little theatre movement early in the twentieth century to found amateur theatre groups in the United States in response to a
movement of independent theatres in Europe. Around the same time,
drama programs in colleges and universities began to be introduced. In
1914, the Carnegie Institute of Technology (now Carnegie Mellon University) became the nation's first degree-granting theatre program.

SPOTLIGHT
Theatre in New York

New York does indeed have a vital theatre scene, but not all of its theatres are Broadway theatres. For the most part, commercial New York theatre can be divided into three basic categories. Though originally the categories were based on the location of the theatres, today the designations are based on audience seating capacity.

Broadway—Seats 500 or more people. Not all Broadway theatres are located on Broadway (or even in the "theatre district"). Example: The Vivian Beaumont Theatre at Lincoln Center is located "uptown" at West 65th Street and classified as a Broadway theatre.

Off-Broadway—Seats 100 to 499 people. Some Off-Broadway theatres are located on Broadway. Example: The Little Shubert Theatre.

Off-Off-Broadway—Seats less than 100 people.

Don't be fooled into thinking that shows produced in Off-Broadway and Off-Off-Broadway theatres are inferior to Broadway shows. As producing plays in Broadway theatre became increasingly costly, Off-Broadway was created as a more cost-effective venue. As Off-Broadway became too costly, Off-Off-Broadway came into being to fill the cost gap. Off-Broadway and Off-Off-Broadway have lower ticket prices and are more likely to house experimental works by new playwrights. Some plays open Off-Broadway and, once they prove themselves as moneymakers, move to Broadway to continue their run. Example: *Avenue Q*, the popular musical featuring Sesame Street-like puppets singing such songs as "The Internet is for Porn" and "It Sucks to Be Me," opened Off-Broadway in 2003, moved to Broadway later that year, and is still running on Broadway today.

In 1935, during the Great Depression, the Federal Theatre Project, part of the Works Progress Administration (WPA) was created to combat unemployment. At one point the project, headed by Hallie Flanagan (1890–1969), employed 10,000 people in 40 states. Many of the productions mounted by the Federal Theatre Project were free to audience members. Flanagan fervently believed that theatre belonged to all—not just to the wealthy and famous: "The ten thousand anonymous men and women—the et ceteras and the and-so-forths, the somebodies who believed it—their

SPOTLIGHT

Margo Jones and the Regional Theatre Movement

Margo Jones was born in 1911 in Livingston, Texas. She attended the Girls' Industrial College of Texas (now Texas Woman's University), where she was a member of the Dramatic Club (the college did not have a drama department). She founded the Houston Community Players and, in 1939, was the only woman to be named one of the twelve

Margo Jones with playwright Tennessee Williams

© John Springer Collection/CORBIS

dreams and deeds were not the end. They were the beginning of a people's theatre in a country whose greatest plays are still to come."

The regional theatre movement surged in post–World War II America due to the efforts of three women who ultimately had such impact on the face of professional theatre in the United States that they were called "The Matriarchs of the American Regional Theatre." These women were Margo Jones, Nina Vance, and Zelda Fichandler (her Arena Stage was mentioned outstanding little theatre directors outside New York City. When World War II began, Jones began teaching at the University of Texas at Austin. In her biography of Jones, Helen Sheehy noted that Jones was known for an unusual grading system: Students in her class either received an A or an F. When the dean attempted to explain the different levels of grading, Jones reportedly said: "Oh no, oh no, darling, you either belong in the theatre or you don't." In 1944, Jones codirected the premiere production of Tennessee Williams' *The Glass Menagerie* on Broadway. She returned to Texas to become the managing director of the first nonprofit professional resident repertory theatre in America, located in Dallas. In her book, *Theatre-in-the-Round*, Jones stated: "My dream for the future is a theatre which is a part of everybody's life, just as the railroad and the airplane are, a theatre in every town providing entertainment for the audience and a decent livelihood along with high artistic ideals for the theatre worker. This is the goal toward which we must now strive, for which all of us who love the theatre must give our energy." Jones died in 1955. In *Regional Theatre: The Revolutionary Stage*, Joseph Wesley Zeigler distinguishes between fact and legend of her untimely demise: "It is known that she had a habit of reading new plays while sitting on the floor in her home. The rug had recently been cleaned with a toxic fluid; apparently Margo fell asleep while reading, inhaled the poisonous fumes, and died. While true, this story is also the stuff of which legends are made: the woman sat on the floor and read and read (fact) and was so consumed by her dedication to new plays (legend)." In recognition of her interest in the development of new plays, today the Margo Jones Award is given annually to the person or theatre in America most dedicated to producing new works.

previously in this chapter). The regional theatre movement exploded in the 1960s with a series of theatres being founded across the country. Award-winning regional theatres in existence today range from coast to coast and include Actors Theatre of Louisville (Kentucky), Intiman Theatre (Seattle, Washington), Goodman Theatre (Chicago, Illinois), and Hartford Stage Company (Connecticut). All of these theatres are members of the League of Resident Theatres (LORT). LORT is a professional theatre association with

Theatre in Colonial America

The first theatre in colonial America was built in Williamsburg, Virginia, in 1716. Williamsburg was the seat of colonial government at the time, and the theatre was built on the green of the colonial governor's dwelling. The theatre was used for amateur performances by community members, as well as by students from the College of William and Mary. In 1745, this building became a courthouse. In 1751, a second theatre was built just outside the city limits. This theatre was refurbished by actor–manager Lewis Hallam in 1752. Due to debts owed by members of his company, Hallam lost ownership of the building, and it was converted into a dwelling house. In 1760, the Hallam company, now managed by David Douglass after the death of Lewis Hallam, decided to return to Williamsburg and build a new theatre. The company performed in this theatre, located very near the capitol building, off and on into the early 1770s.

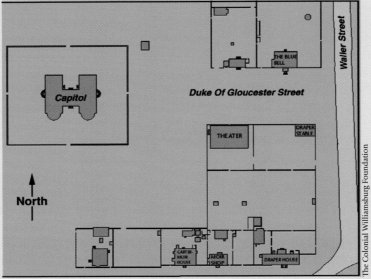

Diagram of Colonial Williamsburg showing the proximity of the third Colonial theatre to the Capitol building.

Theatre in colonial Williamsburg was a place to socialize and make business connections. Both Thomas Jefferson and George Washington attended plays at this "third" Williamsburg theatre. In October 1770, Jefferson attended the theatre nearly every day, noting occasionally in his records: "Pd. For punch at play house 7½ d." In the late 1990s, the Colonial Williamsburg Foundation began an excavation of the site of the third theatre, now called the Douglass Theatre. According to Lisa Fischer, project archeologist: "Being built next to the seat of government would have been a prominent location as compared to northern playhouses, which were often relegated to properties outside city limits."

Though theatres were built and thrived in colonial Virginia, it should not be assumed that theatre was a welcome part of the social fabric of all American colonies. On the contrary, Virginia and Maryland were the

The Colonial Williamsburg Foundation

This 2001 photo shows the excavation of a large pit dug into the ground during the construction of the Douglass Theater in Colonial Williamsburg to accomodate the lower audience seating area. The rectangular feature filled with dark soil and brick rubble visible in the foreground is the remnants of the wall that supported the front of the stage.

only two colonies that never had laws prohibiting theatrical activities. Because it was the Puritans who shut down the theatres in England in 1642, it should come as no surprise to discover that numerous American colonists did not welcome theatres and/or actors in their midst. The first theatre in Boston would not be built until 1794. However, much earlier in Virginia, theatres were located near seats of government, were attended by men of social and political standing, and were buildings of considerable size: According to Fischer, "The Douglass Theatre was one of the largest buildings in Colonial Williamsburg at the time."

over 70 member theatres located across the country. In addition to other stipulations, LORT theatres must be incorporated as nonprofit organizations.

The location of theatres within your state, town or city, and college or university campus has greater significance than might first appear: How far you have to go to see theatre and where those theatres are located can be considered reflections of the significance and importance (or lack thereof) awarded to theatre within a culture. Consider this: In ancient Greece, theatre had both civic and religious importance. The Theatre of Dionysus, in Athens, was built into the hillside of the Acropolis—the summit of the city—near other sites with civic and religious significance such as the Parthenon. In Elizabethan England, public theatres and the sites of other unsavory activities, such as gaming and prostitution, were located outside the city limits, across the Thames River. Throughout history, the location of the performance space has often been indicative of theatre's position within a particular culture.

In what area of your city or town are performance venues found? On a college or university campus? Near an urban or downtown center? In a recently built suburban neighborhood? How might the location of these facilities echo the positioning of theatre and other arts in the cultural and social landscape of your city or town?

CHAPTER SUMMARY

Theatre architecture can be broken down into several basic styles: proscenium, thrust, arena, outdoor amphitheatre, black box, and found space. Regardless of its architectural style, the use of custom configurations can adapt a performance space in endless ways. Sometimes these configurations are based on necessity, and sometimes they are chosen specifically to amplify the message or theme of the play being presented. In addition to considering the interior of the performance space, audience members should note the structure in which the performance space is housed, the location of that structure within the city or town, and the location of the city or town within the context of the country's vast network of theatres. Whether purposeful or happenstance, aspects of the performance space—both interior and exterior—affect the theatre experience. Learning to "read" these factors can greatly enhance an audience member's ability to fully process a performance and the context in which it is staged.

ACTIVITIES

Focus on the Journey and Not the Destination

Where are theatre events held in your city or town? (If you are uncertain, look in the local newspaper or do an online search. If you cannot find any in your town, then search in larger nearby towns and cities.) Do you think that the space is located near its intended audience base? What is the theatre building placed next to? Homeless shelter? Government buildings? Both? How do you get there? Subway? Car? Walk? Find a partner and discuss how these factors might affect audience members. Do you think that your journey to the performance venue affected your last theatre-going experience?

Aesthetics or Practicalities?

In a small group, discuss the following: Choose a play (such as one you have seen or read for this class) and identify pros and cons of staging the play in a large (more than 500 seats) proscenium theatre. Then, identify pros and cons of staging the show in a very intimate (less than 40 seats) thrust or arena theatre. In either extreme, can you imagine ways in which the performance space begins to make an artistic statement on the production? In addition to the aesthetics of space, can you imagine practical reasons that might influence the choice of venue?

The most visible theatre artist is the actor. Although you might have a difficult time providing the names of a handful of directors, playwrights, or designers, the names of numerous professional actors are probably on the tip of your tongue. It is likely that you yourself have acted in a school or community play or, at the very least, know someone who has. Because schools and communities don't typically pay actors, you were an "amateur" actor—though you might have aspirations to one day be a professional. The word "amateur" is derived from the Latin word *amare*, meaning "to love." An amateur does something for the love of doing it—as opposed to doing it for monetary compensation. Today, "amateur" is typically used in opposition to the word "professional." To be a professional at a sport or art usually indicates a certain level of prowess and training and means that the individual is paid to perform or play. It is expected that to be deemed a professional, one should earn their living via that sport or performance. Thus, an amateur is a nonprofessional, and although the word is sometimes used as an insult, it does not necessarily denote that the individual being described is inept or untalented.

Today, there are opportunities for both amateur and professional actors. In this chapter, we will investigate the shift from the predominance of the amateur actor of the classical and medieval periods to the professional actor of Elizabethan times. We will continue to trace the development of acting by discussing the appearance of female actors in seventeenth-century France and in Restoration England. Along the way, we will discuss evolutions in actor training, casting practices, and the actor's position within both the theatre and culture at large.

ACTORS IN THE ANCIENT WORLD

It is predominantly thought that Ancient Greece was the birthplace of the theatre artist known as the actor. Into the sixth century, a dramatic form called a *dithyramb* was popular in Greece. A *dithyramb* was a ritual performance with a chorus and a leader telling, through song, a story typically based on a Greek myth. The leader would take turns alternating storytelling lines with the chorus. It is said that Thespis was the first leader to actually "impersonate" a character—to talk in the first person: "I" instead of "he." In a sense, Thespis "became" the individual in the story. In recognition of his historical step in the development of the actor, the name of Thespis is forever linked with the craft of acting: You may have heard the word *thespian* used as a synonym for "actor." Though this innovation was thought by some to be quite worrisome (Athenian lawmaker Solon deemed acting "deceptively dangerous"), a prize for acting was introduced at the City Dionysia, and Thespis was named the first winner.

Actors rehearsing a Greek comedy.

Theatre in ancient Athens was a religious rite. The festivals at which theatre was presented were civic events honoring gods and goddesses. Participation in these events, whether as playwright, producer, actor, or audience member, was a source of civic and religious pride. Theatrical presentations in Ancient Greece were largely confined to several religious festivals held throughout the year. Because today, depending on where you live, you can see theatre practically 365 days a year, the limited performance schedule of Ancient Greece might seem odd. On the other hand, though you have more opportunities to attend theatre than a citizen of Ancient Greece, it is highly probable that your attendance doesn't have the same religious significance to you that it had to an Ancient Athenian. Plays were important in the religious life of Athenians but not presented on many days during the year. At the City Dionysia, celebrated at the end of March, five days were devoted to performance. As previously stated, Thespis won the first prize for acting at the City Dionysia. A festival called the Lenaia, near the end of January, came to be associated primarily with comedy. Contests at the Lenaia were at first only for comic dramatists and actors, but in 432 BCE competitions began for tragic dramatists and actors.

Perhaps due to the limited performance schedule, most individuals performing in plays in Ancient Greece had a "day job." Although some of the actors may have been paid for their services in the plays, it was not enough for them to make a living acting full time. Beginning in 449 BCE, the leading actors were assigned by lot, whereas secondary actors were probably chosen by the playwright and the leading actor. Only the leading actor was eligible to compete for the acting prize. Chorus members might be chosen well in advance of the festival performance (sometimes being rehearsed for as long as eleven months), but they were still what we would regard as amateurs.

Because lines were both spoken and sung, an actor's voice was of primary importance. Given both the size of the theatres in ancient Greece and the fact that they were outdoors, it would seem obvious that a good voice would be quite important for an actor of the period. Aristotle defined acting as "the right management of the voice to express the various emotions."

Greek actors wearing masks.

For Demosthenes, an admirable actor was "splendid in voice and perfect in memory." The importance of vocal clarity and volume would also be increasingly important, given the fact that actors of the period wore masks, making facial expressions of no importance. Whereas the downside of performing in a mask is the potential for thwarted diction and difficulty with vocal projection, masks lend themselves to performance in a large space (expressions on the mask were much more visible to a huge audience than the actor's face would be) while also allowing actors to more easily play numerous roles. "Doubling," or playing multiple roles, was common during the period, and masks were integral in making distinctions between characters played by the same actor. Little is known of the gestures and stage movements used by actors of the period, but it is assumed, due to the use of masks and costuming practices that included rather bulky large boots, that movement would be minimal by today's standards. Once again, the size of the theatres (sometimes 14,000 to 17,000 people) would indicate that small movements would be useless because they could not be clearly seen by the audience.

As the Roman Empire gained power and exposure to other countries and traditions, the theatre practices of Ancient Greece were incorporated into Roman religious festivals. The status of actors in the theatre of Ancient Rome is debated today, with some scholars asserting that actors were usually slaves purchased by a free man who "managed" the company and others noting that some actors became highly respected, well-paid "stars." After reaching its height in the fourth century CE, theatre began to decline due to forces including the decline of the Roman Empire and the rise of the Christian Church. The latter is not surprising, given ancient theatre's connection to festivals honoring pagan gods. The church even went so far as to forbid actors to partake in such sacraments as communion.

 ACTORS IN THE MEDIEVAL WORLD

One of the main forces driving the decline of theatre in the ancient world, the Christian Church, was, ironically, the very institution responsible for the return of theatre to England and Europe in the Middle Ages, also known as the Medieval Period. As part of the Mass, priests began to use antiphonal or "response" singing passages called tropes. The return of theatre to the Medieval period is usually marked by the introduction of an Easter trope, called *Quem quaeritis*, the earliest of which dates from about 925 CE:

Actors performing in masks for a production of *The Oedipus Plays* at the National Theatre in London.

> Angels: Whom see ye in the tomb, O Christians?
>
> The three Marys: Jesus of Nazareth, the crucified, O Heavenly Beings.
>
> Angels: He is not here, he is risen as he foretold. Go and announce that he is risen from the tomb.

Note that the three Marys and the Angels are not being sung about in a narrative or storytelling fashion (an example of narrative would read: "And then the Angels asked the women whom they were seeking . . . "). The *Quem quaeritis* trope translated from Latin indicates that the clergy are "becoming" the characters in the Easter story. Like Thespis back in Ancient Greece, the priests are now impersonating characters or "acting." Also similar to Thespis and the theatre of the ancient Greeks, acting is once again part of a religious rite or service.

Tropes such as *Quem quaeritis* became increasingly common as the clergy realized that theatre was a valuable tool for teaching biblical stories and morals to largely illiterate parishioners. Eventually, the short tropes became full-blown plays and moved from inside the church to the village streets. Instead of being performed in Latin by priests, these outdoor religious plays began to be performed in the vernacular, or common language, by everyday villagers.

These outdoor religious plays were staged by various trade guilds as well as civic or religious clubs. Staging the plays was a source of civic and religious pride. Many of these events took the form of a series or cycle of numerous short plays covering a wide range of biblical stories from the Creation to Judgment Day. Each trade guild or organization would take on an episode or short play within the cycle. Often the trade guild would be linked in some way to the story of that particular play. For example, the shipwright guild produced the play detailing Noah's construction of the ark.

Although some of the early cycles had relatively small casts, the number of actors required for an entire cycle of plays could be quite large,

Photo © Carol Pratt. Reprinted by permission.

Scene from a recent Folger Consort Production of *The Second Shepherd's Play*, a medieval cycle play.

particularly in the sixteenth century. For a cycle in France in 1536, 494 roles were covered by 300 actors. Actors, for the most part from the working class, were recruited from the townspeople in a number of ways: Heralds might ride through the streets asking for volunteers, or requests for actors might be made from the pulpit of the local church. In some towns, individuals auditioned for a small committee. Most actors were men, but a few were women.

Although most actors in the Medieval period were not paid, they were provided with food and drink at rehearsals. If an actor had to miss work to attend rehearsal, he was expected to pay for a replacement worker. If he could not cover this cost, then the producing guild or club provided payment for the substitute worker. The few actors who were paid during the Medieval period did not make enough to earn a living from acting and had other professions. Acting was a religious and civic duty and not undertaken solely for monetary gain.

With pride of his trade guild and town at stake, individuals acting in the plays took the responsibility seriously. Actors were sometimes required to take oaths regarding dedication to rehearsals and performances. They were sometimes sworn to accept whatever role was assigned to them and to not complain about decisions made by the producing organization. Actors could be fined for missing rehearsals or breaking other rules.

Rehearsal time was minimal—particularly given the fact that many of the cycles took days to perform. For example, in France in 1501, only 48 rehearsals were held for a cycle that took four days to perform. Typically, there were no more than five rehearsals for a play cycle. In contrast, if you were cast in a theatre production at your college or university, it would not be unusual for you to rehearse 25 times for a play with a running time of two hours.

Not all drama throughout the Middle Ages was strictly biblical. Morality plays taught moral lessons and were steeped in church teachings, yet did not feature stories or characters from the Bible. The most popular morality play today (and the one most often produced) is *Everyman* (c. 1495/1510), which features the journey of a common man toward death. The play is allegorical and features characters with names such as Everyman, Death, Good

Deeds, and Kindred. Some theatre scholars believe that morality plays, unlike the more biblically based cycle plays, were staged by professional performers. As the Medieval period progressed, an increasing number of secular or non-religious dramas were produced. One especially popular French play, *Pierre Pathelin*, first produced around 1470, depicts a scheming lawyer outwitted by a seemingly dull-witted peasant. This play had gone through thirty editions by 1600. The rise in secular drama came to its fruition in the drama of Elizabethan England and with it came the advent of fully professional actors.

This 2008 production of *Everyman* at Virginia Wesleyan College mixed medieval and modern elements. Everyman, played by a woman, is seen between Cousin and Kindred.

Courtesy of Travis Malone, WVC Theatre Department.

 ## ACTORS IN ELIZABETHAN ENGLAND

In Ancient Greece and Medieval Europe, actors were largely amateurs. Overall, acting in the ancient world was not viewed as a profession but an activity in which individuals participated with varying frequency. Because theatrical activity in these cultures was religious in nature, actors were taking part in a religious service. During the Elizabethan period, also known as the English Renaissance (Elizabeth I ruled 1558 to 1603 but the period is usually dated from the late fifteenth century through 1642), cultural views regarding the reputations of actors deteriorated greatly, even as actors came to be recognized as professionals and gained greater control over decisions affecting the theatrical enterprise.

The rise of the professional actor was assisted by governmental efforts to control groups of actors wandering the English countryside. The Act for Restraining Vagabonds of 1572 defined the status of actors and restricted the number of licensed companies. To be licensed, a company had to be affiliated with a nobleman or lord. In general, any "masterless man" was an outlaw. Originally, justices of the peace in small provincial towns could license a troupe to play in their town but revisions to the legislation later curtailed that authority. London became the center of theatrical activity. In 1576, James Burbage, a member of a company known as the Earl of Leicester's Men, opened the first theatre building in London: The Theatre. The

SPOTLIGHT
Your Future as an Amateur Actor

If you enjoy acting but are apprehensive or doubtful about trying a career as a professional actor, it doesn't mean that acting can't be an important part of your future. Many people act in theatrical productions throughout their lives while earning a living in another profession. Opportunities for amateur actors exist in practically every community. Check your local newspaper for auditions for community theatre productions. You might also be eligible for auditions at a local college or university (some utilize community members to augment the casting pool, particularly for older roles). Local amateur actors are sometimes sought to serve as extras in films being shot nearby. You could volunteer as an actor at your local church or synagogue.

Aside from the pleasure of doing what you "love" (remember: that's where the word *amateur* comes from!), benefits from acting on a non-professional basis can include establishing friendships and business connections, learning to work as part of a team, having an outlet for personal creativity, and boosting your confidence as a public speaker. Acting can also be a way to support a religious or civic cause that is important to you.

location of The Theatre was, in actuality, outside the city limits. Due to the low reputation of theatre and its perceived association with other vices, public theatres were built across the Thames River alongside bear baiting arenas and whorehouses. Contrast this with the fact that theatres in ancient Athens were located near important civic and religious buildings like the Parthenon! Prostitutes sometimes rented small rooms in Elizabethan theatres called "Lord's Rooms" and met customers there, which did nothing to aid the low reputation of theatres and, by association, actors. However, the advent of permanent theatres dedicated to theatrical activities (previously, plays were performed in spaces such as inns and banquet halls) was crucial to the rise of acting as a profession.

Actors gained considerable power and influence during the Elizabethan era. To contextualize this development, it would be advantageous to better understand the system under which Elizabethan companies were organized. Crucial to our investigation is that Elizabethan companies were repertory companies organized under a sharing plan.

What is a repertory company? True repertory companies have grown increasingly uncommon, so you may have little knowledge of what a repertory company is or how it functions. To make things more confusing, many companies calling themselves repertory companies today don't strictly function as repertory companies in the traditional sense, and a new phrase, "resident company," has come to carry some of the meaning carried by the phrase "repertory company" in Shakespeare's time.

A repertory company is a group of actors that come together to establish themselves as a group for a long period of time. (In Shakespeare's era, "a long period of time" meant many years—perhaps decades—whereas today it might mean a single season.) In this period of time, the company performs a variety of different plays with roles being cast from the actors in the company. Thus, as opposed to coming together to perform a specific play and then disbanding, the group continues working together and performs multiple plays. Instead of having auditions for each individual show, auditions are held once, and then numerous shows are performed by the chosen actors. The few companies today that consist of an ensemble of actors working together for a season or longer describe themselves as "resident companies."

To be a repertory company in the truest sense of the word, a company's plays would be performed "in repertory" (theatre slang: "in rep"), meaning on a rotating basis. This means that instead of performing a single play, such as *Twelfth Night*, night after night for weeks, the company might perform *Twelfth Night* on Thursday, *Antigone* on Friday, and *A Funny Thing Happened on the Way to the Forum* on Saturday.

Repertory companies today tend to receive financial backing from a producing organization. The producing organization makes the artistic and business decisions necessary for the operation of the company. However, in the Elizabethan era, these decisions were made by a group of actors with a vested interest in the company itself. This type of organization is known as a sharing plan, and the group of actors with decision-making power were called "shareholders" or "sharers." Each company had about eight sharers. These men (all actors, whether sharers or not, were men or boys during the Elizabethan period) made decisions regarding play selection and casting, trained apprentices, and tended to business matters, such as leasing theatres for the company to use. Once a sharer, you were in the company until you quit, retired, or died. The group was committed to you, and you were committed to the group.

New works under consideration were required to have roles appropriate for each sharer. Consider what a fundamental impact this must have

SPOTLIGHT

Elizabethan Actors William Shakespeare and Richard Burbage

William Shakespeare

The most famous Elizabethan acting company is the Lord Chamberlain's Men, who later became the King's Men. Their renown is in large part due to the fact that William Shakespeare (1564–1616) was a sharer and wrote his plays for the company. A burgeoning playwright and actor, Shakespeare joined the Lord Chamberlain's Men in 1594. Although it has become theatre legend that Shakespeare was not much of an actor, it is hard to believe that he would have been made a sharer in the company if he did not pull his weight in terms of performance. To be made a sharer, one had to be elected by the full group of shareholders, so we can assume that although he was not the "leading man" of the company, his acting talent was worthy of inclusion. If the complexity and depth of characters populating his plays were not alone sufficient evidence of Shakespeare's familiarity with the craft of acting, the use of theatrical imagery in many of the plays further shows the impact of his acting experience on his playwriting:

> As in a theatre the eyes of men,
> After a well-graced actor leaves the stage,
> Are idly bent on him that enters next,
> Thinking his prattle to be tedious;
> Even so, or with much more contempt, men's eyes
> Did scowl on Richard . . .

Richard II act V, scene ii

Speak the speech I pray you as I pronounced it to you, trippingly on the tongue, but if you mouth it as many of your players do, I had as leif the town-crier spoke my lines.

Hamlet act III, scene ii

All the world's a stage,
And all the men and women merely players;
They have their exists and their entrances,
And one man in his time plays many parts . . .

As You Like It act II, scene vii

Out, out, brief candle!
Life's but a walking shadow, a poor player
That struts and frets his hour upon the stage,
And then is heard no more . . .

Macbeth act V, scene v

As Shakespeare is the most well-known playwright in the world, you have surely heard of him before and likely read or seen one or more of his plays, the most famous of which include *Romeo and Juliet, Macbeth, A Midsummer Night's Dream*, and *Hamlet*. Although Shakespeare's genius is undeniable, it is likely that his writing was, in part, infected by the acting talents and skills of company members such as Richard Burbage, the "leading man" of the Lord Chamberlain's Men.

Given the fact that his father, James, built London's first theatre, it was little surprise when Richard Burbage (c. 1567–1619) showed a propensity for acting. Burbage joined the Lord Chamberlain's Men at the same time as Shakespeare and in the following years gave the premiere performances of the most famous acting roles in the world: Hamlet, Romeo, and Richard III. Along with his brother, Cuthbert, he owned rights in the Globe Theatre and the Blackfriar's Theatre.

Burbage grew so famous as an actor that, along with fellow company member Will Kemp, he was made a character in a play, *Return from Parnassus*, by an unknown author, performed at St. John's College, Cambridge, between 1598 and 1603. In the play, Burbage, who specialized in tragic acting, and Kemp, master of comic acting and Lord Chamberlain's Men sharer for whom Shakespeare created the role of Falstaff, attempt to train two college students in acting. Unfortunately, the "real" Burbage left no acting treatise to enlighten future actors with his methods and theories. He was idealized by seventeenth-century writer Richard Flecknoe as having "had all the parts of an excellent orator, animating his words with speaking, and his speech with acting; his auditors being never more delighted than when he spoke, nor more sorry that when he held his peace. . . ."

© Bettmann/CORBIS

Richard Burbage

SPOTLIGHT
Actor Training in China, India, and Japan

Though this book deals almost exclusively with the Western theatre tradition, theatre also flourishes in other parts of the world. Here are some brief facts regarding non-Western actor training.

In China under the Han Dynasty (206 BCE–221 CE), many types of entertainment flourished both at court and in popular culture venues such as fairs and markets. Known collectively as the "hundred plays," these entertainments included juggling, sword swallowing, tightrope walking, music, mime, and dance. During the Sui Dynasty (581–618 CE), Emperor Yang-Di set up a training school for these entertainers. During his reign, he is said to have staged a festival involving tens of thousands of performers in an area extending over four miles. In 714, Emperor Xuan Zong established a training institute called the Pear Garden. To this day, actors in China refer to themselves as "Students of the Pear Garden."

In Kathakali, a 300-year-old form of Indian dance drama, actors must learn a "gestural language" including more than 500 separate signs. A Kathakali dancer begins training as a child and is not considered mature until he (boys or men perform female roles) has performed a role for about twenty years. In Japan, actors begin training for Kabuki, a theatre form dating back to the early seventeenth century, at a young age (typically 6 or 7 years old) and are almost never judged mature until middle age.

had on playwriting! Today it is more common to select actors, usually by a process called "auditions," based on the needs of the previously chosen script. In Shakespeare's time, scripts would be developed and chosen based on the talents and skills of a company's sharers. Once a sharer had played a particular role, he continued to play it each time his company performed the play. Upon his death or retirement, the actor taking on his "share" (for which the retiring actor would receive payment from the new sharer) would take over the roles he had played.

Sharers did not receive a set salary. After a performance, the sharers would meet and divide the proceeds among themselves. They also shared in the debts of the company, with each being responsible for a share of incurred expense. In addition, each sharer might be assigned one or more apprentices. Theatre companies in this era typically included as many as a half dozen young apprentices. Apprentices, who were boys as young as age ten, lived with their masters, who trained them in addition to providing food and clothing. In return, the masters were paid by the company for the boy's work. Apprentices played the female roles in the plays, typically cast in roles opposite their master. Thus, an apprentice working under the tutelage of Richard Burbage would have performed the roles of Juliet, Desdemona, and Lady Macbeth.

The third category of actor in the Elizabethan acting company was the "hired man." These men were hired at a salary for a set length of time to cover roles not played by sharers and apprentices. Sometimes an actor who began work as a hired man eventually became a sharer. Richard Cowley moved from playing small comic parts as a hired man to being listed as a principal actor and sharer in the company.

Professional actors today tend to work like the hired men of Shakespeare's time, hired at a set wage for a specific length of time. The most common length of time today is a "run of the show" contract. This means that the actor is contracted to stay with the show until it closes. Acting today is a profession sorely lacking in job security. If you are hired on a run of the show contract and the show closes suddenly, then you could be out of work with little or no notice. When the show is over, you are looking for your next gig. Sharers working in Elizabethan companies enjoyed ownership in the theatrical "product" that is not often experienced by today's actor and, in contrast with the vast majority of actors in the ancient and medieval world, were acting to support themselves as opposed to being motivated by civic or religious pride. The change from sharing plan to contract system occurs in Restoration England. First, however, we will discuss developments in acting in seventeenth-century France.

ACTORS IN SEVENTEENTH-CENTURY FRANCE

As the religious drama of the Medieval period began to wane in the early part of the sixteenth century, secular theatre companies began to form in France. The rise of secular drama in that country was complicated by the fact that the *Confrérie de la Passion*, a religious group organized in 1402 to present religious plays, had previously been given a monopoly on

Image © 2008 by Drimi. Used under license from ShutterStock, Inc.

Due to his lasting influence on the theatre, numerous statues of Molière are found in France. This statue stands outside the opera house in Avignon.

theatrical activity in Paris. Even after a decree in 1548 curtailed religious drama, the *Confrérie* retained that control, and theatre companies had to pay them a tax to perform in Paris and a high rental charge to use their theatre, the *Hôtel de Bourgogne*, which was for a time the only theatre in Paris.

Perhaps the most important figure in the French theatre of this period is Molière (1622–1673). Born the son of an upholsterer to the king, Jean-Baptiste Poquelin left school in 1643, changed his name to Molière, and founded an acting company with the Béjart family of actors. Called the *Théâtre Illustre*, the company toured the provinces for numerous years with Molière as the leading actor. Molière was known for his talent in comic roles and soon became an accomplished playwright specializing in comedy. In 1658, Louis XIV granted the company permission to present plays in Paris and to share use of a Paris theatre with another company.

Like Shakespeare, Molière was writing for his own company, so the talents and strengths of the actors greatly influenced his plays. He was also greatly influenced by a type of entertainment that had grown popular during the Italian Renaissance called *commedia dell'arte*. Inspired by *commedia*, Molière filled his plays with exaggerated character types (the title characters in *The Miser* and *The Misanthrope* are examples). In addition, the comic plays for which he is best known require a broad physicality and witty dialogue reminiscent of *commedia*. Perhaps most important, the improvisatory nature of *commedia* required performers in the troupe to stay attuned to each other—to work closely as a team. Likewise, Molière's company was known for excellence in ensemble acting, and Molière, as company manager and coach, was in large part responsible for that reputation.

Theatre legend has it that Molière died onstage while playing the title role in the premiere performance of his play *The Imaginary Invalid*. In actuality, he is thought to have died a few hours after the fourth performance of the play. Despite that fact that he was a favorite of King Louis XIV and his plays were quite popular with the public, the church refused him a Christian burial because he did not repent of being an actor before dying. (This refusal was likely retribution for Molière's play *Tartuffe*, which satirized church corruption. Although the church was successful in banning the play for a time, its production in 1669 had an initial run of 33 performances indicating its popularity with audiences at the irritation of church authorities.) Upon the intervention of Louis XIV, the Archbishop of Paris finally authorized Molière's burial in the parish cemetery on the condition that there be no ceremony and that the burial take place after dark. Though he was buried in the dead of night with no religious ceremony, thousands are said to have walked by torchlight to accompany

Actors performing in Molière's *School for Wives.*

Molière to his grave. After Molière died, his company was combined with several others until eventually the *Comédie Française* was formed and given a monopoly on spoken drama in French. The first national theatre in the world, the *Comédie Française* still exists today. Molière is considered a "patron saint" of sorts to French actors, and the *Comédie Française* is also known as *La Maison de Molière* or "The House of Molière."

The organization of French companies during the seventeenth century was similar to that of Elizabethan acting companies: a basic sharing plan structure with a core group of actors in each company managing the company and sharing in the profits and losses. There was, however, a major difference: French companies included women, and women could become shareholders. Shareholders in the French companies were called *sociétaires.* Upon becoming a *sociétaire*, an actor bound himself to the company for twenty years. When a *sociétaire* retired or died, the remaining *sociétaires* typically elected a replacement from the company's *pensionnaires*, salaried members of the company who played minor roles (similar to the hired men of the Elizabethan companies). Actors at the *Comédie Française* today continue to share in the management of the company, with the actor who has been a *sociétaire* longest functioning as the company head.

The inclusion of women in acting companies in seventeenth-century France and other continental European countries may have been yet another influence of the *commedia dell'arte* troupes, which, as we mentioned previously, included female performers. Perhaps due to its geographical isolation from the rest of Europe and limited exposure to *commedia* troupes, Elizabethan acting companies did not include women. As you will recall, young boys played the female roles in plays such as Shakespeare's *Romeo and Juliet*. Soon, however, the first English actresses were to appear on the professional stage.

SPOTLIGHT

Commedia dell'arte

The theatrical form known as *commedia dell'arte*, meaning "play of professional artists," was immensely popular in Italy between 1550 and 1750. Its popularity spread to other countries as well—particularly France. One of the most distinguishing characteristics of *commedia* is that it is improvised as opposed to being scripted. Actors in *commedia* troupes created stock characters with which they improvised comic sketches around fixed scenarios. These characters were stereotypes with exaggerated personality traits: the witty servant, the lecherous old man, the foolish young lovers. Repeated comic "bits" or routines, called *lazzi*, were included as actors worked their way through the chosen plot outline. For a modern parallel, consider reappearing characters that appear on television shows such as *Saturday Night Live*. Like *commedia* characters, many *SNL* characters are based on exaggerated personality traits and perform repeated comic bits that consistently appear, no matter the particular "storyline" of that week's sketch. Example: At some point in every sketch in which she appeared, Mary Katherine Gallagher, played by Molly Shannon, put her fingers in her armpits and smelled them.

Commedia was performed by troupes comprised of both male and female performers who, originally, traveled the countryside. Theatre historians have hypothesized that *commedia* developed from Greek and Roman mime troupes that also included women. Most women per-

ACTORS IN RESTORATION ENGLAND

In 1642, the Puritans closed the theatres and outlawed all theatrical activities in England, putting professional actors out of work and bringing the golden age of English Renaissance drama to an end. The Globe Theatre was torn down, and the Lord Chamberlain's Men, now known as the King's Men, sold their costumes. The Puritans went on to overthrow King Charles I, and Puritan leader Oliver Cromwell took control of the government. Despite the fact that theatrical activities were illegal during this era known as the Commonwealth period, they did not cease altogether. Performances were given from time to time in various venues such as private homes, ten-

18th-Century engraving of *Commedia dell'arte* actors on stage

forming in *commedia* troupes were married to another member of the company, typically the man playing opposite them. One of these women, Isabella Andreini, became a company head and is lauded by some as "the first great professional actress."

nis courts, and inns. As the Puritans began to lose power, productions were given more openly.

In 1660, Charles II returned to England, and the monarchy was restored to power. The Restoration was a time of great change in English theatre practices and, particularly, acting companies. During the time in which the Puritans had ruled England, royalty and court members had taken refuge in nearby France, where they were exposed to French arts and culture. Upon their return to England, many practices common in French theatre became common in English theatre. One of these practices was the use of female actors. Women were no longer barred from the English stage, and after 1660, it became common practice for female parts to be played by women.

French Print of a *Scene From Molière's*
"Les Fourberies de Scapin"

Illustration of a scene from a
Restoration play. Note the inclusion
of women.

Earlier in this chapter, we established that Elizabethan acting companies and seventeenth-century French theatre companies were organized on a sharing plan. This organizational structure gave actors more power than they had possessed at any previous time in theatre history. Sharers made decisions regarding script selection, casting, and management concerns. They shared in the profits and losses of the company and made what was often a lifelong commitment to the company. Another organizational structure became prevalent in London during the Restoration: the contract system.

Under the contract system, all actors were hired for a set salary for a specified length of time. These wages were augmented by special "benefit performances" held annually for major performers. At this performance, all proceeds would be given to the previously identified actor (or actors—sometimes several more minor performers would share a benefit). Sometimes a higher ticket price would be charged for a benefit performance so the proceeds would be greater than the usual gate proceeds

The position of all actors in companies organized under the contract system is similar to the position of the hired men in Elizabethan companies organized under the sharing plan. Imagine the difference this must have made in the way decisions were reached and in how actors were treated! Powers that had formerly been held by the sharers were now held by businessmen, who often owned the companies and/or the theatres in which they performed. Some of these men, such as Christopher Rich, had no previous theatre experience and were quite unscrupulous in the treatment of actors: Rich was known for withholding salaries and playing favorites among the company. Rich and his son, John, who also went into theatre management, were to remain a dominant part of the London theatre scene until 1767.

Despite the change in London to organization under the contract system, acting companies in the English provinces and in the thirteen colonies that were to become the United States continued to organize under the sharing plan. Over the years, however, that system eroded,

SPOTLIGHT

Restoration Actress Anne Bracegirdle

Anne Bracegirdle (c. 1663–1748) made her acting debut as a child and was the protégé of actor Thomas Betterton and his wife, actress Mary Saunderson Betterton. She excelled in the "clever young female" roles prevalent in the Restoration genre known as "comedy of manners," such as Millamant in *The Way of the World*, a role written for her by playwright William Con-

Anne Bracegirdle

greve. She was also popular for her performances of "breeches roles"—roles in which women dress as men.

Bracegirdle was much beloved by the public and particularly respected for her stellar reputation. That she was called "the celebrated virgin" undoubtedly underscores the public's association of promiscuity with actors left over from the Elizabethan period as well as an inclination to assess women in terms of their sexuality, which some might argue continues today (hence the obsession with the Paris Hilton "sex tapes," among other lurid "news" stories covered in contemporary media).

In addition to her skill as an actor, Bracegirdle played a part in theatre management. When Betterton left the Drury Lane company managed by businessman Christopher Rich in protest of Rich's poor treatment of actors, Bracegirdle accompanied him and became comanager of the new company at Lincoln's Inn Fields. She retired in 1707 at the height of her fame.

Although today it is assumed that women have "equal opportunity" in terms of a theatre career, one must look at theatre history to identify the steps that made such access possible. The talents and popularity of Restoration actresses such as Anne Bracegirdle and female playwrights of the period such as Aphra Behn (1640-1689) paved the way for women working in these fields today. By understanding that progression, women theatre artists today can better determine how to help future generations.

and today theatre companies organized under a sharing plan are rare. It is most common today for actors to work as lone artists, becoming part of a company for the run of a single show or perhaps a season and then looking for the next audition.

 ## CHAPTER SUMMARY

The prevalence of the amateur actor in ancient Greece and the medieval period gave way to the dominance of the professional actor of the Elizabethan era. At the same time, the organization of Elizabethan acting companies under the sharing plan gave actors greater control by giving them company ownership. Though Elizabethan companies did not include women, women were company members in seventeenth-century France and could become shareholders. While the *Comédie Française* still operates under a sharing plan, it is the organizational system dominant in Restoration England, the contract system, which is the most common organization system for acting companies today.

 ## ACTIVITIES

Does This Repertory Company Run "in Rep"?

Find an existing company with the word "repertory" in its name (via an online search, newspaper listings, or other method of inquiry). Look at the production schedule for this company (most are posted online as well as available in a brochure from the box office). Do the plays run one at a time or "in rep"? Is this group a resident company (meaning it consists of a core group of actors appearing in every show), or do actors appear on a "run of the show" basis?

Create Your Own Commedia Character ("Live from Theatre 101: It's Saturday Night")

Choose a personality trait that intrigues you in some way. Some examples: conceit, kindness, intelligence, enthusiasm. Begin to imagine a character driven by that particular trait. Give your character a name. Find a partner and with them brainstorm a potential signature *lazzi* (repeated comic bit) for your character. After focusing on your character's development with a partner (and helping generate ideas for your partner's character), share your character's name, dominant personality trait, and *lazzi* with the class. As a class or in a smaller group, choose two to three characters developed by the class to be placed in a scene with each other. Cast classmates to play the characters and place them in a simple improvised scene (such as the three characters waiting at a bus stop). Let the scene play until each character has had a chance to perform his or her signature *lazzi* at least once—and maybe twice!

"Professional" vs. "Famous"

Although some professional actors are quite famous, many individuals earn a living by acting, yet never become well-known. Someone sitting next to you in a classroom or on the bus may, in fact, be a professional actor. Choose one or two classmates and discuss the following together: Is it assumed that a professional actor who is not famous has "failed" as an actor? Why? Would we have the same expectation of fame from someone pursuing a career in law or a physical therapy? What other assumptions or expectations do you have regarding individuals pursuing a career in acting?

The Craft of the Actor

Student actors rehearse a scene.

SPOTLIGHT

The Astor Place Riot

On May 10, 1849, in New York City, the National Guard was called out to quell the increasingly violent gathering of an estimated twenty thousand people outside a theatre during a performance of *Macbeth*. Ultimately, 22 people were killed and many more wounded in what would come to be known as the Astor Place Riot. This event was the culmination of conflicts of class and nation as crystallized in the acting styles and personas of two of the most popular actors of the time.

American actor Edwin Forrest and English actor William Charles Macready had become emblematic of a growing

Charles Macready as Macbeth.

© Historical Picture Archive/CORBIS

schism between two factions: Forrest's fans were working-class American "Bowery Boys," whereas Macready's supporters included poets, aristocrats, and upper-class elite. Macready's approach to acting was thoughtful, subtle, and intellectual, whereas Forrest was known for his physical, emotional, and unsophisticated performances. For years, the actors had been competing with one another. They often played the same roles in the same towns (sometimes even on the same night). Loyalty to the American-born Forrest, coupled with a growing sense of nationalism and frustration over economic theatre practices, led to tremendous dissatisfaction among lower-middle-class American audiences.

The site of the riot, the Astor Place Opera House, opened in 1847 as a place for upper-class patrons to watch theatre and opera without

In Chapter 7, we traced historical developments in the status of the actor within the world of theatre as well as within larger social and cultural contexts. We will now focus on the craft of acting as learned and practiced today. Simply stated, an actor's job is to bring a character from the script to life. Through the rehearsal process, as coached by the director, an actor makes physical, vocal, and psychological choices unique to, and appropriate for, the character or characters being portrayed. Each choice is carefully having to tolerate the theatre habits of working-class attendees used to shouting at the stage, throwing fruit, and in general disrupting performances. Not only did box seats at the Astor Place Opera House have to be retained for the entire season (far more money than working-class audiences could afford to spend at one time) but the entire pit, formerly filled with backless benches, had been replaced with armchairs, which could only be purchased by subscription. A dress code required the purchase of expensive clothes, which in turn required the use of a carriage to avoid dragging one's clothes through the muddy New York streets. These practices, among others, were conscious efforts to keep working-class audiences out of Astor Place. Macready's willingness to appear at Astor Place cemented, in the minds of the American working class, his depiction as an icon of highbrow, stuffy, European snobbery.

Edwin Forrest as Richard III.

© CORBIS

The Astor Place Riot was brought about by an intricate interweaving of national, political, and economic issues with passionate feelings on the part of audiences regarding actors, styles of acting, and the accessibility of theatre to the working class. It is, perhaps, difficult for college students today to imagine a world in which theatre is so much at the heart of contemporary debate.

crafted to efficiently communicate the specifics of the character to the audience. As an introduction to the work of the actor, this chapter will focus on dominant styles of acting and the actor's place within the audition and rehearsal process.

Today, the dominant acting style in the United States is psychologically based, whereas European and Asian models emphasize physicality. The psychological approach is sometimes called "realistic," and the physical approach is often associated with nonrealism. Although these are not the only two approaches to acting and are not mutually exclusive (actors can train in both and most, if not all, actors rely on psychological, vocal, and physical choices to develop a character), we will speak of these two approaches as distinct entities to provide a basic introduction to acting theory and technique.

It is obvious that knowledge of prevalent acting styles and approaches to training is important to the would-be actor, but it can also be beneficial to the nonactor. It strengthens the ability to understand and critique performances. It facilitates the interpretation of not only theatre but other art forms as well, and it provides the information necessary to contextualize art styles within the era in which they appear. Although perhaps not commonly the topic of casual conversation today, there have been periods in history in which acting styles were a major topic of discussion within dominant culture—even a battleground for national pride as in the case of the Astor Place Riot.

HOW ACTORS TRAIN: THE PSYCHOLOGICAL APPROACH

The psychological approach to acting is most closely linked to Russian actor and director Constantin Stanislavski (1865–1938). Stanislavski developed his innovative acting theories in opposition to the more "declamatory," artificial style that was prevalent at the time. His new, more subtle, and "believable" acting style better suited the realistic and naturalistic genres of playwriting and production emerging at the turn of the century. In 1898, Stanislavski cofounded the Moscow Art Theatre, which was to become the home of his developing methods. Several books by Stanislavski present his evolving theories. Three of these books make up a trilogy considered so basic to actor training as to be called the actor's "ABCs": *An Actor Prepares*, *Building a Character*, and *Creating a Role*. The first of these to be published, *An Actor Prepares*, published in 1936, is one of the premiere acting treatises in the world and continues to be utilized as a textbook in many beginning acting classes.

An Actor Prepares sets forth the idea that the goal of the actor is "to live the part" of the character: "The very best

Constantin Stanislavski

Photofest

that can happen is to have the actor completely carried away by the play. Then regardless of his own will he lives the part, not noticing how he feels, not thinking about what he does, and it all moves of its own accord, subconsciously and intuitively." To prepare for submersion in the character, actors are to carefully study what Stanislavski calls the "given circumstances" of the play. Given circumstances include "the story of the play, its facts, events, epoch, time and place of action, conditions of life," the actors' and the director's interpretation, the sets, lighting, costumes, properties, and sound effects.

Once the given circumstances are known, the actor uses "if" as a tool to tap into the imagination and place themselves within the skin of the character. The actor asks herself: "If I were this character and if this happened to me, what would I do?" Stanislavski said, "If acts as a lever to lift us out of the world of actuality into the realm of imagination." If is a powerful, essential tool in actor training. In recognition of its importance within the psychological approach to acting, it is sometimes referred to as "the magic if." By utilizing if to become the character and, therefore, placing themselves within the given circumstances, Stanislavski believed that actors will unconsciously create onstage action that has "an inner justification" and is "logical, coherent and real." The assumption behind the Stanislavski approach to acting is that what happens onstage should be driven by what is going on internally within the character.

Perhaps two of the most well-known terms associated with the Stanislavski system of actor training are "beat" and "objective." Chances are that if you have taken an acting class, you have been exposed to at least one of these concepts. According to theatre lore, "beat" is actually a misinterpreted pronunciation of the word "bit," due to the heavy accents of the early Russian teachers of the Stanislasvki system in the United States. To further complicate matters, some students heard the word "bead" being said. Stanislavski's writings, as translated into English, use the word "unit" instead. It is, perhaps, a happy accident that pronunciation made the precise word being used unclear. Both "beat" and "bead" have some interesting connotations in this usage: If you have studied music, you know that a beat is an important unit of musical measure. Beats combine to make measures, and measures combine to make scores. Likewise, a "bead" is a small unit that, when strung together with other beads, becomes part of a larger whole: a necklace.

Whether called "unit," "bead," or "beat," the concept is the same: In the preparation of a role, an actor must divide his part into small sections. Each beat or unit has its own creative objective or goal. By identifying the objective, the actor identifies what the character is doing in the scene. When

SPOTLIGHT

Uta Hagen

Uta Hagen (1919–2004) made her debut as a professional actress at age 18. Her big break came when she was cast on Broadway as Nina in a production of Anton Chekov's *The Seagull*, starring the famous Lunt family. While working in a 1947 play directed by Group Theatre member Harold Clurman, Hagen began to note the difference between hiding behind a character's "mask" and letting herself "evolve" in the character. She went on to explore this dichotomy

Uta Hagen.

with Herbert Berghof, founder of HB Studio in New York City. She later married Berghof and taught at HB Studio until her death. Her famous students include Matthew Broderick, Liza Minnelli, Whoopi Goldberg, and Amanda Peet.

Hagen's *Respect for Acting*, published in 1973, continues to be utilized in acting classes today.

Beginning actors find the book an engaging, "easy read," covering topics ranging from the theoretical (Does an actor "present" or "represent" a character?) to the practical (How do I make myself cry onstage?). In *Respect for Acting*, Hagen presents her "object exercises": a series of ten exercises designed to assist actors in creating organic, believable onstage performances. The first object exercise challenges

stating an objective, an actor speaks from the point of view of the character: "I wish to . . . ." Examples: "I wish to threaten her." Or " I want to console him." In these examples, "I" is the character the actor is playing. The objective is stated from that character's point of view. The "her" or "him" refers to another character in the scene. Note that "threaten" and "console" are verbs. Stanislavski said that the objective should be expressed by a verb and not a noun: "Every objective must carry in itself the germ of action." Verbs are active, whereas nouns are static. When selecting the objective of each unit, the actor must carefully select verbs that work together to support the super objective, which is "the essential idea, the core, which provided the impetus for the writing of a play."

the actor to re-create onstage two believable minutes of their own lives. To do so, Hagen stated that actors must first answer the following questions (closely related to Stanislavski's concept of Given Circumstances):

Who am I?	Character.
What time is it?	Century, year, season, day, minute.
Where am I?	Country, city, neighborhood, house, room, area of room.
What surrounds me?	Animate and inanimate objects.
What are the given circumstances?	Past, present, future, and the events.
What is my relationship?	Relation to total events, other characters, and to things.
What do I want?	Character, main and immediate objectives.
What's in my way?	Obstacles.
What do I do to get what I want?	The action: physical and verbal.

As the exercise makes clear, Hagen's book continues the tradition of the psychological approach to acting in the United States.

In the 1920s, two members of the Moscow Art Theatre, Maria Ouspenskaya and Richard Boleslavski, began teaching the Stanislavski system in the United States. American actor Stella Adler studied with Ouspenskaya and Boleslavski and became a founding member of an American company called The Group Theatre. A primary focus of The Group Theatre was to further the methods of Stanislavski. In 1934, Adler and Harold Clurman, also a founding member of The Group, went to France to study directly with Stanislavski. Eventually, an Americanized version of the Stanislavski system developed. This Americanized system came to be known as "The Method." When differences of opinion regarding "The Method" caused dissent in The Group Theatre, several individuals left the company and began working with another company called The Actors Studio. Both The Group Theatre and The Actors Studio are known for their association with, and development of, method acting.

In *An Actor Prepares,* Stanislavski deemed the actor's imagination, as stimulated by an identification and understanding of the given circumstances and use of "the magic if," as crucial to the actor's ability to "live the part." If in their own lives actors had gone through a similar experience to one undergone by the character, Stanislavski's technique of "emotion memory" assisted in developing full recall of past emotions associated with the experience and encouraged actors to use them onstage: "Just as your visual memory can reconstruct an inner image of some forgotten thing, place or person, your emotion memory can bring back feelings you have already experienced. They may seem to be beyond recall, when suddenly a suggestion, a thought, a familiar object will bring them back full force." Method acting builds on Stanislavski's principle of emotion memory. In method acting, the actor's emotions and the process of exploring and reliving those emotions are given primacy. Let's say, for example, that an actor is playing a murderer. Hopefully, the actor has never killed anyone. However, the actor searches his past for an instance in which he, personally, felt great betrayal and rage. Through rehearsal exercises, the actor begins to relive those emotions. As this process is sometimes quite traumatic, it is recommended that method actors use only memories that are at least seven years old and work in the presence of a qualified instructor. The actor imagines, in great detail, the room in which this moment in the past took place. Through sensory work, he tries try to place himself back in that memory and experience the rage and betrayal again. Then, when running the scene in the play, he tries to bring that rage and pain directly onstage.

In addition to development of a systematized psychological approach to acting, Stanislavski also recognized the importance of the development of the actor's physicality. In American training programs, however, it is the psychological elements of the Stanislavski system that are emphasized, and actors wishing to train the body usually look to other methods. In the next section, we will identify several physical approaches to actor training.

 ## HOW ACTORS TRAIN: THE PHYSICAL APPROACH

An alternative approach to the psychologically based actor training prevalent in the United States today is one that begins with and emphasizes physicality. Two of the most famous international proponents of this approach to performance are Eugenio Barba and Tadashi Suzuki.

Eugenio Barba's life story is as interesting and as international as his approach to theatre. Though he was born in Italy in 1936, he settled in Norway in 1954. There he joined the Norwegian Merchant Marines, which gave him an opportunity to travel to Asia, a source of inspiration for many of his future ideas about theatre. In 1961, he began studying theatre in Poland under the famous experimental director and theorist Jerzy Grotowski. A trip to the Kathakali school in Cheruthuruthy, India, in 1963 helped him construct the rest of his foundation for his earliest theatrical explorations. In 1964 he founded the Odin Teatret in Oslo, but he moved the company to Holstebro, Denmark, two years later. Since its inception, the company has regularly employed performers from all over the world, leading to a remarkable diversity in production. In 1979, Barba founded the International School for Theatre Anthropology (ISTA), which is dedicated to exploring the connections between Eastern and Western performance styles and practices. In addition to his work at ISTA, Barba has taught his approach to theatre throughout Europe, Asia, North America, and Latin America and has published several important books on theatre, including *The Secret Art of the Performer* and *The Paper Canoe*.

© Lindsay Hebberd/CORBIS

Odissi dance helped shape Barba's concept of "extra-daily behavior."

Barba's approach to actor training evolved over the course of many years as he synthesized and personalized an amazing array of techniques and theories from such Asian sources as Noh, Kyogen, and Topeng and from European theorists and performers like Jean-Louis Barrault, Dario Fo, Etienne Decroux, and from Grotowski and Grotowski's famous actor and collaborator, Ryszard Cieslak. As Barba worked with this rich array of source material, he was not primarily looking for a set of skills that a performer had to master to perform. Instead, he was seeking a way of expanding a performer's process, allowing the performer to refine and test the range of his means of expression. In so doing, the performer could be prepared to reveal the provocative tension between the creation of the character and the experience of performing the character. Because of the emphasis on process and on personal cultivation, some performers have trained with Barba for over twenty years.

The principle of "extra-daily behavior" is a key tool for Barba and his performers. Whereas Stanislavski and his followers were interested in helping the actor appear to live life onstage, Barba is more interested in a heightened form of physicality. He looks for ways to intensify the performer's presence by energizing the body in ways we don't typically see

The physicality of Noh theatre influences the work of Tadashi Suzuki.

offstage. In daily life, people attempt to execute tasks using a minimum of energy. Onstage, however, it may be more interesting to see an expanded range of motion, the parts of the body moving at different speeds, with different tensions, or in different directions as in Odissi dance or Western mime, or a performer in the kind of precarious or "luxury balance" associated with Eastern forms like Kathakali and Western forms like ballet. These techniques exceed our daily habits and help to locate what Barba calls the "preexpressive" impulse underlying a performed action. Such performance strategies create a "dilated," or highly expressive and energized, body that is engaging to watch and that exudes presence. Character and performer converge in novel ways through this heightened form of physicality, thus creating a dynamic and moving experience for the audience.

Tadashi Suzuki is another theorist and director who has formulated a physical approach to actor training. Suzuki, who was born in Japan in 1939, makes an interesting point of comparison with Barba because although both men approach character from the outside and work in and both draw on ideas from Eastern cultures, their approach to the cultural source of inspiration differs. Barba might be called "acultural" in his explorations. He looks across cultures, draws comparisons, but ultimately disconnects techniques from their original contexts. Suzuki, on the other hand, maintains an interest in the cultural associations connected to his choices—he wants to commingle traditional techniques and their symbolic values with modern sensibilities—and continues to examine these instead of regarding the performance techniques in isolation. His "intercultural" method aligns with the ideas connected to postmodernism that you will find in Chapter 13. He allows disparate voices to coexist in his work—Noh inspired walking is backed by contemporary pop song while a chorus is added to a play by Chekhov—without synthesizing them into a smooth whole. He allows the gaps to show in his work and asks the audience to think about what they might mean.

The Suzuki method is a very precise training program that emphasizes a demanding set of physical exercises that allow the performer to harness the power of space and rhythm. A teacher or master breaks down and demonstrates the exercises, which Suzuki calls *kunren*, meaning disciplines in Japanese, to a group of students or disciples. The exercises concern different ways of walking, stamping or stomping, stopping, and centering or balancing that are derived from Noh theatre's walking and from Kabuki theatre's *mie*, or frozen poses. The exercises are largely silent, as the method suggests one learns through the body, not through verbal, discursive, and communal discussion. The teacher is an unquestioned authority, and the performer must humbly submit to and accept corrections from the teacher. There is also an emphasis on calm and steady breath, as evidence of a union of the external and internal, though the exercises don't address these directly. Actors must find these individually as they perform the disciplines. From repeated and dedicated practice of the exercises, a performer gains a detailed body awareness and inner concentration that are valued across cultures. The method provides the actor with the tools necessary to explore texts from a variety of times and places and to work with directors with a range of visions. In productions he has directed himself, actors trained with the Suzuki method have performed everything from Greek tragedy to Anton Chekhov to Stephen Sondheim.

Tadashi Suzuki

Since Suzuki's ideas were first translated into English into the late 1970s, the Suzuki method has been taught throughout the West, notably by the company Frank in Australia and the SITI Company in the United States, as well as by Suzuki himself at the University of Wisconsin in Milwaukee, the Juilliard School, and the University of California at San Diego. Ellen Lauren, one of the cofounders of the SITI Company, whom Suzuki has called the best teacher of his method, teaches these ideas at Columbia University.

AUDITIONS

The process in which actors compete for roles in a play or company is called "auditions." Some generalities about the audition process remain the same whether the actor is professional or nonprofessional and whether the organization holding auditions is a repertory company or a university. Let's focus on what you might expect if you were to attend an audition at your college or university, and along the way we will identify ways in which professional auditions might differ.

SPOTLIGHT

Anne Bogart and the Viewpoints

The Viewpoints is a method of actor training, ensemble building, and creating new work most regularly associated with director Anne Bogart and the SITI Company that she founded with Tadashi Suzuki in 1992. The Viewpoints are intended to be both practical and philosophical, as well as creating a route toward understanding, physical awareness, and collaboration.

In *The Viewpoints Book*, coauthored by Bogart and director Tina Landau, the authors note that the inventor of the Viewpoints is Mary Overlie, a choreographer with whom Bogart worked at New York University. Overlie, they wrote, came up with the Viewpoints to help structure improvisation in dance. The six viewpoints Overlie discovered are space, shape, time, emotion, movement, and story. As Bogart and Landau began experimenting with how these techniques for dance could be applied to theatre, they identified nine Physical Viewpoints—spatial rela-

Anne Bogart's 2006 production of bobrauschenbergamerica at the American Repertory Theatre is representative of her lively visual style, full of striking physical and spatial relationships. Kelly Maurer (above), Leon Ingulsrud, Akiko Aizawa.

Photo by Michael Brosilow, courtesy of and reprinted by permission of SITI Company.

tionship, kinesthetic response, shape, gesture, repetition, architecture, tempo, duration, and topography—and five Vocal Viewpoints—pitch, dynamic, acceleration/deceleration, silence, and timbre.

Whereas American actors are trained to focus on psychology while creating character, the Viewpoints provide an alternative or additional emphasis on matters of time and space and encourage ongoing, even daily, practice of its principles. Instead of figuring out what a character, or perhaps more realistically what a director, wants the Viewpoints encourage mutual engagement from the entire ensemble as the team figures out together what the production wants and how that can be realized in time and space.

Bogart and Landau proposed a series of increasingly complicated exercises that allow practitioners to explore what the Viewpoints have to offer. Following is a sample exercise from *The Viewpoints Book* playing with the Viewpoint of Spatial Relationship:

> The group moves around the space in any tempo, including starts and stops. . . . Notice when you start to feel something happen. Work with more extreme spatial relationships. Go radically close to someone: touch them, hear their breathing, smell them. Then work with someone far away from you: feel the tension, increase it, make it more taut. In this exercise the only goal is to maintain extreme proximity or distance, to live in this state of aliveness, to be sensitive to when it dies and nothing is happening, and start the occurrence again simply by moving closer or farther away from another body.

As you can see from this exercise, actors working with Viewpoints, begin with the physical—with the movement of the body in space and in relationship to other bodies—but from the physical the emotional develops. Tension and intensity result from physical spatial relationships, rather than having to be manufactured internally in performance and thrust outward. The Viewpoints allow something to occur on stage rather than making it occur. Invention results from the collaboration of those around the performer and the force of the physical world. They free the actor to be awake with all the senses while on stage and to create from the vibrant range of choices that such awareness provides.

Bogart herself has used these techniques with great success in texts authored by contemporary artists such as Charles Mee and Naomi Iizuka and in classic texts by Shakespeare and August Strindberg. Among her awards are two Obies, a Bessie, and a Guggenheim Fellowship. In addition to her own work as a director, Bogart teaches at Columbia University, where she runs the Graduate Directing Program.

Student actors at West Georgia University in a recent production of Suzan-Lori Parks' *365 Days/365 Plays*.

Courtesy of Alan Yeong

Auditions are typically announced via newspaper or Web site. Professional actors look for audition notices in trade papers and/or through the Actors' Equity Web site. Actors' Equity is the labor union for professional actors. Often, Equity auditions are closed to nonprofessional actors. In an educational setting, auditions are typically open to all interested students and sometimes community people as well. A good way to find out about audition opportunities at your college or university is by checking bulletin boards in the theatre and/or fine arts building. More than likely, there will be a special bulletin board called "The Call Board" on which flyers regarding all acting opportunities are posted. Read each audition flyer carefully, as it typically provides important information—not the least of which is where and when auditions are to be held.

The audition flyer should provide information regarding whether or not the auditions are for a specific play or a group of plays. At some large campuses, multiple shows are often being cast at the same time, whereas on a smaller campus, auditions are typically for a single production to be held that semester. Although not usually required, reading the play, or plays, prior to auditions is advisable if you wish to be as competitive as possible. You might be asked to bring a head shot (an 8 × 10 black-and-white photo of yourself) and a resume. The flyer should also tell you what you might be asked to do at the audition. Audition activities can include doing prepared monologues, cold readings, singing, dancing and other movement, and improvisations. If you might be asked to move or dance, you will want to wear clothing that will not prohibit your doing so.

Prepared monologues are short solo passages, typically not directly from the show being cast, that actors memorize in advance and perform for the individual casting the show—typically the director of the play. Sometimes actors are given a time limit such as two minutes for these pieces. An actor serious about being cast has carefully crafted and polished a prepared monologue. Often these pieces are the product of the actor's work in acting classes. Professional actors typically have numerous prepared monologues (as well as 16 bars of a song) ready to go on a moment's notice. The monologues are chosen by the actor to showcase his or her range and talents and to highlight for the director qualities that might make the actor suitable for a particular role in the show or shows being cast.

Whether or not you are asked to do a prepared monologue, you will likely eventually be asked to read from the script of the play being cast. These readings are sometimes called "cold readings," meaning you've not had the chance to prepare but are asked to make choices regarding motivation, objective, and tactics on the spot. Of course, if you've read the play being cast, you are hopefully familiar with it (remember, we said that reading the play in advance gives you an advantage!). Occasionally, you might be asked at an audition to do a reading completely cold—one that you have never seen before. In these instances, the director is usually assessing your instincts and ability to make creative decisions in the moment.

In a college or university setting, the initial phase of auditions is an "open call." This means that anyone interested in auditioning for the play is invited to attend. As the process of casting continues, the phase known as "callbacks" begins. In this phase, the director invites individuals to read for particular roles in the play. To attend callbacks, you must be invited or "called back" by the director. Sometimes callbacks are handled in a single session, but it is not unusual, particularly in larger institutions, for callbacks to last several days.

Eventually, the director makes cast selections, and a "cast list" is posted. The cast list provides the names of the actors that have been cast as well as their assigned roles. It often also provides the date and time of the initial reading of the script (called a "readthrough"), as well as the first rehearsal and instructions on when and where to report for costume measurements, where to pick up a script, and other important information.

PRE-REHEARSAL AND OUTSIDE REHEARSAL WORK

Once an actor is cast in a role, rehearsals may start almost immediately or there may be an interval of several weeks or more. If actors have time before rehearsals begin, they have an opportunity to prepare for rehearsal; if rehearsals begin right away these activities may take place alongside or in addition to rehearsals. An actor's choice of prerehearsal and outside of rehearsal activity has much to do with the role in which the actor has been cast, the type of director, and personal preferences.

Actors must spend time outside rehearsal with the text of the play. In professional theatres it is usual for actors to be "off-book"—or to have

SPOTLIGHT

Where Actors Train: Conservatory or University?

In the previous chapter, we identified apprenticeship as the primary source of actor training during Shakespeare's time. Although not as common as in the Elizabethan era, and certainly not as formalized, apprenticeship remains a source of actor training today. Some companies, such as the Milwaukee Repertory Theatre, have slots specified as apprentice or intern positions. Competition for these positions is so fierce, however, that those chosen have often already completed a training program in a conservatory or a university. Today, would-be actors typically train in one of those two settings.

A conservatory approach to actor training is one in which individuals spend one to two years taking specialized classes. These classes typically focus on speech, voice, movement, and acting technique, with specialty courses in areas such as dance, stage combat, and script analysis. When the range of courses offered by the conservatory are completed, the student often earns a "certificate of completion" or, if the conservatory is accredited, a bachelor's degree or master's degree in acting. An example of a conservatory with a degree program is the American Conservatory Theatre (ACT), in San Francisco. Auditions for the program are held annually. In addition to the regular conservatory program, ACT offers a summer training program lasting almost two months that is attended by numerous college students.

memorized all their lines—before the first rehearsal. Many directors at the college level also require this of their actors. Memorization techniques can be quite specific to each actor and might include "running lines" with a friend or creating a recording of the lines (and the cues—in addition to knowing what to say the actor must know when to say it) and listening to them repeatedly. In addition to memorization, most actors engage in some kind of script analysis. One method that many actors find effective is based on the ideas of Stanislavski described earlier. Actors analyzing scripts in this way go through the play, looking for beats. Any time there is a change in the action of the play that affects their character—in terms of what they want, how they will try to get it, or even how important attaining this goal becomes—they will draw a line in the script. Breaking the script up into these smaller sections makes the daunting task of getting to know the plot and their character's role within it

Many students pursue actor training while undertaking a degree within a college or university setting. Colleges and universities across the United States offer classes ranging from basic acting techniques to advanced acting to improvisation. Some students take these classes while pursuing degrees in other disciplines, whereas others choose to major in theatre or acting. A significant difference between training in a conservatory and training in a college or university is that, in the former, students take classes almost exclusively in acting and/or theatre. In a college or university, a student also takes the standard general studies curriculum required for a college degree.

Of course, acting classes can also be offered outside a conservatory or university environment. These classes might be associated with the techniques of a particular master teacher, such as Uta Hagen's HB Studio in New York City. In other areas, an acting class might be offered by the local parks and recreation department or area arts center. We should perhaps clarify that an individual isn't required to have any training at all to work as an actor. Untrained or "raw" talent does occasionally work professionally—sometimes quite successfully. However, the intense competition for roles in the current market does not make this approach advisable.

much more manageable. They may also name beats and highlight important words within beats. (And of course, an actor looks up the definition and pronunciation of any unfamiliar words!) If working with a director who approaches rehearsals collaboratively, an actor will have more ideas about the play and the characters based on this kind of homework. The actor will then be more prepared to enter into a creative partnership with the director.

Actors also spend time inside and outside rehearsal doing imaginative work. It takes considerable imagination to live within the given circumstances of the play and to employ the "magic if" as described earlier. Actors may use music from the period in which the play is set to help spark their imaginations or look at paintings and sculptures to get their creative juices flowing. They may also research aspects of their character. If the play is set in seventeenth-century France, they may choose to learn more about the

(a)

(b)

Photo © Michal Daniel, 2002

Photo © Michal Daniel, 2002

Many film actors also appear in threatre productions. Shown here are Jimmy Smits, Julia Stiles, and Zach Braff in *Twelfth Night* at the Public Theatre (above); and Angela Bassett and Alec Baldwin in *Macbeth* (below) also at the Public Theatre.

(a)

(b)

Photo © Michal Daniel, 2007

Photo © Michal Daniel, 2007

social and cultural context in which the play is happening. If their character is based on an historical figure, reading a biography may prove useful. When characters aren't drawn from the pages of history, actors will sometimes create their own character biographies, imagining pivotal moments in their characters' lives that are not covered in the script. Other actors may seek opportunities to interview people who live lives similar to their character's or they may seek to experience something a character has by visiting important locations—a fancy hotel, a mountain cabin, or a hospital. A great many actors find that watching movie versions of the play in which they are cast is not helpful. This may close down their imagining of what their character can be instead of opening up new possibilities.

Physical activity can also prepare an actor for a role. Sometimes actors are asked to do things on stage that are well outside their regular skills. If a play requires a particular kind of dancing, sword fighting, juggling, or a variety of other physical tasks, the actor may need to practice these on her own or with the help of some of the theatre professionals like a dance choreographer or fight choreographer. Another kind of specialist who may help an actor with the physical components of a role is the voice coach. If dialects will be used in the show, an actor may require expert help in pronouncing the words of the script correctly. Even if the manner of the character's speech is very similar to the actor's own, a voice coach may help an actor sustain volume, play with speed and rhythm, or a variety of other vocal techniques that will help make the actor's portrayal of the character unique, appropriate, and understandable for the audience.

Another type of physical preparation may involve transformation. Film actors are regularly required to gain and lose weight—think of Renee Zellwegger in the Bridget Jones films or Christian Bale in *The Machinist*. Although it is less common for stage actors, particularly at the college level, to have to meet such a demand, they may work on their bodies in other ways. An actor who is going to be playing a soldier may choose to run or lift weights in an effort to shape the body and to have an insight into the physical demands of the character's life. Or if an actor is playing a character with physical challenges—a limp, or blindness, for example, the actor may choose to simulate this condition outside rehearsal so that their physicality will better mesh with the character's.

Although the bulk of the actor's work takes place in rehearsal, there are a variety of options for enhancing and even accelerating that work before and outside rehearsal. Some actors find that this kind of preparation feeds them creatively so that new choices and options open to them. Others find that this kind of work can be meaningful distraction, that while their consciousness is devoted to historical research or while their bodies are being challenged at the gym, another part of their brain can kick on, readying them to make new leaps with their characters when they are in the presence of other actors and the director.

 THE ACTOR IN REHEARSAL

Rehearsals typically take place five days a week for a period of several weeks prior to performance. The dynamics of each rehearsal period are different, just as the dynamics of each of your college classes is different. These dynamics can be affected by a number of factors, such as the subject matter, the time of day and time of year in which the class meets, the personality and experience of the instructor, your personality and experience, and the individual personalities and experiences of the other students. If you are to maximize your experience in a given class, you must learn to adapt to its unique qualities.

Learning to work as a team is a basic element of the rehearsal process for actors. Particularly in the early part of the rehearsal period, it is not uncommon for actors to do improvisations or acting exercises designed to facilitate greater trust and intimacy among the group. One such exercise is the Trust Walk. Actors break into pairs. One places a blindfold over her eyes and allows the other to lead her around the rehearsal space, through the building, outside, and perhaps into other buildings. The actor tries to keep a relaxed body and an open mind. She notes the particular leadership style of her partner and, whether or not it comfortably suits her style as a follower, adapts accordingly. She pays attention to stimuli provided by the senses: the gentle hum of a nearby fan, the harsh quality of the rocks underneath the feet. After fifteen minutes or so have passed, the partners change places. The formerly blindfolded actor is now "leading" her fellow actor. The exercise continues as above and concludes with a discussion between the partners and, ultimately, with the whole group. Though relatively simple in form, exercises such as Trust Walk can greatly enhance the camaraderie of the group and quickly highlight potential trouble spots as well as reveal to actors their own idiosyncrasies. For some individuals, such inner revelations and growing self-awareness are one of the most rewarding aspects of acting.

Once rehearsals are well underway, the work of actors focuses on two major areas: blocking and characterization. "Blocking" refers to the on-stage movement of actors. Some directors "give" actors their blocking, This means that the director spends a rehearsal or two, typically early in the rehearsal period, telling actors where and when the characters move, sit, and stand. On the opposite extreme, some directors never give or set blocking but encourage actors to vary the character's movement. Perhaps most common is the choice to let the actor experiment with blocking for several rehearsals—sometimes even several weeks of rehearsals—and eventually "set" movements that the director wishes to keep. With this method, actors have more creative input in the final product.

Although one might assume that actors would prefer to assist in creating the blocking for the character or characters they are playing, there are actors who prefer to be given blocking from the director in the early stages of the rehearsal process. Some feel "lost" when given too many choices and would rather spend their energies animating movement that they know the director prefers. Another asset to the preblocked option is that it is quicker, and sometimes when trying to put a show together time is of the essence. On the other hand, when the director is the sole creator of the movement, the blocking is limited to his or her vision of/for the character. This leaves a valuable resource untapped: the actor's vision of the character. Ultimately, the actor knows the character in a way that the director cannot, and the director "sees" the stage movement in a way that the actor cannot. Perhaps for those reasons, many actors and directors believe that the most productive approach to blocking is a collaborative one.

In terms of characterization, actors typically devote time and energy in the rehearsal period to developing unique (not like the last character the actor played) and appropriate (within the world of the play and in the context of the director's vision) choices. The style of acting featured in the play determines the way in which these choices are made. When utilizing a realistic style of acting, actors tend to deal with psychological choices. It is common for actors working in this style to focus on "What does my character want?" The answer to this question is typically called the character's objective or goal. "Why does my character want this?" is called the character's motivation. "What does my character do to get what she wants?" identifies tactics or methods utilized by this character. "How important is this goal to my character?" deals with stakes. In addition to the psychological choices, actors would make physical choices that seem appropriate to the character. Factors such as age, gender, occupation, and economic class would be considered when developing physicality. Working within a nonrealistic style of acting often means focusing more exclusively on physical explorations such as those detailed earlier in this chapter.

As performances near, a series of rehearsals begin that are called technical or "tech" rehearsals. These rehearsals introduce elements such as lighting, costumes, and properties. By the time tech rehearsals begin, the creative work of the actor is largely at an end, and the actor shifts his energy to more practical concerns. For example, now that the show is being

SPOTLIGHT
Theatrical Superstitions

Actors and other "theatre people" can be quite superstitious. Here are some of the most common theatrical superstitions involving rehearsal and performance:

Never wish an actor "good luck" in terms of his or her performance. Instead, say, "Break a leg." This practice might have derived from the idea that to wish someone good luck is to part with it yourself (which would be particularly bad for the performance if the person uttering the phrase was another actor in the show) or it could have developed from the belief that to wish someone good luck alerts evil spirits as to the importance of the upcoming endeavor, which might prove detrimental to that effort. Another theory behind this tradition is that because actors must bend the legs to bow and in earlier times "break" was sometimes used for the word "bend," "break a leg" meant wishing actors so much audience applause that they would have to bow numerous times.

It is bad luck to say the word *Macbeth* in a theatre. Instead, actors refer to Shakespeare's masterpiece as "The Scottish play." This tradition is linked to a series of misfortunes (both documented and undocumented) associated with companies performing the play (an example: the Astor Place Riot discussed earlier in this chapter took place during a performance of *Macbeth*). Some actors won't even say a line from the play while in a theatre and believe that it is bad luck to use any properties, set pieces, or costumes that have been associated with a production of *Macbeth*.

Most theatres have a "ghost light." The ghost light is a light onstage that remains illuminated when the theatre is empty. Practically, this light ensures that the last person out of the theatre can see to exit safely and the first person to return to the theatre can see to enter safely. However, legend has it that this light is related to spirits in the theatre. Some believe that it is left on to keep evil spirits out of the space, and some believe that it is left on to provide illumination for the plays that spirits perform in the absence of the company.

run with costumes, a fast clothing change might need to be polished. Running the show under the given lighting design might mean that actors have to adjust blocking to ensure that they remain visible to the audience. If the play is a "period piece" (meaning it takes place in another era), although it is likely that the actor has been working in a "rehearsal skirt" for weeks, the weight, style, and fabric of the actual costume might necessitate some changes in movement. Once tech rehearsals begin, character development takes a back seat while the actor deals with more practical performance, matters. A good actor, however, eventually adjusts to the physical means of performance, and creative choices once again come to the fore. Hopefully, this adjustment is made prior to opening night!

 ## CHAPTER SUMMARY

For the purposes of introduction, contemporary actor training can be divided into two main categories: The dominant system in America foregrounds the psychological aspects of characterization and is built on the teachings of Constantin Stanislavski. The dominant system in Europe and Asia emphasizes physicality. Its practitioners include Eugenio Barba and Tadashi Suzuki. Today, actors usually train in a conservatory or university setting. Through the audition process, actors aim to demonstrate their abilities and readiness to perform in a given production. Once cast, actors undertake necessary "homework," such as memorization, script analysis and research, and physical and vocal preparations. Once rehearsals begin, actors focus on areas such as teambuilding, blocking, and characterization. They work closely with the director to make vocal, physical, and psychological choices appropriate to each character. In tech rehearsals, actors must deal with practical matters, such as costuming and lighting concerns, but ultimately focus returns to the communication of "character" to audience.

 ## ACTIVITIES

The Counting Game

With a group of five to seven classmates, try this exercise: Form a circle. Make the circle smaller and smaller until your shoulders touch the shoulders of the students next to you. Close your eyes. After a few breaths, someone in the circle is to say, "One." Then another individual is to say "Two" and then another "Three," and so on. Individuals are to speak in random order with no preplanning. If two people say the next number at the same time, the counting begins again with "One." Why do you think this game is commonly used in actor warm-up sessions prior to rehearsal and performance? What skills are required to play this game well? What skills might you learn even while playing it poorly?

What's My Objective?

Choose a partner. Take three small slips of paper and, on each, write an objective. Use verbs when phrasing objectives, use the first person (refer to yourself as "I"), and include the object of the action (your partner as the "him" or "her"). Examples: "I wish to humiliate him." "I want to worship her." "I want to beg him." Fold up the slips of paper and place them in a pile on a nearby desk or chair.

Decide who will play A and who will play B and commit the following lines to memory:

A: What time is it?

B: I don't know.

A: You don't have any idea?

B: Sorry.

Getting up on your feet, run the preceding short scene several times. Each time, select a different objective from the pile of slips. Don't let yourself say "no" to any objective you might select—try your best to make it work. Don't tell your partner ahead of time which objective you have chosen. Does your chosen objective impact how you say the lines? Does your partner's objective impact how you respond to their lines?

Catch

With a ball and a partner, practice playing catch. How can you exert more or less energy as you throw and catch the ball? Find ways to alter your balance as you throw and catch. Does this make the game harder? Funnier? Which parts of your body are tense? Which are relaxed? Now turn on some music. Repeat the exercise by playing with the rhythm and tempo of the music. Repeat again playing against the rhythm and tempo of the music. Now join another group. Play catch while the other group watches and vice versa. Which version of the game was most interesting to watch?

Dance Anthropology

Look for pictures online of dancers from different parts of the world. Observe the relationships between their arms and legs, faces and hands, and other parts of the body. Do the parts of their bodies form straight lines, curves, or a mixture? Where is the tension in their bodies? What kind of balance do they have? What similarities and differences do the dancers from different places have regarding these topics? Which dancers do you find most interesting? Why?

The Vision
of the Designer

Courtesy of Thomas Swarr

Designers create the appropriate onstage environment for a play—and much expertise is required to do so. For this scene in *Gint* at Elizabethtown College, lighting designer Barry L. Fritz utilized ellipsoidal reflector spotlights with a glass gobo to create the lightening bolt and traditional steel gobos for the clouds. A gobo is a patterned piece of metal or other material placed on a lighting instrument.

In Chapter 1, director and designer Julie Taymor was featured as an artist who brings together numerous art forms in a creative vision uniquely her own. She is perhaps best known for her staging of the animated film *The Lion King* as a Broadway musical. Taymor not only directed the musical, she also designed costumes, puppets, and masks as well as developed additional lyrics and music. *The Lion King* opened on Broadway in November 1997 and is still playing—with over 4,000 performances. In 1998, Taymor's work on *The Lion King* won Tony Awards for Best Costume Design and Best Direction of a Musical (the first ever won by a female director).

How does a designer approach source material so popular and well known (*The Lion King* was for several years the highest grossing animated film of all time and, subsequently, one of the best-selling videotapes of all time) and, instead of merely rehashing the story, create something just as beloved yet uniquely distinct from the original? In *The Lion King: Pride Rock on Broadway*, Taymor acknowledged that the first challenge in the process was "to maintain the integrity of my own style, while incorporating it into one of the most beloved stories in recent history . . ." She wondered, "The film's imagery is so identifiable and ingrained in the audience's minds. With preconceptions about what the characters should look and sound like, would they accept variations on a theme?" Yet Taymor boldly proceeded, and the rest is Broadway history.

Such is the power of the designer's vision. Theatrical designers work with a variety of materials—space, light, fabric, and sound, to name just a few. Despite the unique demands of their media, set, lighting, costume, and sound designers share many aspects of their process and ways of thinking. This chapter explores the four major design areas and proposes ways that students can employ this knowledge while watching and interpreting a play. We will discuss generalities of the design process and the importance of production concept to the work of the designer. Then we will explore each of the four main areas and introduce the technicians and crew members necessary to bring a design to fruition. Finally, we will investigate the tech rehearsal process and the ins and outs of running a production.

GETTING STARTED: PRODUCTION CONCEPT

A designer's creative work on a production begins with the script. A designer reads the script multiple—perhaps even countless—times. The initial read is to get a sense of the story. Further reading provides opportunity

Courtesy of Shawn D. Irish

Tennessee Williams' *Night of the Iguana* is set on the veranda of a Mexican hotel. The script specifies that several guest rooms open up onto the veranda—which is the main playing space for the actors. This production at the University Theatre, University of Arkansas, featured scenic design by Shawn D. Irish and lighting design by D. Andrew Gibbs. Note the use of gobos to create dappled light as if the area were shaded by trees.

to analyze the script. Designers are typically trained in script analysis and conversant with dramatic structure. Understanding a play's structure can provide clues as to potential shapes that the visual and aural world of the play could or should take. The genre of the play—musical, tragedy, comedy—also affects the visual and aural world. For example, tragedies end unhappily and typically deal with "darker" aspects of the human condition. In production, this "darkness" can be conveyed not only by the text but also through the production design: The visual world created for a tragedy is, more often than not, rather stark and austere. The color palette is typically not as bright and "cheerful" as one chosen for a comedy. Selected music will be more somber than that of a comedy.

More reading might bring specific images to the designer's mind—inspirations that designers will note. References to time of year, time of day, geographical location, the era in which the play is set, the socioeconomic status of the characters, and related information will receive attention. A script set in the parking lot of a convenience store in rural Mississippi in 1990 is bound to inspire different images and ideas than one set in a Russian palace during the final days of Tsar Nicholas II. Each designer will make

SPOTLIGHT

"Seeing" and Interpreting Design

Even if you've seen many plays, you might have to consciously develop your ability to notice and interpret theatrical design. The following terms address common design elements. Familiarity with these terms can assist you in processing the visual and aural world of the production:

Line –A line connects two points. It can be long or short, thick or thin, curvy, angled or straight.

Shape – A line that encloses a space creates a shape.

Mass – The three-dimensional aspect of a shape. Consider not only a single mass but also its proportion and proximity to others onstage. Look for repetition as well as masses that seem distinctly different.

Position—The relative location of various masses.

Color – Pay attention to the color of individual elements as well as the overall color palette utilized within the production. Particularly note variations from the overall palette.

Texture – Not only fabric has texture: Lighting can be textured (with gobos, which will be discussed later in the chapter), and scenic devices can have texture. It can be argued that sound has texture as well.

Until you get the hang of it, you may have to really work at seeing what's onstage. For example, let's say that the lead character is wear-

notes on internal references regarding their specific design area. A remark made by a character in Act 1 regarding how embarrassed she is to have to wear such an old winter coat will be of prime importance to the costume designer. An offstage gunshot in Act 3 is crucial information for the sound designer. Frequent changes in locations depicted in the play need to be considered by the scenic designer. It might mean that the use of highly detailed sets could be problematic.

As analysis of the script progresses, the designer undertakes research as necessary. Though designers with graduate degrees in their discipline have studied history and period style (clothing, architecture, furniture), further ing a dress in Act 2. Though it might be a true statement, it doesn't make for a very interesting analysis in your next paper for this class. Is it a sheath or a ball gown? Silk or denim? Does it show off the neckline, the leg, or virtually nothing? Is it plain or fancy? Is it heavy and layered or light and floaty? Is it loaded with sequins or virtually unadorned? Designed for a cold or warm climate? What color is it? Does it look expensive? How does it compare to other costumes worn by the same character? How does it compare to the costumes of other characters? Instead of noting simply, "There was a chair onstage" in the opening scene, give the chair more note: Is it made of rough pine or steel? Could the average woman pick it up and move it by herself? Is it bigger than everything else on stage or much smaller? How does it make the individuals who use it sit? Do they have to keep a straight back? Do they sink into the chair? Does the ringing phone sound particularly ominous? Musical? Lyrical? Staccato or legato? Is the pitch uncomfortably high? Did the sound "jar" or surprise you? If so, how might that choice have been purposeful or otherwise supported what was going on in that particular scene?

Learning to note and process the layers of choices a designer makes can help you to more fully engage in and appreciate the totality of the fictive world depicted onstage and more accurately interpret the intended meaning of a given performance. These creative choices and others are what transform a script—a literary art form—into the immediate, ephemeral art form of live theatre.

research is often needed to investigate the play at hand. For example, a sound designer might need to investigate Baroque German composers to select appropriate background music for the party scene of a play set in early eighteenth-century Weimar. In addition, designers sometimes study the production history of the play. The lighting designer of *Death of a Salesman* may wish to research Jo Mielziner's original lighting design to more fully understand the premiere staging of the play and make a more informed decision regarding how to approach the design differently.

Weeks, months, or perhaps even a year or more prior to the show's opening, its director, designers, and other production staff begin to meet regularly to discuss the play and to develop a unique creative approach for this particular production of it. These meetings are called production conferences. Production conferences give the director and designers an opportunity to inspire each other, work collaboratively, and ensure that, for example, the color palette for costumes works well when lit by the selected lighting gels and doesn't clash with the paint colors of the set. Perhaps most importantly, production conferences are integral to the development and implementation of a unified production concept. The unique creative approach to the production—called the production concept—can be reached in a variety of ways. Sometimes, the director comes to the first production meeting with a strong sense of the production concept already developed. Alternately, the director and the designers can develop a production concept collaboratively through group discussion and reflection. Either way, once the production concept has been articulated, it is crucial that everyone involved in the production commit to it and work to unify the production under its auspices.

To more fully understand what is meant by "production concept," it is important to realize that not all productions of *Death of a Salesman* are, could, or should be the same. Part of what makes theatre such a vital art form is that no two productions of a script are exactly alike. Each group of theatre artists creates a unique interpretation of a script. One company might wish to perform *Death of a Salesman* as an homage to its 1950s milieu. Another might interpret the play as a commentary on corporate greed and stage the play amid the Enron Corporation crisis of the early twenty-first century. A feminist interpretation might wish to draw attention to the lack of female depictions onstage.

Once a production concept is selected, each designer works within their selected media to create a design. That design will be articulated on paper and then handed off to the appropriate theatre technicians for construction and full articulation. Each design area has a specific domain under its purview. Next, we will investigate the discrete areas of scenic, lighting, costume, and sound design.

SCENIC DESIGN

The scenic designer (sometimes called a set designer) is responsible for the visual appearance of scenery and stage properties such as furniture and decorative elements. Nowadays, scenic designers almost always hold a bachelor or master of fine arts degree. Courses within these degrees include

(a)

(b)

Robert Shoquist served as scenic designer for *Sweeney Todd* at Northwestern University in 2008. Pictured here are (a), a front elevation with details regarding color palette and finishes and (b), a photograph of the finished set production.

general theatre history and script analysis along with specialty courses in design, period style, scenic painting, lighting, computer graphics, and drawing and rendering.

If the play being staged is a realistic one and the chosen production concept reinforces that realism, then the scenic design typically provides important clues to audience members about the time period and place in which the play is set. For example, a room with rows of wooden desks and chairs, manual typewriters and rotary-dial phones quickly communicates to us a work environment of the twentieth century. If the script and/or the production concept is nonrealistic, then it is likely that the scenic design will emphasize the mood or theme of the production. A set design featuring numerous clock faces ranging in size from two to twelve feet and painted in neon colors would ready us for a fantastical production in which the concept of time, or the passage of time, is probably a primary focus. In both realistic and nonrealistic productions, it is important that the designer create an onstage environment that supports and communicates the production concept agreed on by the director and the other designers.

Several practical considerations must be weighed in the development of a scenic design. The designer must create a design that can be built within the budget allowed and in the time available. The designer must consider the demands of the performance space (the various kinds of spaces—proscenium, arena, thrust—and their peculiarities were discussed in detail in an earlier chapter). Awareness of the construction schedule for other shows being produced in the same facility and/or by the same company can also affect the design.

A scenic designer presents the design in several ways. The very early stages typically use thumbnail sketches to convey ideas to other members of the production team. These small drawings, usually made in pencil, communicate general ideas but very little detail. As the design process progresses, the designer will make renderings or color sketches. These are typically done to scale and provide much more detail. Next, might come a three-dimensional model. The designer could use a computer drafting program to provide an interactive model detailing the view of the stage from various seats in the auditorium (called a sight line drawing). A ground plan (the set as viewed from a vantage point above the stage) is created to show the location of all scenery and properties. Before the scenery is built, this ground plan is often taped out on the floor so that the director and the actors can rehearse with an awareness of the location of major pieces of scenery.

The scene shop foreman or master carpenter, sometimes under the supervision of a technical director, is responsible for overseeing the construction of the set by a crew of stage carpenters and the painting of the set by scenic painters. Though some of the basic skills required and tools utilized are the same, theatrical carpentry and scene painting differ from "normal" carpentry and painting in both the materials utilized and the level of care taken with "finish work." Unlike walls in your house (which are framed and covered with sheetrock to be sturdy and snug), walls onstage are typically created with flats. To create a flat, a lightweight frame is made of wood or tubing. Muslin is stretched over the frame and stapled. Sizing is then used to shrink the muslin taut against the frame. The flat can then be joined together and painted similarly to an ordinary wall. When viewed by the audience, this wall might be 12 or more yards away. This distance affects the level of detail work utilized in its completion—it doesn't make sense to spend time on details that will not be visible to the audience.

As previously mentioned, set dressings or decorative props such as curtains and lamps are included in the scenic design. Often, a properties master is put in charge of gathering or constructing these larger items as well as "hand props." A hand prop is a small item carried onstage by an actor such as a book or a bottle.

LIGHTING DESIGN

Lighting, if done well, is arguably one of the least noticeable elements of most productions. Light is a medium that can be difficult to "see" unless one is trained to do so. Indeed, we typically take lighting for granted unless experiencing an extreme (complete darkness or blinding glare). A skilled lighting designer takes this intangible medium and makes it an integral, expressive element of the artistic event. Numerous colleges and universities offer a master of fine arts in lighting design. In addition to studying dramatic literature and history, a student in one of these programs is likely to take courses in period research as well as drafting and rendering in both traditional media and new media (such as digital imaging and computer-aided design or CAD).

On the most basic level, a lighting design provides basic illumination of the stage: In a darkened auditorium, it enables us to see what's going on onstage. However, a talented lighting designer can do much more. She creates mood and atmosphere. She helps the audience focus attention on the appropriate part of the stage picture. A lighting design can help to communicate time of day, season, and location. Through special effect lighting (in lighting parlance called a "special"), the designer may single out a particular moment onstage. The design reinforces the general production

(a)

(b)

Lee Fiskness served as lighting designer for *Sweeney Todd* at Northwestern University in 2008. Pictured here are (a), a model of the set as lit for a particular scene and (b) a representative photograph of lights as they appeared in production.

concept espoused by the director and the other designers and thereby creates unity within the production.

Several elements of light can be controlled, and the lighting designer works with these in the design. The first is the quantity or intensity of light. As previously mentioned, the level of light can range from darkness to painful brightness, with countless variations between the two extremes. Another manipulative quality of light is distribution. Where onstage does the light fall? What is the size of the area onstage being lit? Is this area sharply defined or does the light fade gently into darkness? How long does one area stay lit before the lighting changes or "moves"? Color is another way in which light can be controlled. Even light that appears colorless or "natural" onstage must be manipulated to do so.

Numerous pieces of equipment are utilized to achieve these manipulations. The basic lighting instruments used in theatrical lighting are ellipsoidals, Fresnels, and followspots. The ellipsoidal reflector spotlight provides hard-edged light capable of traveling long distances. The Fresnel spotlight provides softer light often used to "fill in" light provided by ellipsoidals. Both are connected to a dimmer to control the intensity of light to each instrument. Followspots are high-intensity lights mounted on stands and operated by technicians. They are used to "follow" a particular actor onstage and are most often utilized in musicals.

The lighting designer articulates a design through specialized paperwork detailing information as to where each light is to be hung, what kind of light should be hung there, which part of the stage each should illuminate (called "focus"), how each light should be colored, and a list of cues (when and how the lighting should change). In professional theatres and large colleges and universities, an assistant lighting designer often aids the designer in creating this paperwork. The master electrician supervises the electricians in the implementation of the lighting design. Implementation includes hanging and focusing each light as well as applying color media (often called "gels" because in olden days they were made out of gelatin).

COSTUME DESIGN

The costume designer is in charge of the visual appearance of actors onstage, including not only clothing but also hair and makeup. Costume designers often hold a bachelor or master of fine arts degree. Curriculum for an MFA in costume design usually includes general theatre history and script analysis along with specialized courses in costume history, stage

SPOTLIGHT

Virtual Reality Techniques and Theatre Production

In the 1990s, the University Theatre program at the University of Kansas explored applications of virtual reality (VR) techniques to theatre production. Beyond the now relatively common use of computer drafting and rendering in the early design process, designers and production staff utilized computers, specialized software, and equipment such as headsets and "sunglasses" to create onstage environments mixing traditional and virtual elements. When taken as a whole, the four shows produced over the course of the decade in association with the department's Institute for the Exploration of Virtual Realities can be considered representative of the range of possibilities for the utilization of modern technologies in theatre design.

In *The Adding Machine*, by Elmer Rice, produced in 1992, computer-generated images were used to create settings for the play such as an office. The "Boss" was played by an offstage actor, whose image was projected into the office setting, creating a much larger-than-life Boss

Mr. Zero and his boss in the 1992 University of Kansas production of *The Adding Machine*.

Photo courtesy of the University of Kansas Theatre.

looming over the worker character (aptly named Zero), played by an onstage actor of average size. For 1996's production of Arthur Kopit's *Wings*, each audience member wore a head-mounted display (HMD). When wearing the HMD, audience members could see live actors on the stage and images projected onto the rear projection screens behind the actors in addition to images appearing on the video screens inside their HMD. David G. Fraser's *Tesla Electric*, produced in 1998, featured a departure from real-time computer-generated images (and the subsequent limitation on detail necessary to facilitate the real-time experience) and instead created highly detailed, photo-realistic "sets," which were placed on 35 mm slides and rear projected onto a very wide panoramic triple screen. Live actors performed in front of the screen. Stereo imaging was utilized, and audience members wore special 3-D sunglasses. With 1999's production of *Machinal*, by Sophie Treadwell, a return to real-time graphics was enhanced by the utilization of digital light processing projectors, advances in computer workstations and VR software, and a variety of live and recorded VR images.

Photo courtesy of the University of Kansas Theatre

Audience member wearing a head-mounted display.

You might assume that VR technology would most appropriately enhance a new play or script but the four scripts mentioned range in age considerably. Three of the four focus on the advent of new technologies and subsequent angst and concern. Both *The Adding Machine*, written in 1923, and *Machinal*, written in 1928, deal with increasing mechanization in the early twentieth century. Both are expressionistic plays featuring main characters driven to murder by a dehumanized society. *Tesla Electric*, first published in 1998, focuses on the life and career of inventor Nikola Tesla. A contemporary of Thomas Edison, Tesla's work proved important in the development of technological advances such as AC power and radio. The fourth play, *Wings*, written in 1979, depicts a main character, Emily Stilson, suffering a stroke and struggling to recover. The script juxtaposes the world around Emily (both as it "really" is and as she perceives it) with her inner dialogue. The play's focus on issues of perception was an impetus behind its selection for exploration via VR techniques. According to Mark Reaney, designer/technologist for the productions, "The unifying factor in our choice of shows was the requirement for some expressionistic or fantastic elements—either psychological, magical or supernatural."

In recent years, KU theatre has continued to explore the use of VR technology in productions such as the Mozart opera *The Magic Flute* (2003) and a children's theatre event called *Dinosaurus* (2001). Though some critics have charged that VR "upstages" live actors, draws unnecessary attention to production elements, and undermines the unique "immediacy" of theatre, others have lauded its potential to augment the ways in which an audience interacts with performance and bring about important advances in theatre technology. Reaney says, "Our underlying mission is to introduce today's media into productions speaking to a modern audience. Or, as Robert Edmund Jones said back in the 1940s: 'The business of workers in the theatre is, as I see it, to express a timeless theme by means of the tools of one's own time.'"

makeup, figure drawing and rendering techniques, tailoring, and pattern drafting. Students of costume design might also take courses in making hats (called millinery), masks, jewelry, or wigs. Knowledge of textile science is useful as well.

When developing costumes for a production, the designer has multiple goals. Of course, one of these goals is to create a design that unifies

Courtesy of Izumi Inaba

Courtesy of Izumi Inaba

Image by Izumi Inaba

Izumba Inada served as costume designer for *Sweeney Todd* at Northwestern University in 2008. Pictured here are two of her costume renderings and a shot of the finished costumes in production.

the show. The costumes should reflect the overall production concept agreed on by the show's director and the other designers. If the production concept is based in realism, the costumes should reflect the time and place in which the play is set. Last, each costume should communicate significant aspects of the character wearing it. A costume can give an audience member important clues regarding the character's age, occupation, economic status, and mood. Costume changes throughout the play can also alert audience members to changes in the character. A character that is brightly and flamboyantly dressed in the beginning of the play and suddenly appears in a demure black suit draws our attention. Such a change should only be utilized when meaningful and purposeful. If, as audience members, we see such a change, we can trust that we should pay attention to it.

Aside from these creative aspects of costume design, there are practical considerations for the designer. The amount of money available for costumes is often a huge factor in how the design is articulated. Budget size will affect the design possibilities in numerous ways from the types of fabric that can be used to the size of the construction staff that can be hired. The number of costumes required by a show will determine how much money per costume the designer can spend. The time period in which the play is set, as well as clothing styles during that period and the economic status of the characters, are powerful influences: Costumes for a production set in the past 100 years in the United States might be purchased at a local thrift store or "pulled" from the theatre company's stock, but nineteenth-century ball gowns will likely have to be made from scratch from yards and yards of expensive fabrics. Costumes for some shows can be rented from online costume companies. This can be a pricey alternative, but cheaper sometimes than constructing costumes. On the other hand, if a company constructs the costumes, then, after the show has closed, the company can add them to their wardrobe stock, potentially making a future production cheaper to costume.

Ultimately, costume designers create drawings of each costume. These drawings are called renderings. A rendering usually includes a front and back view of each costume and/or it might include all costume designs for a particular character on the same page. Some designers are so skilled at the rendering process that the resulting drawing is practically a work of art. Occasionally, theatre companies will post design renderings for a production in the lobby area for audience members to peruse at intermission or prior to the show.

At this point in the design process in professional companies and larger colleges and universities, the costume shop manager steps in and brings the design to fruition. The manager oversees the pulling of costumes from stock and/or the construction of costumes as per the designer's design. He collects measurement sheets on each actor in addition to creating a costume calendar with deadlines for shopping, construction, and fittings. In large facilities, the costume shop manager oversees numerous individuals with various specialties such as pattern making, cutting, stitching, and draping. In smaller companies, he often does this work personally or with a much smaller staff.

In terms of makeup for the production, except for the smallest of theatre spaces, actors always wear makeup to avoid looking "washed out" and colorless under theatrical lighting. Every actor should know how to apply the basic "corrective makeup" (makeup used to make the face appear three-dimensional and natural onstage). When "character makeup" (such as that utilized to make an actor look much older) or "special-effect makeup" (such as to make someone look bruised or bleeding) is required, a designer typically creates a makeup design rendering much like a costume rendering. Hair design is treated similarly.

SOUND DESIGN

Technological innovations have greatly altered sound design in recent years. MFA programs in sound design are now offered at some colleges and universities. In addition to theatre history and dramatic literature studies typical of any graduate degree in a theatre-related field, coursework in sound design usually includes advanced audio production and technology, electrical and computer engineering, and electives such as computer music and music theory.

Sound design for a production can be divided into several categories. The sound designer is responsible for creating internal sound effects within a script. These might include a ringing telephone or a doorbell. Sometimes, these effects are created "live" (meaning a sound running crew member generates the sound on cue at each performance). If not, then the sound will be recorded and played back at performance by a running crew member.

Let's say the sound required is a phone ringing. Seems pretty straightforward, but getting the desired sound cue might not be quite so simple. The designer must consider the time period and geographical location in which the play is set. The sound of a ringing phone has changed

Page	Cue	In	Out	What it is	Source	Pre Set Vol	Vol Adj	Spk	Notes
	A	SM Calls		Pre Show					
5	B	Call With Lights	X Fade in Cue C	Shadow Play	CD 1 Track 1			All 4	Chakra 6
5	C	SM Calls with Tower		Tower Rumble	Comp Row 2			Start in all 4 fade to back two	Row 1 on Comp
5	D	SM Calls	Fade out Tower		Comp Row 2			Start in all 4 fade to back two	X Fade From Cue C
5	E	SM Calls		Intro Music	CD 1 Track 2			All 4	Wanderlust King
5	F	SM Calls		Wind	MD			Start in all 4 fade to back two	X Fade From Cue E
5	G	SM Calls		Officers Madness	CD 1 Track 3			All 4	X Fade From F
5	H		Fades out completely when Officer Hacks table		CD 1				
6	I	"Should I"		Parents Enter	CD 1 Track 4			All 4	Fade up
6	J	Fade ends on Father's enter		Parent Enter	CD 1				
9	K	Called w/ Lights		Tango	CD 1 Track 5			All 4	Fade up
9	L	Fade out Complete on exits		Tango	CD 1			All 4	

Daniel Runyan, sound designer for a 2008 production of August Strindberg's *The Dream Play* at Boise State University, created this cue sheet for the sound board operator to use when running the show. From left to right, the columns provide the page number in the script on which the cue is heard, an assigned letter to identify the cue, the prompt to begin the cue (usually either the stage Manager's "go," a line in the script, or a visual cue from the stage), the prompt to end the cue (if necessary), what the cue "is" (music, wind, etc.), the source of the cue (usually a CD, mini disc or computer), columns to note volume levels and any required changes to those levels as the sound runs, the speakers from which the sound should emanate, and, finally, a place for other notes regarding that cue. As you can see, there are seven sound cues on p. 5 alone (the first page of the script). There were over 50 sound cues in the production.

significantly in the past twenty years, and, for example, a ringing phone in London sounds different from a ringing phone in New York. Once the designer has completed research and knows what kind of ring is needed, numerous sound effect electronic archives (available on CD or online) could be consulted to locate the precise sound. If not available, the designer may have to create the sound utilizing a synthesizer or other audio design technique.

Once the cue is located or created, the designer records it for use in the production. In the not too distant past, this meant recording each cue onto a cassette tape. The sound operator sat in the booth with a stack of cassette tapes, each of which had to be cued up prior to the show each night and then carefully placed in the order in which they were to be played during the show. The advent and accessibility of CD burners meant that a single CD could be created that held all sound cues required in the production in the order in which they were to be played. Nowadays, electronic sound files are run from a computer and sound board.

In addition to sound effects called for by the script, the designer often creates and/or gathers music to be played prior to the show, at intermission, and/or as the audience exits the performance space. This music is selected purposefully to reinforce themes present within the text and to amplify the show's chosen production concept. Listening to this music carefully can provide audience members with important clues in the meaning-making or interpretive process.

Although few "straight plays" (theatre parlance for nonmusical productions) have a musical score playing underneath their action in the way that most films have, sound design for the theatre has been influenced by familiarity with this cinematic convention. Most audience members (and arguably many or most sound designers) have seen more films than they have plays. With increasing frequency, sound designers are playing music underneath scenes to enhance the tension or assist in communication of the desired mood.

Sound design can also include amplification of the actors' voices. Though in most performance spaces actors can project their voices adequately without artificial techniques, sometimes amplification is necessary due to the size of the space, the nature of the production (one singing voice trying to balance against a large chorus), or the nature of the other sound effects required for the show. In these instances, the sound designer must include this amplification in the design as well as within the sound portion of the production budget. Like other designers, the sound designer works within the constraints of budget, time, and available equipment in the development of a plan for the production. If the theatre does not own equipment such as wireless microphones, these will have to be rented or purchased.

SPOTLIGHT

Design and Tech Terms

Tech theatre utilizes specialized language. Here are some samples:

Batten—A metal pipe or length of wood from which scenery or lights are hung.

Bump—Abruptly ending a light or sound cue.

Cyclorama or "cyc"— A large expanse of cloth used to surround the stage.

Drop—A large piece of cloth hung from the top of the stage. Often painted.

Fade—Gradually taking out a light or sound cue.

Flat—A lightweight frame of wood or tubing with muslin or other material covering the frame.

Fly loft—A large area above the stage large enough for drops and other pieces of scenery to be hidden from audience sight when "flown" up.

Gel—Color media placed on a lighting instrument to color the light coming from that instrument. Originally, these media were made of gelatin, but they are now made of synthetic materials. "Gel" is also used as a verb: To gel a light is the act of inserting the color media.

TECH REHEARSALS

During a performance, audience members are immersed in the onstage fictive world. You might not have considered that there is another world backstage, without which this immersion would not be possible. If theatre technicians do their jobs well, they are invisible. This "invisibility" is the result of a series of rehearsals focusing on technical elements. These rehearsals are called technical rehearsals or "tech." During the technical rehearsal process, numerous backstage workers coordinate, practice, and refine the technical elements and their execution. The goal

Gobo—A patterned piece of metal or other material placed on a lighting instrument. Creates a pattern or textured quality to the light coming from that instrument.

Grid—A metal frame attached to ceiling (or fly loft) of theatre from which lights or scenery can be hung.

Legs—Stage drapes (usually black) used to mask the backstage area (these keep the audience members from seeing "behind the scenes").

Practical—A lighting effect executed during the show by an actor onstage, such as turning a bedside lamp on or off.

Revolve—Circular portion of stage floor (or platform built on the stage floor) that can be turned or "revolved" by electrical or manual means.

Scrim—Drop made from see-through fabric.

Special—Shortened form of "special effect." Example: Red lights that come on as a character is supposed to be burning at the stake would be described as a "special."

Strike—To take a prop or scenic piece offstage is to "strike" it. Strike is also the name of an event held following the final performance. At this event, the set is torn down, and costumes, props, and lighting equipment are put away.

of tech rehearsals is to create a backstage life that works smoothly and efficiently. In essence, the very active world of backstage "disappears" into the fictive world depicted onstage. Tech elements should never draw attention to themselves. Instead, they support and enhance the onstage world. By the time the audience sees the play, the technical elements appear to work effortlessly, but hundreds of hours are spent reaching that point.

The stage manager is a major player in the tech process. Throughout the entire rehearsal process for the play, the stage manager assists the director with administrative tasks, such as contacting actors for costume fittings,

The Stage Manager directly interacts with all members of the production team. These photos chronicle the work of Katie Schultz as Stage Manager of *Something's Afoot* at Emporia State University in 2008.

Image by James R. Garvey, courtesy of Emporia State University Office of Public Affairs and Marketing.

Shultz prepares the rehearsal room. Note that the set has been taped out on the floor. In the background, we see the director talking to the actors.

Image by James R. Garvey, courtesy of Emporia State University Office of Public Affairs and Marketing.

Schultz reviews the progress of a special effect with a construction crew member.

setting up the rehearsal room, and keeping the prompt book. She serves as a liaison with designers and other production staff. For example, if in rehearsal the director decides to add a prop to a scene, the stage manager will pass that information along to the prop master. In professional theatres, the stage manager must be a member of the actor's union: Actor's Equity. In educational theatre, the stage manager often doubles as the assistant director.

At tech, the stage manager becomes the coordinator of all technical elements and "calls" the show. This means she sits in the control booth or backstage on a headset and tells the technicians in charge of lighting and sound (usually also on headset) when each cue should "go" or occur. A "cue" calls for a change (usually in lighting or sound). A production can contain hundreds of cues. It is imperative that the stage manager be organized, attentive, and responsible. A sense of humor, the ability to stay calm

Image by James R. Garvey, courtesy of Emporia State University Office of Public Affairs and Marketing.

Schultz consults with the director during a rehearsal break.

Image by James R. Garvey, courtesy of Emporia State University Office of Public Affairs and Marketing.

Schultz confers with the costume designer on raincoats being used in a key scene in the play.

Image by James R. Garvey, courtesy of Emporia State University Office of Public Affairs and Marketing.

Shultz reviews rehearsal notes with the technical director as members of the construction crew work on a stair railing.

Image by James R. Garvey, courtesy of Emporia State University Office of Public Affairs and Marketing.

Schultz reviews rehearsal notes with the costume designer and costume shop manager.

during times of tension, and good people skills are also quite an asset. A skilled stage manager is worth her weight in gold.

There are several different types of technical rehearsals. Early on, the stage manager will meet with the designers and talk through the timing of cues, scene changes, and costume changes. The stage manager will record this information in the prompt book and reference it to call the show. This early tech meeting is called "paper tech." Once the scenery is in place and the lights are hung and focused, sometimes a "dry tech" is held. Dry tech is a tech rehearsal without the actors. Sometimes a dry tech is divided by area: each scene shift is run in order, each lighting cue is run in order, then each sound cue is run in order. Or all cues can be run in the order in which they occur in the show (light cue, sound cue, scene change). When performers are added, dry tech becomes "wet tech." For the remainder of this

Schultz reviews microphone assignments with the sound board operator.

Image by James R. Garvey, courtesy of Emporia State University Office of Public Affairs and Marketing.

Schultz and the director at dress rehearsal.

Image by James R. Garvey, courtesy of Emporia State University Office of Public Affairs and Marketing.

An actor receives safety instructions regarding an entrance.

Image by James R. Garvey, courtesy of Emporia State University Office of Public Affairs and Marketing.

Manager Schultz "calls the show."

Image by James R. Garvey, courtesy of Emporia State University Office of Public Affairs and Marketing.

chapter, we will shorten the phrase "wet tech" to "tech." A cue-to-cue tech means that the actors are instructed to start a few lines prior to a line that triggers the calling of a cue. They start there and continue until the cue is called. If the cue is executed smoothly, then the actors are instructed to jump to a few lines prior to the next cue. If not, then the same cue is run repeatedly until it is sufficiently rehearsed. Eventually, all cues for the show have been practiced. A running tech means that the actors run the entire show, and the cues are called as the show unfolds. The actors are stopped when needed and can be instructed to repeat a section if necessary. Once costumes are added to the tech process (the first techs usually focus on lights, scenery, and sound), techs are called dress rehearsals. Earlier, there might have been a "dress parade," which gives the director and costume designer an opportunity to see all the costumes on the actors and request any desired changes.

The various technicians necessary in the running of a show are called "running crew." Running crew members are integral to the success of a production. The qualities necessary in a crew member or "techie" are responsibility, dedication, levelheadedness, and the ability to refrain from talking backstage. Each crew member is usually assigned to one of the four basic design areas.

The scenery running crew executes scene changes. Dressed in black, they can sometimes be seen onstage between acts of the play moving furniture and props. Their work backstage includes maintaining prop tables (backstage tables on which props are organized and stored until needed onstage), setting up the stage preshow, and mopping the floor. The lighting running crew typically includes one or more lighting board operators and possibly a follow spot operator. The costume crew includes dressers (particularly important for fast costume changes), individuals to assist with makeup application and hairstyling, and individuals to iron, launder, and repair costumes as necessary. Sound crew members operate the CD player and execute any "live" cues.

During tech rehearsals, the director and designers typically watch the show from the audience and provide notes for the stage manager and crew members regarding everything from how to tighten cues to necessary sound level changes. Sometimes this "tweaking" continues through opening night and into the run of the show. If the show has a long run, it is possible that the designers might attend a performance again several months later and provide similar feedback. The designer has a vested interest in ensuring that the production continues to be true to his or her creative vision and the production concept.

CHAPTER SUMMARY

Scenic, lighting, costume, and sound designers utilize design elements to develop the visual and aural world for a production while working collaboratively to unify the show according to the chosen production concept. Once their creative vision has been articulated on paper, numerous technicians work to construct the necessary materials and articulate the design. In tech rehearsals, the running crew—headed by the stage manager—spends many hours working to ensure an efficient and smooth backstage execution of the design plans and, ultimately, a seamless incorporation of the technical elements into the performance.

ACTIVITIES

Finding the Parameters

Read a short script (Jean-Paul Sartre's *No Exit* and William Saroyan's *Hello Out There* are two examples—ask your instructor for other suggestions). Note ideas that come to you regarding interpretive choices you might make as a scene designer for the play. These ideas can be expressed as words, phrases, or complete sentences, as well as sketches. Once you have that list completed, reread the piece and note textual references to setting, lighting, costume, and sound requirements. What is specified in the script? What research might be necessary to meet these specifications? As a designer, would you want to vary from the style described in the script? Why? How might you justify that variance?

Once you have completed both your "creative" list and your requirements list, compare them to lists for the same play made by other students in the class. Are the requirements lists similar? Do the creative lists vary from interpretation to interpretation? How might you refine your design ideas after seeing the lists of others?

YOU'VE GOT THE LOOK

In the following photos, you see the same performer in costume and makeup for several different roles. Find a partner and create a list of words or phrases to describe each character's "look." What assumptions might you make about each particular character? What ideas do you get as to the occupation, social status, temperament, personality traits, and disposition of each character? If you and your partner disagree, discuss that particular point further. Are there cultural influences that might affect a particular audience member's interpretation?

LOCATION, LOCATION, LOCATION

Choose a television sitcom with which you are quite familiar. Identify several of the most common sets utilized on the show. (Albeit an "old" example, it's likely that you've seen one or more episodes of the sitcom *Friends,* still running in syndication. For *Friends*, common sets could be identified as the coffee shop, Monica's apartment, and Joey's apartment.) Spend several minutes listing, from memory, details of one of these locations as depicted on the show (Monica's apartment is brightly lit, has purple walls with turquoise accents, the two main seating areas are the dining table—with mismatched chairs—and the comfy couch/armchair area near the television, a brightly colored poster is positioned above the television). Then, watch an episode of the show and check your memory. What details did you miss? Add those to your list. Read over this newly revised description of the set. Have you ever given the set this much thought? How might your interpretation of the show and the characters be different if this set was drastically altered (for example, what if Monica's apartment featured steel-colored walls, stark, minimalist furniture, and dim, cool lighting?)? Does the set as depicted enhance the comedic aspects of the sitcom? If so, how? If not, why do you think it doesn't?

Shifts in Theatrical Design

© Photostage

Today's technology allows lighting designers to create amazing visual effects as in this 2008 production of *A Midsumer's Night's Dream* at the Royal Shakespeare Company, Stratford-upon-Avon, England.

Changes in technology directly affect everyday life. Twenty-five years ago, most people did not own a personal computer; today college lecture halls are filled with almost as many laptops as students. We expect information, entertainment, and access to our friends and families to be no more than a keystroke or two away—even when we are supposed to be occupied with another task, like listening to a professor's lecture and taking notes. We navigate Web sites and screens fluidly, hardly blinking as our mouse clicks and our attention shifts from details about Italian Renaissance visual culture to a new friend request on Facebook. As part of our daily routine, we process information and stimuli that we see and hear in ways unimaginable just a generation ago.

The history of theatrical design—set, costume, light, and sound design—has also been profoundly affected by the changes in technology that have shaped society as a whole. Theatre design is, in many respects, about focusing the ways we see and hear. The tools we use to process information and perceive stimuli outside the theatre are inevitably brought inside. Sometimes we need to get past the habitual ways of seeing and hearing in everyday life that these tools condition us to use to heighten our perceptions in an aesthetic context.

We will look at four moments when the ways people see and hear changed: as perspective painting was introduced; when gas and electrical

© Photostage

An audience in Berlin sits riveted by the spectacle of Eugene O'Neill's *Hairy Ape*. The play examines the plight of the working man as industrial technology changes the world around him.

lighting became available; when photography sparked a vogue for realism in the theatre and in costume in particular; and when digital sound became established. As we do so, we'll place these developments within the broader histories of each design element, consider what kinds of theatrical spectacle were possible at these times, how these images and sounds were created, and how the technological capabilities and emphases of each theatre reveal fundamental aspects of each culture's perception of itself.

PERSPECTIVE PAINTING AND RENAISSANCE SCENIC DESIGN

In today's theatre, a specific artist called a scenic or set designer is responsible for the visual appearance of a production's scenery and stage properties. In addition, in some theatres, the scenic designer may also define the playing space, choosing how to arrange the stage/audience configuration in a flexible space or deciding how much of a proscenium theatre's stage space will be used in the show. But theatre was not always made this way. For several centuries, set design was indirectly the job of the playwright. The play's author didn't necessarily build platforms or paint scenery (though Aristotle credited Sophocles with introducing the art form in the fifth century BCE), but he did help audiences imagine where the play was set through his words. In these periods, a generalized playing space—one that could represent many different places—was the main acting area, and usually it was embellished with only minimal detail or a few small objects or structures beyond the words chosen by playwrights and spoken by actors. In the ancient Greek theatres the *skene* or stage house provided the main playing background, whereas *periaktoi*, or three-sided paintings, or *pinakes*, the forerunners of today's painted flats, might add further detail. In the early forms of medieval theatre staged inside churches, the *platea* was an empty playing space to which more particularized "mansions," small scenic structures representing particular locales that were simultaneously visible, might be added. In the Elizabethan and Spanish Golden Age public theatres of the sixteenth and seventeenth centuries, we continued to find a generalized playing space to which a few scenic properties like thrones, beds, and tapestries might be added to indicate a specific location. When Prospero conjured a storm at sea to buffet a ship full of men in Shakespeare's final play, *The Tempest*, for example, there would not have been a giant replica of a ship on stage at the Globe. Instead, the décor would have been spoken and the scene painted with words.

© Photostage

The reconstruction of Shakespeare's Globe in London provides a prime example of generalized playing space.

Italian artists were responsible for instigating changes that would eventually transform painting and the ways people were taught to see the world throughout Europe. In the first quarter of the fifteenth century, Fillipo Brunelleschi and Masaccio systemized the evolving art of perspective painting. By the beginning of the next century, Italian painters had mastered single-point perspective on the canvas, thus conveying depth and featuring imagery that receded to a vanishing point on the horizon. It was not long before this technique was applied in the theatre.

Perspective painting may have been used in the theatre in the last quarter of the fifteenth century, but historians are certain it was in use in 1508. That year Pellegrino da San Daniele painted the scenery for Ariosto's *The Casket* in Ferrara, Italy. He placed houses in front of a painted backdrop and thus established the style for scenic design. In 1545 Sebastiano Serlio published the second part of his *Architettura*, a treatise on architecture that included sections on the theatre. In *Architettura*, Serlio disseminated his typical settings for tragedy and comedy, which painters could then copy onto a backdrop, hang at the back of a playing space, and adorn with three sets of angled "wings" that, along with a steeply raked or angled floor, helped the viewer's vision recede toward a vanishing point. The idea that scenery ought to be created specifically for each new production is one that does not arise until the advent of realism in the nineteenth century demanded such detail and individuality. In fact, generality and universality were values held in high regard for many years. The use of "stock scenery"— generalized pieces owned by a company that could be reused for many plays— continued, and satisfied audiences, for centuries.

It is important to note that a particular viewer had the best vantage on the vanishing point: the ruler, who was seated at the center of the audience. Artists painted with this spot and this person in mind. The designer would then base lines and angles exactly on this position. No one else in the theatre would have a perfect view of the stage and its scenery. A viewer would instantly recognize the ways sight was skewed

In this example of perspective painting, "The Annunciation," (c. 1475–1485) note the way that the artist, Antoniazzo Romano, creates the illusion of depth with the lines of the floor tiles and the scale of images in the foreground vs. the background.

© Burstein Collection/CORBIS

and would need to imaginatively see through the perfect vision of the ruler's eyes. Thus the power structures and political order were mirrored in the painted scenery and audience arrangement.

In *Theatre Histories*, Phillip Zarilli et al., argued that the dominance of perspective painting on stage was directly linked to another important new technology: the printing press. They wrote, "By the 1630s, literate Europeans had been looking for a hundred years at the pages of books and pamphlets that organized their vision according to the laws of perspective. How 'natural' then to expect that stage scenery should mirror that reality."

The visual technology of perspective painting was strongly connected to a change in theatre architecture that also defines this period of theatre history: the development of the proscenium arch. As we discussed when we investigated performance spaces, the proscenium arrangement is the most familiar theatrical configuration used today.

The oldest surviving theatre with a proscenium arch is the Teatro Farnese in Parma, Italy. The theatre, designed by Giovan Battista Aleotti, was completed in 1618. Scholars believe that the theatre in the Uffizi palace in Florence preceded the Teatro Farnese in the use of the proscenium arch by thirty-two years, but that theatre was destroyed in

The Metropolitan Museum of Art, Harris Brisbande Dick Fund, 1937 (37.37.23) Image © The Metropolitan Museum of Art.

Le Sorti Di Francesco Marcolino Da Forli

The pit and stage, with the world's oldest surviving proscenium arch, seen from the audience benches at the Teatro Farnese, Parma.

the eighteenth century. How Aleotti arrived at his design, and Bernardo Buontalenti before him in Florence, is a subject of debate. Some scholars think the proscenium arch developed from the arches used in street pageants; others suggest the recreations of Roman stages that featured multiple doorways were the inspiration; still others say the proscenium derived directly from perspective painting.[1] Perspective stage painting, with its receding, central view, was often flanked by side units. When perspective created a finite view—as opposed to the simultaneous settings of the medieval theatre with numerous mansions surrounding an empty playing space— that view seemed to demand a frame. The frame both kept the audience from seeing what was offstage, such as machinery for creating special effects, and focused their view on the stage picture and the fiction it represented. Though we cannot say for sure, it is logical to suggest that theatre architecture and scenic design developed in relation to each other.

GAS LIGHTING, ELECTRICITY, AND THE DEVELOPMENT OF LIGHTING DESIGN IN THE NINETEENTH CENTURY

Light has always been an essential element of theatre, but theatre artists have not always been completely in control of this powerful tool. In several periods of theatre history, basic illumination of the stage was a challenge. That first hurdle had to be crossed before designers could turn their attention to fundamentals of contemporary lighting design like focusing audience attention and creating mood and atmosphere.

When theatre was staged partially or entirely outdoors, as it was from the classical periods until around 1600 in many parts of Europe, playwrights could consider the cycles of natural light available to them and avoid scenic effects running contrary to the daylight in which their plays would be presented, but many were not concerned with such matters. Examples from Shakespeare's plays demonstrate that he was willing to draw on the audience's imagination to create a scene different from the natural one surrounding audience members. The Elizabethan public theatres were partially open-air structures where performances usually began around 2 p.m. In the first act of *Hamlet*, the ghost of Hamlet's father appears on the battlements of Elsinore castle as the night watchmen are on duty. The idea that stage lighting could or should accurately depict environmental lighting conditions is a very modern one.

Meanwhile, in the Elizabethan private theatres, smaller indoor structures, candlelight was used. Though candles could sometimes be dimmed, illumination was hardly precise. Furthermore, in indoor theatres, candle-laden chandeliers lit the audience as well as the actors on stage. The "mystic chasm" envisioned by Richard Wagner in the nineteenth century, which created a gulf separating the stage world and the audience's world, was not yet available to theatre artists due to the limitations in lighting.

The eighteenth century saw some improvements in theatrical lighting. By midcentury, candles were appended to "ladders" behind the side wings, and these lights could be dimmed with small shields that blocked the light source. Footlights, which had been in use in the previous century, could also be dimmed by lowering them beneath the stage. In addition to direction and brightness, Phillipe Jacques DeLoutherbourg, a celebrated French designer who came to England to work at the Drury Lane Theatre under famous actor–manager David Garrick, was able to manipulate color through his use of colored silk screens that filtered the light.

During the nineteenth century, the technology of the Industrial Revolution was applied to the theatre. Some historians argue that the popularity of melodrama, with its emphasis on stage spectacle and special effects, accelerated these technological innovations. Though the melodramatic works so very popular in the nineteenth century seldom hold the stage today—one would be very hard-pressed to find a production of the era's most popular play, George Aiken's adaptation of Harriet Beecher Stowe's *Uncle Tom's Cabin*—the innovations they ushered in are still used in the contemporary theatre.

SPOTLIGHT
Henry Irving

A Portrait of Henry Irving.

© Hulton-Deutsch Collection/CORBIS

Henry Irving (1838–1905) was one of the most successful and important actor–managers in England in the late nineteenth century. Irving was tremendously popular as a performer of melodrama and had a wonderful stage partner in his leading lady, Ellen Terry (1847–1928). He was also the first English performer to be knighted. But Irving deserves a prominent place in the history of theatrical design for his work that advanced pictorial realism and for his exploration of the possibilities for stage lighting.

Throughout the nineteenth century, demands for stage spectacle grew. Melodrama depended on spectacle as a form, and its growing audiences sought more and greater effects. One change Irving made was eliminating the grooved scenery that had dominated scenic practice for 200 years. (This kind of scenery was attached to and also moved along grooves that were a permanent part of the stage floor. Other grooves were located overhead.) Instead Irving used "free plantation" scenery, which meant set pieces could be placed wherever designers and directors desired. Designers and directors were free to think outside the grooves that had dictated the placement of scenery and the look of the stage picture. Irving also used a front stage curtain, which meant set changes could be masked from the audience's view, thus offering the chance for surprise. In addition, he employed archeologists to help him perfect historical detail and famous painters to create the most stunning work possible.

Irving also experimented with the new advances in stage lighting. Irving used gas lighting in his theatre and sought unprecedented control of its possibilities. He broke up the footlights into smaller sections, each of which used differed colors, used masking pieces at the front of the stage to keep stage light on stage, and darkened the lights in the house, thus separating the stage and audience worlds. He was also interested in harmonizing all technical and design elements, and as such he anticipated the work of the modern director.

In 1816, Philadelphia's Chestnut Street Theatre became the first in the world to employ gas lighting in its interior. It was in use in most theatres in the Northeast by the 1820s. For the first time in theatre history, the stage could be lighted as brightly or as dimly as desired, but it wasn't without problems. Gas lighting was expensive, it smelled bad if it wasn't properly ventilated, and its intense heat made it dangerous.

The Chestnut Street Theatre, as seen from the exterior around 1800. In 1816 the theatre would become the first in the world to use gas lighting in its interior.

© Bettmann/CORBIS

Another innovation in lighting arrived in 1816 when Thomas Drummond invented the limelight (cylinders of compressed hydrogen and oxygen were directed against a column of lime to heat it to incandescence). At first its rays were used for creating atmospheric effects such as sunlight and moonlight, but eventually it became used as a follow spot to emphasize starring performers. This explains the popular use of the terms "limelight" and "spotlight" today.

Thomas Edison invented the electric incandescent lamp in 1879. By 1881, the Savoy Theatre in London, and by 1900 almost all East Coast American theatres, had followed suit. Electric light was more flexible and controllable than gas light or candlelight, and of course it was much safer. Nevertheless, one of the worst fires in American theatre history occurred after the invention of electric light. In 1903, 602 people died in the Iroquois Theatre Fire in Chicago. An arc light shorted out, the asbestos fire curtain disappeared after the fire and may not have been the flame retardant material asbestos at all, the door to the auditorium had locks that eliminated the possibility of quick exit, and the theatre was housing almost 200 more people than the seating capacity for the show. All these factors led to a horrible disaster.

It is well worth noting that advances in lighting also coincided with a time of self-definition for a large group of theatregoers. Middle- and working-class viewers filled the seats in nineteenth-century theatres. These audiences were hungry for melodramatic spectacle, which arguably drove theatre managers to find innovations in lighting. But melodramatic spectacle, with its clearly defined good guys and bad guys, averted disasters, and happy endings, also helped viewers craft, or become co-opted into, new codes of morality and ideals of social respectability. As lighting innovations were changing the way audiences saw the stage, the shows in which they were being used were also changing the ways the audiences saw themselves and the world.

Photo © Michal Daniel, 2004

Since the beginning of theatre, costumes have added to the visual excitement of the art form. This continues into the twenty-first century as this production of *The Pirates of Penzance* makes clear.

of Europe, costume design (particularly in public theatres) did not appear as a regular part of theatrical production until late in the nineteenth century, and even at that late date, it was often undertaken by a theatre artist who had other tasks in production like directing, set design, or acting.

Long before costume was consciously designed, it was often an important visual element. Although playing spaces remained general in parts of Europe from the medieval period through the early nineteenth century either because of neutral playing spaces or through scenic backdrops that were reused for a wide variety of shows, costumes were sometimes the most visually spectacular things on the stage. But it was not until realism dominated the stage that costume and character matched consistently. Prior to the nineteenth century, most characters (there were exceptions) wore contemporary garments, regardless of the period in which the play was set. Thanks to the universalizing tendencies of neoclassicism, differences in places and time periods were deemed largely unimportant visually. Furthermore, actors, who frequently chose their own costumes, wanted the most sumptuous garments possible to demonstrate their status as performers. Though company wardrobes were available to the performers from which to choose costumes, the more prosperous performers shunned the wardrobes in favor of their own garments.

In the second half of the eighteenth century, guides to dress such as *Recuil des Habillements* and *The Dress and Habits of the Peoples of England*, began to provide historical detail about the history of garments for theatre practitioners in England. At the same time in France, artists at the Comedie Francais, such as the performers Mlle Clarion and H.L. Lekain, became interested in creating costumes particular to a role, but many actors rejected the new ideas about stage dress until the turn of the nineteenth century.

During the early nineteenth century interest in scenic spectacle, historical accuracy, and "local color" increased sharply. The generalized idealism of neoclassicism was out, and more detailed and individual representations were in as romanticism and melodrama, forms we will investigate in Chapter 11, came to dominate the stage. As the century wore on, and realism became an increasingly popular theatrical style, playwrights became more diligent in adding details about their characters' dress and integrating these details into the narrative. Henrik Ibsen's (1828–1906) *A Doll's House* (1879) provides a prime example. The play tells the story of Nora, a young wife and mother, who is coming to terms with consequences of a lie she told to save her husband's life. When Torvald, her husband, became ill, Nora forged her dead father's signature on a bank note to get the money to take Torvald to Italy. When Krogstad discovers her crime, he blackmails her, hoping to protect his job at the bank her husband manages. Nora begins the play dressed as respectable lady of the period, but as her hysteria mounts when she thinks she will soon be revealed to her husband and society at large, she dons an Italian peasant's shawl and dancing costume. There is a practical reason for the costume change: Nora and Torvald are to attend a masquerade party. But the details of her costume—its Italian roots recall the specifics of her crime, and her husband relishes seeing her bare shoulders while she dances a wild, sensual Italian dance, which like the crime itself, goes against the rules of deportment for a lady of her standing—help to move the plot toward its climax. To stage the play, one must create a very specific costume.

When scholars look to explain the development of realism, the writing style that *A Doll's House* did much to establish, they sometimes examine the technological advances of the mid-nineteenth century. One such development that coincides with the establishment of realism as a major theatrical style is the invention of photography in 1839. Photography allowed artists to capture an exact, detailed representation of the world around them. It also required a very particularly physical process—involving light, material objects, and chemicals. Photography emphasized the material aspects of existence in a given moment. The precise, comprehensive, and materially oriented account that a photograph could provide gave playwrights an intriguing new form to emulate. Although it would be incorrect to say

SPOTLIGHT

The First Generations of American Costume Design: Aline Bernstein and Irene Sharaff

Perhaps one of the most interesting facts about the history of costume design in the United States is that it really hasn't been written. Countless pages have been devoted to the history of playwriting, directing, producing, and scene design, but very little has been written about American costumers—particularly prior to the 1950s. Even locating the names of the first generation of American costume designers is a challenge.

There are several reasons for this strange phenomenon. First, for many years, one person designed all aspects of a production. Even though realism was making the demand for historical accuracy widespread in the last years of the nineteenth century and the early years of the twentieth century, this did not yet mean separate specialists were designated for each design area. At first some directors and producers simply did the work themselves (we will discuss the work of Georg II

Aline Bernstein's costume design for the premiere of Lillian Hellman's *Children's Hour* on Broadway in 1934.

and David Belasco in the next chapter), and sometimes stars commissioned designers to create costumes just for them, while the rest of the production was more or less "undesigned." Examples of this latter phenomenon include Edwin Forrest hiring Jackson Allen (1176–1853), Edwin Booth hiring (Thomas Joyce 1821–1873), and Viola Allen hiring H. A. Ogden (1856–1922). It was not until an actors strike in 1919 that a producer was required to purchase costumes for all the performers in a production. This date provides a turning point in the history of costume design. The contractual obligation and scale of the task made the costume designer a necessary part of the artistic staff of many theatres.

In his work chronicling the history of theatrical design since 1945 for *The Cambridge History of American Theatre*, Ronn Smith noted that at the turn of the century only one percent of the programs from New York stage productions featured a costume designer; by the end of the 1940s the number had reached 50 percent. The 1930s and 1940s provided two other landmarks in American costume design history: costume designers were allowed to join the United Scenic Artists Association, the American union for stage designers, in 1936 (but they were not allowed to vote on union issues until 1966), and in 1947 the Tony Awards added a category for Best Costume Design.

Irene Sharaff's costume design for the premiere of *West Side Story* on Broadway in 1959.

Aline Bernstein (1880–1955) was one of the artists who rose to prominence as a costume (and set) designer in the early years of the twentieth century. She was born in New York City, but in her childhood travelled the acting circuit with her mother and her father, who was an actor. In her teens, after both parents died, she lived with her aunt, who ran a theatrical boarding house in New York City, and later studied painting at the New York School of Applied Design. Though she married a Wall Street broker in 1902 and had two children shortly thereafter, she did not divorce herself from the life of the theatre. She volunteered backstage at the Henry Street Settlement, where she met Alice and Irene Lewisohn, who produced plays. Between 1915 and 1924 she designed costumes for fifteen shows for the Lewisohn sisters at their famous Neighborhood Playhouse. Bernstein also designed for the acclaimed actress, director, and producer Eva La Gallienne at the Civic Repertory Theatre and designed the costumes for *The Children's Hour*, Lillian Hellman's first play, in 1934. Beyond these early accomplishments, Bernstein helped establish the Costume Institute at the Metropolitan Museum of Art and continued designing steadily into her seventies. She was seventy when she won the Tony Award for costuming the opera *Regina* in 1951.

In the early years of American costume design, it was standard practice for designers to promote the work and careers of their assistants. Bernstein's assistant at the Civic Repertory Theatre was Irene Sharaff (1910–1993). Sharaff, who was born in Boston and artistically trained in New York and Paris, went on to a stellar career on her own in costume design for theatre and film. Among her career highlights onstage are *The Boys from Syracuse* (1939), *A Tree Grows in Brooklyn* (1951), *The King and I* (1952), *Candide* (1957), *West Side Story* (1959), *Funny Girl* (1964), and *Sweet Charity* (1966). Her film highlights include Academy Awards for all the following films: *An American in Paris* (1951), *The King and I* (1956), *West Side Story* (1961), *Cleopatra* (1963), and *Who's Afraid of Virginia Woolf?* (1966). She was nominated for twelve more Academy Awards. In 1993, the Theatre Development Fund named its Lifetime Achievement Award in Costume after its first recipient: Irene Sharaff.

Three different twentieth-century costume designers interpret the details of Nora's dancing costume in *A Doll's House.*

BAM/Photofest

Photofest

Photofest

that photography changed the way costumes were made in the nineteenth century, it is not unreasonable to suggest that photography eventually changed the way plays were made. As playwrights sought a new level of detail in their writing to capture the particulars of material existence, the costumes used to visualize this writing also demanded a new level of detail. In the following decades a theatre's production staff included specific artists—costume designers—to imagine and facilitate the creation of these stage garments. Such garments were made with detailed choices, which would play a major part in the telling of a specific dramatic story.

SPOTLIGHT

Darron L. West

Darron L. West (1966–) is one of the contemporary theatre's most innovative and hardworking sound designers. Though his field is the newest in the theatre, he's already shaking up the way the art is practiced.

West, the son of a minister, grew up in Kentucky, played drums and bass guitar in garage rock bands, worked a great deal in radio as a DJ and studio engineer, and was inspired by the advent of multichannel cinema sound (and participated in a summer youth theatre program, where he took a role in *Bye Bye, Birdie* and caught the theatre bug) before majoring in broadcasting and minoring in theatre at Western Kentucky University. In his freshman year of college, the school was getting ready to produce *Foxfire*, which included many recordings of a singer in a band. Knowing about his radio and sound engineering experience, one of the professors suggested he serve as the play's sound designer, a job that West didn't know existed at that point in his education. After designing every production staged during the rest of his undergraduate years and earning his degree, the technical director at the school

Darron L. West at work.

Courtesy of Darron West

helped West land his first professional job—as resident sound designer at the illustrious Williamstown Theatre Festival in 1989. He then spent a season as resident designer at the Alabama Shakespeare Festival before going back to Kentucky to work at the Actors Theatre of Louisville, where he collaborated with a variety of artists, including Tina Landau, Lee Blessing, Jose Rivera, Marcus Stern, and Jon Jory. During the 1991–92 season, he met director Anne Bogart while working on Eduardo Muchado's *Eye of the Hurricane*.

Soon after, he joined Bogart's SITI Company and moved to New York. Bogart's working method, The Viewpoints, makes sound a vital, integral part of each production. When West works with Bogart, he is there for the entire rehearsal period, not just to introduce a design during the technical rehearsals right before a show opens. He sets up computers and samplers in the rehearsal room and creates a soundtrack for the show as the actors are creating their roles. As Bogart told Steven Drukman of *American Theatre*, "Darron is the best dramaturg I have ever encountered. When he is sitting to the left of me in rehearsals, he is looking out for the play and what the play is trying to tell us at every moment." In a 1999 interview with David Barbour for *Live Design*, West echoed Bogart's assessment of his function, "Good designers should function as dramaturgs. You're trying to tell the story, too— you're just using a different tool. The best designers can carry on a conversation with the director about the play, not about whether you should use a clarinet or not. If you're talking about the play, then the play will tell you musically what's it's supposed to be."

West has found an extraordinary collaborator in Anne Bogart, and through their work together, he has challenged the still nascent paradigm of how a sound designer works. But West has also worked with a host of other directors and companies as a freelance designer—on Broadway, Off-Broadway, in regional theatres all over the country, and internationally. His work has been nominated for and won numerous awards, including those from the American Theatre Wing, the Barrymore Award, the Obie, the Drama Desk, and the Louise Lortell Award. He is currently based in New York City, where he is Design Associate for the New York Theatre Workshop and where he continues to thrive as a company member and resident sound designer for Anne Bogart's SITI Company.

DIGITAL TECHNOLOGY AND THE TWENTIETH-CENTURY LAUNCH OF SOUND DESIGN

Music has been an important part of theatre since its inception in the West—Greek choruses provided lyrical, musical interludes throughout the performance—and sound effects have an equally long theatrical history, but sound design as a formalized practice and a discrete theatrical design area is a very new phenomenon. It is so new that its history is still being written (and teased apart from related developments in film), but some important dates in the 1990s are emerging as signposts. In 1991, John Gromada earned an Obie for his sound design for an Off-Broadway production of Sophie Treadwell's play, *Machinal*. (Sound design would not become an award category for the Tonys until 2008.) In 1993, the Yale School of Drama admitted its first class of sound designers. Also in 1993 a standard labor contract was created by the stagehands' union, IATSE, for Broadway and Broadway-tour sound designers.

Emile Berline created the first microphone, a telephone transmitter, for Alexander Graham Bell in 1876, and Albert Edison made the first recording of the human voice in 1877, but many argue that it is the advent of digital sound, which occurred in the 1990s, that has made the sound designer a necessity in the design process. Sound designers are not just limited to recording and amplifying sound with the aid of these two earlier inventions. In the digital era, sound can be manipulated and captured in ways previously unimaginable. Sound design is a field that is evolving by the minute. Consider the example of Apple's GarageBand software, introduced in 2004 and already in version 4 by 2008. Other options for sound designers include Soundtrack Pro, also from Apple, and Audacity, which is free to download from SourceForge.net. In this regard, sound design echoes larger cultural patterns: rapid change is a hallmark of early twenty-first-century life, as is the intervention of global corporations, like Apple, into virtually every aspect of existence.

CHAPTER SUMMARY

The study of these four moments in the history of the theatre reveals that although the potential for theatre spectacle and sound have changed radically over time, embracing broader cultural and technological shifts, something fundamental to the nature of theatre has remained the same.

Contemporary theatrical spectacle has the potential to sharpen audience perception.

The visual spectacle of the theatre is used to intensify our perceptions. Sound in the theatre does likewise. Whether it uses a painted backdrop, colored light, detailed and purposefully designed costumes, or digitally enhanced sound, the technology of the theatre takes us places we can't go on our own and reveals to us things we hadn't quite been able to understand, visualize, and articulate.

ACTIVITIES

Photography, the Internet, and Theatrical Style

If photography, a major nineteenth-century invention, coincided with realism and realistic production technique, how might the Internet, a contemporary invention, affect the way art is made today? How could theatre artists learn from the way people use the Internet? How does the Internet affect the way we process image, story, and sound? When does the Internet isolate people and ideas and when does it connect them? Collect images or sound clips to aid your discussion of these questions with a partner or group.

Deleted Scenes

Many DVDs include deleted scenes in their selection of bonus materials. Find a DVD that offers this feature and pay particular attention to sound in a couple of scenes. Many times the deleted scenes have not yet been under-scored. Watching these scenes you get a clear sense of the function of sound in film. Now go back to the movie and watch any regular scene. Discuss the different ways you were affected by a scene without music or additional sound and one with this addition. Then discuss a play you have read or seen for class. If you saw the play, how was sound used in the production? How would different music, different sound effects, or a different method of amplification change the message and experience of the play? If the play you're discussing is one you've only read, what choices would you make for this play in terms of music, sound effects, and amplification?

The Rise of the Director

DUKE GEO. II OF SAXE-MEININGEN & WIFE   3484-13

Georg II, Duke of Saxe-Meiningen, with his wife and collaborator, Ellen Franz. Georg II is often called the first modern director.

As the nineteenth century unfolded, theatre producers and audiences became increasingly interested in detail, accuracy, and specificity in performance, as we discussed in the last chapter. With this demand, and changes in dramatic writing style, came the need for a single person to coordinate the visual and verbal elements of the theatre and to unify them into a compelling, and sometimes spectacular, whole. Jobs that had, through the history of Western theatre, been distributed to other theatre artists were now centralized in the hands of the modern director. This chapter looks at the ways Madame Vestris, Richard Wagner, Georg II, Duke of Saxe-Meinigen, Andre Antoine, and Constantin Stanislavsky shaped modern understandings of the work of the director. The chapter also considers playwrights representative of the styles that facilitated that need for the director: Dion Boucicault (melodrama), Victor Hugo (romanticism), and Anton Chekhov (realism). Finally we'll look at some of the ways European ideas about directing took shape in the United States in the early twentieth century.

THE WORK OF THE DIRECTOR EMERGES: MADAME VESTRIS

Long before anyone was called "the director" in the theatre, people were performing the tasks we now regularly associate with that role. Before we look at the artists usually identified as the first directors, it will be helpful to look back a generation to the work of Madame Vestris. When we see the kind of work for which she became famous, it will help us understand what changed in the late nineteenth century.

Madame Vestris was born Lucia Elizabetta Bartalozzi in 1797. She married at age sixteen and began acting at age eighteen. Though we will be looking at her work as a theatre manager, she was also well known for her work as an actress. She was one of the most popular performers of light comedy and burlesque, then understood as a light satirical form without today's implications of striptease, until she retired at age fifty-seven.

Her most innovative work came in the 1830s while she managed London's Olympic Theatre. Her productions were groundbreaking, thanks to her care with all the visual aspects of production. Madame Vestris was very particular about harmonizing all the design elements: she coordinated set, costumes, and props. She became famous for her use of the box set, which she embellished with real furniture and other domestic items. Though she was associated with the exaggerated form of burlesque, she replaced the typical outlandish costumes, as they would have been out of sync with her carefully crafted domestic interiors. Instead she used costumes that were

SPOTLIGHT
The Box Set

The box set, which gives the sense of three walls surrounding an open living space, first appeared in Italy in the late seventeenth century. Fabrizio Carini Motto described its use in Mantua in his *Construction of Theatres and Theatrical Machinery*. But this particular way of designing stage space is generally associated with the late nineteenth century and the growing realistic impulse in theatre production at the time. When painted scenery was still in vogue, domestic stage space generally had little in common with real rooms. Actors acted before paintings decorated with tables and chairs, for example. But the box set made stage space three dimensional, an effect enhanced when real tables, chairs, and other household objects were used within it. Madame Vestris was some sixty years ahead of popular English theatrical practice in her scenic techniques: the box set would not become commonplace in England until the Bancrofts made it popular near the end of the nineteenth century, when realistic playwriting had also become prevalent. But once the slowly evolving box set became popular, it stayed popular—it is in fact still commonly used for realistic interiors on stage today.

Photo courtesy of the University of Kansas Theatre.

The box set, which first became popular in the nineteenth century, is still regularly used today. This box set was designed for a 2008 production of *A Flea in her Ear* at the University of Kansas.

reminiscent of everyday life. Though her work precedes the work of the great directors later in the century, the impulses she harnessed—specificity, care with detail, and unification of detail into a harmonious visual whole— signal a change in the way theatre looked and was made.

RICHARD WAGNER: THE THEORY OF THE TOTAL ARTWORK

While Madame Vestris put her ideas into practice on the stage in England, Richard Wagner (1813–1883), the great composer, would soon explore some similar concepts theoretically. Wagner was very familiar with the theatre—his stepfather and his siblings worked in theatre—but some of his most influential ideas were formulated while he was exiled from Germany for his part in the revolution of 1848. During these twelve years, he voiced two of the most important ideas that shape modern understandings of the work of the director.

Though much of the early history of directing is linked to realism, Wagner was vehemently opposed to realism. He believed that dramatists should forge myths, not slavishly recount domestic detail. Instead of dwelling on surfaces, he wanted to tap submerged impulses as, he believed, this would lead the artist to an idealized, magical world. He also advocated for the

Photofest

Richard Wagner translated his theatrical theories to the stage in his operas. The Metropolitan Opera produced his great work, *The Ring of the Nibelungen*, for PBS.

power music held, as opposed to the spoken word. Musical performers were subject to far greater control by the composer than actors are by the dramatist. According to Wagner, the author/composer should hold all authority over the art, unifying all parts of the performance into a well-integrated whole that he called the *Gesamtkunstwerk*, which is translated as total artwork. Finally, Wagner advocated a separation between the world of the audience and the world of the stage that we discussed in Chapter 5. He argued that "a mystic chasm" was needed between these two planes. When he designed his Festival Theatre at Bayreuth, he concealed the orchestra pit beneath the stage. He did not allow musicians to tune their instruments in the pit to further the illusion and also forbade applause during the show. As a last touch, now quite familiar to contemporary theatergoers, he darkened the auditorium. In sum, Wagner insisted on a unified artwork, controlled by a central, authoritative figure. He solidified theatrical illusion so that audience could feel that they were peering into a world separate from their own.

ROMANTICISM AND THE SOLITARY GENIUS

As our study of Wagner demonstrated, the rise of the modern director has roots beyond realism. Another nonrealistic form that contributed to the development of directing is romanticism. Romanticism developed in Germany in the early nineteenth century. Theatregoers first came to know romanticism from the fate tragedies popular between 1810 and 1820 such as Zacharias Werner's (1768–1823) *The Twenty-fourth of February* (1809) and from Ludwig Tieck's (1173–1853) productions of Shakespeare. Shakespeare became a role model for romantic writers who were looking to escape the structural bonds of neoclassicism that we will discuss next. The theory of romanticism spread through the essays of August Wilhelm Schlegel (1767–1845). Romanticism celebrated nature and other unspoiled places and peoples; emphasized the spiritual, extreme states of emotion, and other forms of heightened experience; valorized rebellion; and suggested that the highest truth might be glimpsed through art.

A tenet of romanticism particularly pertinent to the work of the director is described by Oscar Brockett, perhaps the preeminent American theatre historian, as follows:

> Only an exceptional imagination can perceive the final unity behind the apparently endless diversity of existence, and only the artist–genius and the philosopher has this. The artist is a truly superior being capable of providing guidance for others willing to listen.

"Wanderer Above the Sea of Fog" by Caspar David Friedrich, captures the isolation of the romantic genius.

© The Gallery Collection/CORBIS

These ideas suggested that unity was important, and only a superior artistic consciousness—like that of a director—might lead others toward it. Though the director would emerge later in the nineteenth century, the ideas of romanticism smoothed the way for this artistic transition.

Romanticism also thrived in France. Many historians date French romanticism from the opening night of Victor Hugo's (1802–1885) play *Hernani* in 1830. The title character is an outlaw who loves a beautiful woman, Dona Sol. She is also pursued by the king and by her guardian, but it is Hernani who wins her love. Just when a happy ending seems to be eminent, her guardian reminds Hernani of a debt he pledged for his assistance in the past. Hernani is required to kill himself at the guardian's request. Dona Sol then joins him in death.

In the play, Hugo violates many of the rules of neoclassicism. Neoclassicism was set up as the opposite of romanticism because of its rigid attachment to order. Hugo ignored neoclassic verse form and the unities of time and place, mixed the comic and tragic, showed death and violence onstage, and threatened ideas

Erich Lessing/Art Resource, NY

"Illustration of the Hernani riots at the Comedie Francaise in 1830" about how noble characters were expected to behave. And if what was happening on stage wasn't revolutionary enough, Hugo made sure what was happening in the house would be incendiary too. Hugo bought many tickets throughout the house for the opening performance, choosing not to rely on the *claqueurs*, or those the theatre placed in the audience to applaud at the right times, and distributed the tickets to young men like Theophile Gautier, a future poet of some renown. Gautier came to the play in pea green pants and a pink doublet that he'd had specially tailored for the occasion so as to shock the conservatives in the audience, those the romantic youth called "Romans," with his dress. Old and young clashed over things onstage and off—paintings of the first night show the disagreements Hugo sparked escalating to physical violence. So even though *Hernani* does not feature a solitary artistic genius willing to drive others into the future, one might argue that it is Hugo himself who embodies this romantic quality through his daring play and the drama he helped to create offstage that accompanied it.

POPULAR SPECTACLE: NINETEENTH-CENTURY MELODRAMA AND DION BOUCICAULT

The nineteenth century saw the birth of one of the most popular dramatic forms of all time—the melodrama. During this period, vast numbers of people were moving from the country to the city to find work and to earn more money. They spent some of this money on entertainment, and melodrama was the ideal vehicle for this new urban class. Melodrama was fast-paced, exciting, and easy to understand. The lines between good and evil were clearly drawn, and virtue was ultimately rewarded, whereas vice was punished. Deep, complicated characters were foreign to melodrama. Instead of placing high demands on the audience's intellect, writers and producers worked to generate emotional responses through the use of musical underscoring, broad acting styles, and vibrant spectacle. Spectacle was in fact a major component of melodrama's popularity, and one of the things that ties the form to the development of the modern director. With the complicated visual effects that the scripts demanded came the need for an artist to oversee and coordinate these effects—a task now associated with the director. Also important was comic relief. Many plays featured a comic sidekick, whose antics gave a reprieve from the emotional intensity. In many respects, melodrama functioned much like television functions today. It had enormous mass popularity as it simultaneously responded to

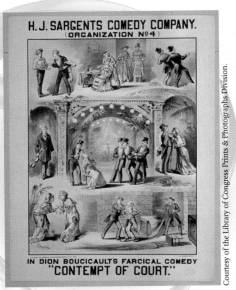

H. J. SARGENTS COMEDY COMPANY.
(ORGANIZATION No 4)

IN DION BOUCICAULT'S FARCICAL COMEDY
"CONTEMPT OF COURT."

Courtesy of the Library of Congress Prints & Photographs Division.

In Dion Boucicault's Farcical Comedy *Contempt of Court.*

and helped to define the artistic tastes and morality of the era.

While August von Kotzebue's *Misanthropy and Repentance* (1789) is sometimes called the first melodrama, it was Charles Rene Guilbert de Pixerecourt's plays a decade later like *Victor, or The Child of the Forest* (1798) and *Coelina* (1800) that helped shape melodrama into an easily recognizable form with the characteristic features described earlier. In the United States, Dion Boucicault (1822–1890) did much to popularize the form.

Dion Boucicault was born Dionysius Lardner Boursiquot in Dublin. When he began acting—he had great success as a comic performer—he called himself Lee Morton, but when he began writing plays in 1841, he settled on the name for which he is now famous. Boucicault lived in France from 1844 to 1848, and it was there that he learned how to create in the melodramatic form. He spent most of the 1850s writing, acting, and managing in the United States, while during the next decade he divided his time between the United States and England. Among his famous plays are *The Corsican Brothers* (1852), *The Poor of New York* (1857), *The Octoroon* (1859), and *Colleen Bawn* (1860).

Boucicault's scripts were very popular. He had the wise idea of charging a percentage of each evening's proceeds when other theatres wanted to produce his work. This innovation created the foundation of the royalty system, which would make playwriting a more lucrative endeavor, especially after copyright was established in 1886.

DUKE OF SAXE-MEININGEN: THE FIRST MODERN DIRECTOR?

Georg II, a German aristocrat, became the Duke of Saxe-Meiningen in 1866. Almost as soon as he came to the throne, he set about improving the thirty-year-old court theatre. Georg II had very specific ideas about the kind of theatre he wanted to see, thanks to his exposure to theatrical innovations in London, Berlin, and Coburg-Gotha. He also had two able assistants in Ludwig Chronegk, a comic actor the duke hired as a director who arranged the company's famous tours, and in Ellen Franz, an actress who

SPOTLIGHT

Goethe's Rules for Actors

© Bettmann/CORBIS

When historians are looking for the first director, they sometimes name a German who preceded Georg II, Duke of Saxe-Meiningen: Johann Wolfgang Friedrich von Goethe. In 1808, Goethe's secretary, Eckermann, compiled the ninety-one rules for actors he established while working at the Weimar Court Theatre, clearly indicating that he had an authoritative system guiding his work with actors. Goethe's aesthetic was based on beauty, stateliness, and order and his rules are aimed at realizing this goal. Some of his rules provide wise guidelines, even for contemporary actors, such as his Recitation & Declamation, #20: "The words which I utter must be brought out with energy and liveliest expression, so that I seem to experience each emotional impulse as actually present," and Recitation & Declamation, #28: "The declaimer is free to select his own stops, pauses, and so forth; but he must guard against destroying the true meaning, which he can do by this means just as easily as by an omitted or badly expressed word." Other rules, however, suggest a style far too formal for most contemporary stage work such as Posture and Movement of the Body on the Stage, #39: "Accordingly, it is mistaken naturalness for the actors to play to each other as if no third person were present; they should never play in profile, nor turn their backs to the audience." Finally some other guidelines will strike contemporary readers as humorous, such as Avoiding Bad Habits, # 74: "The actor should never allow his handkerchief to be seen on stage, still less blow his nose, still less spit. It is terrible to be reminded of these physical necessities within a work of art."

Perhaps Goethe would have made further theatrical innovation and wrested the title of first director away from Georg II if he hadn't retired in 1817. He quit in a huff when he was unable to prevent a dog from performing on the stage he had worked so hard to make beautiful and orderly. A trained poodle, along with his master, an actor called Karsten, had taken much of Germany by storm. Caroline Jagemann, the troublemaking leading actress in Goethe's company and also the mistress of the Duke of Weimar, was anxious for the poodle to perform. Jagemann implored her boyfriend to let the poodle take the stage at Weimar, so the duke overruled Goethe.

SPOTLIGHT

The Nineteenth-Century International Star

Though the Duke of Saxe-Meiningen was known for creating a strong ensemble and that feature of his theatre helped pave the way toward realistic production, star performers were extremely popular throughout most of the nineteenth century. International theatre stars had never been truly possible before the nineteenth century. Railroads and steamships, which aided travel and touring, and photography, which allowed the mass circulation of images in newspapers and other publications, came together to help create these global acting sensations. Millions flocked to the theatre to see these celebrities, even though the actors usually performed in their native languages. Following are photos and brief biographical sketches of some of the performers who burned so brightly as they trod the boards between 1800 and 1900.

Sarah Bernhardt (1844–1923) was the greatest French actress of the nineteenth century and probably the century's biggest international star. She began performing when she was eighteen and joined the Comedie Francais, the preeminent French theatre company, just ten years later. She stayed at the Comedie Francais until 1880, when she left to tour internationally. Bernhardt was especially known for her magnetic depictions of passion, rage, and death.

Sarah Bernhardt

Eleanora Duse (1859–1924) was the greatest Italian actress of the nineteenth century. She started performing as a child. By the time she was in her twenties, she had formed her own company, which toured the world. Though she had officially retired when she was 50, she returned to the stage in 1921 and died while on tour in Pittsburgh. She was known for subtle, complex performances that she created through her own physicality, not through the aid of makeup or other forms of theatrical magic.

Eleanora Duse

Henry Irving (1838–1905) was one of the most acclaimed English actors of the nineteenth century, in addition to his technical innovations that we discussed in Chapter 10. Irving (born Henry Brodribb) started acting at eighteen and played in the provinces for ten years before making his name as an actor and manager in London. For twenty years Irving managed the Lyceum, which he made the most prominent theatre in London. He was excellent in both melodrama and Shakespearean tragedy. Though he remained based in London, he toured throughout England and visited the United States eight times.

Actor Henry Irving

Ellen Terry (1847–1928) came from a famous family of English actors and continued to build her family's legacy as Henry Irving's leading lady as well as through her management of the Imperial Theatre. Her timing and vocal command helped her create masterful versions of Shakespeare's female characters.

Actress Ellen Terry

Edwin Booth (1833–1893) began his theatrical career in his childhood by going on tours with his father, Junius Brutus Booth. He debuted in Boston in 1849, toured in his native United States and internationally in the early 1850s, and became established as a star in New York by the mid-1850s. He was especially well known for his productions of Shakespeare. His *Hamlet* played for 100 nights, setting a record for the show that would hold until the twentieth century. When his brother assassinated Abraham Lincoln, he did leave the stage for a while, but he came back in 1869 and opened the Booth Theatre in New York. Though he went bankrupt in 1874, he continued to take star roles in other people's productions until he retired in 1891.

Actor Edwin Booth

would eventually marry the duke but who also chose the plays the company would perform, adapted them, and did vocal coaching for the other actors.

The Meiningen Players had several trademark qualities under the leadership of Georg II, Chronegk, and Franz. First, the Meiningen Players did not rely on star performers. Instead, unknown actors—some beginners and some more seasoned performers who never attained fame—were rehearsed carefully and for long periods, sometimes for several months. The company had no set deadlines, so they worked until the material was ready. They were coached in vocal delivery and given very specific blocking for each moment in the show. Particularly effective were the Meiningen's highly choreographed and elaborate crowd scenes. Second, Georg II designed the set, costumes, and properties with meticulous care. His work was extremely detailed using authentic materials and construction methods, and because he was making all the choices and was making them specifically for each show, the visual elements of the show were completely unified. Georg II had complete authority, and his detailed work made total illusion in the theatre a viable possibility.

Touring was a significant part of the Meiningen Players' influence. For the first eight years of their work, the Meiningen Players stayed at home, but from 1874 to 1890, they toured extensively, visiting some thirty-eight cities in England, Holland, Belgium, Austria, Sweden, Denmark, and Russia. After 2,600 performances across Europe, they were the most respected and well-known company currently in operation, and their high standards became goals to which others aspired.

THE INDEPENDENT THEATRE MOVEMENT: ANDRE ANTOINE AND THE THEATRE LIBRE

Among the members of the audience for an 1888 performance of the Meiningen Players in London was a young Frenchman named Andre Antoine. Antoine had worked as a clerk in a gas company to support himself while he took small roles with professional companies and performed with an amateur group in Paris. But his trip to England, where he also saw the work of Henry Irving, proved inspirational for the artist who had, the year before, founded his own company, the Theatre Libre.

The Theatre Libre was a revolutionary force in the late-nineteenth-century theatre. When his amateur group refused to produce the kind of work he was interested in doing, he broke off on his own. Antoine was interested in the work of naturalist writers like Emile Zola. Naturalism was an extreme form of realism that was particularly interested in detailed environments and how such environments shaped character. Antoine gave this idea physical and spatial form. He was one of the first artists to demand strict observance of the "fourth wall." Actors were not allowed to acknowledge the presence of the audience. He arranged stage rooms as though they were rooms in real life, full of actualistic details as such as beef carcasses for a play called *The Butchers*. He insisted that each play have a distinct setting. His high standards left him constantly in debt, but nevertheless he managed to tour with his company to five other countries. In his wake, others—including Otto Brahm at the Freie Bühne in Germany and J. T. Grein at the Independent Theatre in London—sought to employ realistic production principles as they staged the new naturalistic and realistic dramas that were sweeping through Europe and revolutionizing theatre.

CONSTANTIN STANISLAVSKI, ANTON CHEKHOV, AND THE MOSCOW ART THEATRE

The Independent Theatre Movement came to Russia in the 1890s. Throughout the nineteenth century, the Russian theatre primarily relied on eighteenth-century theatre practices. But in 1885 and 1890, the Meiningen Players visited the country, showing new possibilities for theatrical production. In 1898 Constantin Stanislavski and Vladimir Nemirovich-Danchenko founded the Moscow Art Theatre, Russia's own independent theatre.

From the start, the Moscow Art Theatre differed from the independent theatres in England and Europe. The company was fully professional, and the repertoire consisted primarily of Russian playwrights. When the MAT figured out how to produce the work of the great realist playwright Anton Chekhov successfully, both the company and artist immediately hurdled into international prominence.

Chekhov, who had trained as a doctor, began writing vaudeville sketches and short comic plays. His full-length play, *The Seagull*, premiered at the Alexandrinsky Theatre in St. Petersburg in 1896. It was a disaster because the actors hadn't memorized their lines and didn't understand this new kind of play would not work with the melodramatic performance techniques—declamatory speech, bodies always facing the audience, all action staged right at the footlights—that were the norm. *The Seagull*, like Chekhov's other three major plays (*Uncle Vanya*, 1899; *The Three Sisters*, 1901; *The Cherry Orchard*, 1904), features a detailed portrait of Russia's

SPOTLIGHT

Realism and Revolutionary Ideas in the Nineteenth Century

The connections between theatrical form and the history of ideas are particularly clear when it comes to realism. As we discussed in Chapter 10, realism came to the fore in the late nineteenth century. Typical features of realistic production include dialogue emulating everyday speech, cause-to-effect plots affected by environmental factors as well as the heredity of the characters, three-dimensional functional objects on stage, and observance of the fourth wall. Eventually psychologically motivated acting was added to the mix. These artistic traits are directly linked to some of the radical shifts in various forms of intellectual activity and scientific discovery that occurred in the nineteenth century.

The father of modern sociology, **Auguste Comte** (1798–1857), believed that social problems could be studied in a scientific manner. By carefully observing the world and studying it in detail, solutions might be found. In realistic drama, the playwright was a meticulous reporter of contemporary issues. Through this hybrid of artistic and scientific investigation, audiences had the opportunity to contemplate the world around them in new ways.

Charles Darwin's (1809–1892) ideas connect to realism through his interest in the environment's effect on different species. Darwin wrote about the concept of natural selection. When plants and animals

landowning class. Set in rural Russia, the play's many characters are frequently bored with their lives and talk around and over each other about the conditions in which they find themselves. These particular characters are struggling artists looking for love. Though at first it may seem like very little happens in the play, the clearly drawn characters have deep, rich emotional lives, and a layered, nuanced picture of a time and place at once particular and universal, emerges.

Though Chekhov had sworn off playwriting after the debacle in St. Petersburg, he did allow the fledgling MAT to remount the play. When Chekhov's particular style was paired with Constantin Stanislavski's ideas about acting and character development, theatrical magic occurred. In Chapter 8 we discussed Stanislavski's ideas about acting, but it is well worth reviewing some of the highlights here. His work directing actors at can adapt to their environment, they stand a better chance of survival. Realistic playwrights were interested in the way environments—domestic, social, and cultural—might shape a character's personality and choices. Environment exerts tremendous pressure on characters in realistic drama.

Karl Marx (1818–1883) also connects to realism through the ways he argued that the material conditions under which people live might affect them. An earlier worldview might be summarized by Rene Descartes' idea—"I think therefore I am." Marx argued that people think as a result of how they live—if they have enough to eat or a warm place to sleep. Marx's ideas provided further inspiration for how the physical world and its conditions might affect a character.

Sigmund Freud (1856–1939) had a tremendous influence on both realistic and nonrealistic drama. His ideas about the ego (the central part of the psyche or self), superego (the psyche's source of control and morality), and id (the pleasure-seeking part of the psyche that often conflicts with the regulatory superego) were of great use to writers seeking to create characters driven by hidden motivations that the characters themselves might not initially understand. Meanwhile, his theories about dreams would inspire writers looking for an alternative to realistic writing and its attention to everyday experience.

the MAT served as a laboratory for his theory, and this theory has had a tremendous influence on the way many subsequent directors continue to work with actors today.

Stanislavski encouraged actors to observe reality in great detail. Because Chekhov's plays were highly detailed and intimate accounts, the two paired beautifully. Further, Chekhov gave more emphasis to character than plot. He carefully rendered each character, and these characters are vibrant because of what they say and feel, not because of what they do. Stanislavski's use of the magic if—if I were this person in this situation, I would. . . .—and his theory of emotion memory—which encouraged actors to import analogous situations from their own experience into the creation of character—served Chekhov's character-heavy plays very well. Finally, Stanislavski's desire that actors work within given circumstances—

© Austrian Archives/CORBIS

Anton Chekhov with Cast of *The Seagull* at the Moscow Art Theatre

meticulously drawn by Chekhov—to find a throughline and motivation for their characters also meshed well. Stanislavski's many ideas made it possible for actors to move past inspiration in performance to something that was carefully crafted and capable of occurring at each performance, not just when an actor was "on." Beyond crowd control and rehearsal practices, Stanislavski developed a system that helped actors interpret their characters. We see in Stanislavski the emergence of the director as a primary interpreter of character and one who helps the actor reach similar insights that can be reproduced at each and every performance for the audience.

EARLY TWENTIETH-CENTURY AMERICAN DIRECTORS AND THE RESHAPING OF NINETEENTH-CENTURY TRENDS

By the dawn of the twentieth century many of our current expectations about the work of the director were in place. Thanks to ideas and practice of people like Madame Vestris, Richard Wagner, Georg II, Andre Antoine, and Constantin Stanislavski, the following tasks and qualities were commonly thought of as belonging to the director: coordination and unification of the visual aspects of productions, authoritative leadership of the artistic team, interpretation of a playwright's text, and coaching of actors. Though these ideas were developed in England and Europe, they were soon imitated in the United States. At the end of the nineteenth century, Edwin Booth (discussed earlier in the stars spotlight), Augustin Daly (1836–1899), and Steele Mackaye (1842–1894) did much to bring European trends across the Atlantic.

Portrait of David Belasco.

David Belasco was one of the major American directors of the early twentieth century. Also an actor and a playwright, Belasco became famous for his meticulously detailed productions over which he held complete control and for coaching his actors with precision. Among his memorable stagings were *The Easiest Way* (1909), for which he reproduced a boarding house on stage with all the items he had purchased from an actual boarding house, and *The Governor's Lady* (1912), for which he created a Childs Restaurant on stage with the help of the food chain. Though he didn't tend to cast famous performers, they gained fame thanks to his work with them. He chose actors carefully for each part and then helped them make the most of their roles.

Belasco also put an American stamp on the idea of director as a powerful leader through his battle with the Syndicate. The Syndicate was a theatre management organization that controlled the American theatre in the early years of the twentieth century. By dictating what would play along the major routes between large cities, they controlled touring. Generally they insisted that shows appeal to the largest possible number of people and contain stars. In so doing, they curtailed experimentation and innovation. But Belasco was developing his own following for his incredibly realistic and well-acted productions and wanted to go on tour. Even though he refused to give the exclusive rights to his shows to the Syndicate, his popularity and audience demand forced them to cave and let him tour along their routes. Historians regard the Syndicate's failure to control Belasco as one of the first signs that their reign was ending. Belasco's success heralds the power the director would wield in American theatres of the twentieth and twenty-first centuries.

Meanwhile, the European independent theatre movement found an American expression in the Little Theatre Movement that started around 1912. Imitating the work of Antoine and Theatre Libre, Stanislavski and the Moscow Art Theatre, and others, some fifty groups sprang up around the country. Some of the most significant of these theatres were the Chicago Little Theatre, the Provincetown Players, and the Washington Square Players. Though the actors were usually amateurs, the theatres employed professional directors. The theatres are a major part of American theatre history thanks to their ability to pave the way for different kinds of scripts and production choices that would expand American theatrical tastes later in the century.

CHAPTER SUMMARY

The nineteenth century was a time of great change. People were on the move—from the country to the city and across large stretches of landscape thanks to innovations in transportation. Ideas were moving quickly too—philosophy and art were changing rapidly and in radically new directions, and instruments of mass communication like the newspaper were thriving. Melodrama, romanticism, and realism in the theatre developed almost on top of one another. (A technological upstart, film, entered the scene in the late nineteenth century. By the 1910s silent movies were challenging almost all forms of live popular entertainment, a condition that would only intensify with the advent of the talkies in 1927.) No wonder, then, that people in the theatre were looking for someone to lead them, to make sense of things, and to pull a variety of forces into a coherent whole. That someone was called the director. As we'll read in the next chapter this job has continued to develop into a fascinating field of theatre practice, with myriad approaches and stars all its own.

ACTIVITIES

Stars on Stage

Recast a play you have seen for class or cast a play you have read for class with movie or television stars. What are the advantages and disadvantages of casting these celebrities? Compare your cast list with a partner's.

A Romantic *Gesamtkunstwerk*

Study the painting *Abbey in the Oakwood* by Caspar David Friedrich. Find a piece of music that illustrates the mood of the painting. Then find a second piece of music that creates a very different feeling. What are the advantages of reinforcing image with sound? What are the advantages of working against artistic and sensory unification? If you were directing a play, would you aim toward unification at all times, or can you think of situations when it might be useful to create contrasts? Share your music and thoughts with a partner.

Making History

Who won the most recent Tony Awards for Best Direction of a Musical and Best Direction of a Play? Google these recent prize-winning directors and write a short spotlight of your own about the artist you think sounds most interesting and what s/he is contributing to the development of the role of the director.

The Work of the Director

Notice how director Heiner Goebbels uses height, stacking images atop one another, as he builds his stage picture.

It is an interesting contradiction: directors are some of the most powerful artists in the contemporary theatre, and yet few have immediately recognizable faces, even by seasoned, sophisticated playgoers. Take a recent example in New York City. International directing visionary Heiner Goebbels attended the U.S. premiere of his music theater piece, *Eraritjaritjaka*, in July 2006. It had already received rave reviews around the world, as had his *Hashirigaki*, which played three years earlier at the renowned Brooklyn Academy of Music. Yet Mr. Goebbels could walk almost entirely unnoticed through the lobby of Lincoln Center's Rose Theatre, whereas Dianne Wiest, the Oscar, Emmy, and Golden Globe-winning actress, who did a stint on television's *Law and Order*, but who was merely present to see the show, turned many heads and inspired lots of excited whispering as she entered the theatre and took her seat. For better or for worse, actors, even the high-brow and mature variety, have a kind of celebrity that acclaimed directors do not.

And yet it is the director who, in virtually every context in the contemporary theatre, makes the bulk of the decisions about how a play looks and sounds on stage. Directors are the interpretive guides for the actors, design team, and audience. As we will see in this chapter, they have tremendous artistic and managerial oversight over the productions on which they work.

DIRECTOR AND THE TEXT
Finding a Show / Letting a Show Find You

The director's job begins when she or he becomes "attached" to a script. This sounds straightforward, but there is actually considerable variety in how this happens, depending on the theatre in which the play will be performed and the stature of the director. In academic theatres, it is not uncommon for the director to choose the script to direct. In this kind of situation, directors becomes "attached" to the script when they find one that excites them. When they find a script with a story they want to tell, with characters to whom they are drawn, with images they want to physicalize, and with ideas they want to explore, they probably realize that they have found a strong candidate for their next project. The director will also take into consideration the script's educational value—if it represents a particular historical period, introduces student audiences to an important voice in playwriting, or offers the kinds of challenges that the student actors in the department need. Beyond the immediate show, the director will also weigh the larger needs and constraints of the theatre program. For example, an entire season of Shakespeare is uncommon in most academic theatres. A season usually features variety in terms of playwriting style, period, and genre. A director will also need to evaluate the current casting pool. If a program has many more female students than male—quite a common occurrence at the college level—some shows may be difficult to cast. Or if a cast makes specific demands in terms of race, this may be easier to accommodate in some

French theater director Ariane Mnouchkine, at the "Indiana" theater.

parts of the country than others. In community and professional theatres, scripts are often chosen for a season by a company's artistic director or advisory board—perhaps on a given theme, reflecting recent hits in New York, or featuring the winners of prizes such as the Pulitzer or the Tony— and directors are then chosen or hired to direct each show. If the system works well, directors are paired with material for which they are suited. A person with little interest or experience in musical theatre would not be ideal for a new production of *South Pacific*, for example, but perhaps that person's tastes and worldview might be ideal for an absurdist classic from Samuel Beckett. But a director who is well known and highly regarded may have the opportunity to recommend a play title in these kinds of theatres as well, thus ensuring a perfect match.

Early Interpretive Work

Once a director and script are paired, the director begins the interpretive work. Such work may take place many months before rehearsals begin. In Chapter 9 we noted that designers read the script multiple times in the first phase of their work. The director's first task is also reading the script—and then rereading it over and over again. As directors read, they typically look for a number of things. First, they read for story. Most scripts tell a story, so directors identify the story the playwright seeks to tell, and then they analyze how they tell that story. They look at dramatic structure and how the

In order to create a compelling scene, such as this one from Rupert Gould's 2007 production of *The Glass Menagerie* at London's Apollo Theatre, a director must read for and imagine story, character, and image.

© Photostage

rhythms of that structure might best be brought to life on stage. Second, directors read for character. Whereas actors using an internal approach to character building will consider their character's superobjective and beat objectives, directors look at these issues for all the characters in the script. If a director prefers a more physical approach to character or seeks to combine a physical and psychological approach, the director may look for defining gestures for a character or think about other ways an actor might give the character a particular bodily shape. Third, directors read for image. They look for the visual and aural cues that writers place within the text—recurring colors, repeated references to an object, or the frequent use of sounds or words—that might spark a designer's interest as s/he gives the script material and physical form on stage.

To make this more concrete, we'll look at Tennessee Williams's play, *The Glass Menagerie*. *The Glass Menagerie* is a memory play. Tom, the play's narrator, reflects back on his life in a ramshackle St. Louis apartment with his flamboyant mother, Amanda, and his reclusive sister, Laura. As a director reads for story, she or he will trace Tom's decision to abandon his family. The director will be concerned with understanding how the family got to be in the financial and emotional situation they are in, why Jim O'Connor comes to dinner, and how Jim's presence in the home intensifies the conflicts that have long been brewing. As a director reads for character, he or she will be interested in understanding what drives each character. The director will want to understand Amanda's youth and probe her tales of her many "gentleman callers." The director will seek to understand why Amanda is so driven to snare a beau for Laura. When considering Laura, the director will explore the imaginative world Laura creates through her glass figurines and her interpretation of her past interactions with the most popular boy in high school, Jim O'Connor. Laura needs to retreat to her protected realm, and the director will analyze the steps Laura takes to do so. Tom, meanwhile, is increasingly hungry for freedom. He is an outsider and a poet, and he chafes under his mother's (and his sister's) needs and demands. Tom seeks to escape all that binds him. As a director reads for image, the focus is likely to be on glass (including but not limited to Laura's animal collection) and the way it breaks; the unicorn; the phonograph records left behind by the absent father; light—from the dance hall, the sparkling glass, as a result of the power outage, and from the candles at the play's end; the photograph of the father on the mantle; and the blue roses of Laura's nickname. Story and character objective provide a structure to the play, but so too does this network of recurring, evocative images that are both visual and aural.

It is worth noting that different directors will prioritize story, character, and image in different ways. Some begin with image and leave story until later. Others find ways of combining categories. When, for example, they are reading for character, they may begin visualizing the physical gestures and repeated movement patterns that will translate their ideas into visual images. Directors may also read differently when approaching different scripts. A realistic play by Henrik Ibsen is fundamentally different from one of Bertolt Brecht's epic theatre works, and thus it may behoove a director to read these scripts using different tactics. Regardless of how they read, as they read, directors are moving toward a concept or organizing idea for the production.

Directorial Strategies

Directors who work with scripts preauthored by a playwright tend to have one of three main goals as they formulate a concept and start to move from prerehearsal to rehearsal work: (1) some seek to translate faithfully a playwright's vision from page to stage; (2) some attempt to make a playwright's vision speak clearly to a contemporary audience and are willing to emphasize and deemphasize certain aspects of the text to make that happen; and (3) some view the playwright's words as a springboard to creating their own unique version of the play that may be radically different from what the script's author imagined.[1] Directors whose work is representative of these three approaches are Elia Kazan, Bartlett Sher, and JoAnne Akalaitis.

Elia Kazan is one of the most famous American directors of the middle part of the twentieth century. Kazan is especially well regarded for his work on the premieres of Tennessee Williams's major plays like *A Streetcar Named Desire* and *Cat on a Hot Tin Roof* as well as the premieres of Arthur Miller's *All My Sons* and *Death of a Salesman*. Kazan, in collaboration with designer Jo Mielziner, created a stage style that dominated the American theatre from the 1940s through the 1960s. The plays of Williams and Miller are sometimes called selective or modified realism. Although characters and

The original cast in a scene from *A Streetcar Named Desire*, directed by Elia Kazan in 1947.

situations are recognizable in selective realism, elements of the dramatic world and its expression exceed the realistic, delving into something more poetic. In his review of the original production of *Cat on a Hot Tin Roof*, Eric Bentley wrote that the dramatic world Kazan crafted is "a view of man's exterior that is also a view of his interior." Williams and Miller were both interested in outsiders who longed to express themselves in the face of demands for conformity. Kazan was able to use a psychological approach to character as well as Mielziner's fluid, fragmented, yet formal settings to give voice and shape to the ideas animating the playwrights' scripts.

Bartlett Sher is currently the artistic director of the Intiman Theatre in Seattle. He directs there as well as in major New York City venues like Lincoln Center (where his direction has earned him a Tony Award) and the Metropolitan Opera. At the Intiman, Sher created the American Cycle. Each year, for five years, the theatre produced an American classic, either written for or adapted to the stage, with the goal to "produce great art, cultivate curiosity, advocate for literacy, encourage an informed citizenry and understand interconnectedness." (www.Intiman.org) In 2004, he directed Thornton Wilder's *Our Town*. Sher reinvigorated this longtime staple of American theatre by using a multiracial cast. This choice allowed him to make the classic story seem immediate and personal to a more diverse audience. In 2006, his *Awake and Sing* gained popular and critical praise, including a Tony nomination for best direction. Sher succeeded in making Odets's Depression-era story feel vital through a set design that eloquently

Two scenes from Bart Sher's 2004 production of *Our Town* at the Intiman Theatre in Seattle.

clarified the experience of the characters. Throughout the show, the walls of the apartment disintegrated very slowly, eventually erasing the family's protection from the cruelty of the outside world. Also in 2007, when he directed the *Barber of Seville* at the Met, he created a "passerelle," a walkway connecting stage and audience that literally brought the story of the opera immediately into the world of the audience. In 2008, his revival of *South Pacific* was a critical and popular hit. It also earned him his first Tony Award.

Joanne Akalaitis was the first and only woman chosen to head the venerable Public Theatre in New York City. In her brief and stormy tenure there, she directed several classic texts, including Shakespeare's *Cymbeline*, John Ford's *'Tis Pity She's a Whore*, and Georg Buchner's *Woyzeck*—all of which were radically reset and reimagined to fit Akalaitis's unique theatrical vision. But perhaps her most controversial staging was the 1984 production of Samuel Beckett's *Endgame* at the American Repertory Theatre in

A scene from Joanne Akalaitis's controversial 1984 staging of Samuel Beckett's *Endgame*.

Photo © Paula Court

Richard Foreman wrote and directed *Deep Trance Behavior in Potatoland*. The 2008 production received critical praise for its perception-altering images.

Cambridge, Massachusetts. As part of his absurdist aesthetic Beckett designated generalized places and universal characters. Akalaitis chose to particularize place and character, setting her version of the play in an abandoned subway station after a nuclear holocaust and featuring characters who were homeless people. In addition, portions of the dialogue were taped, and famous composer Phillip Glass contributed music for the production. Beckett, enraged over what he viewed as fundamental changes to his work, attempted to have the production closed.

Directors also sometimes direct texts that they have created. Directors who work this way include Richard Foreman and Mary Zimmerman. Richard Foreman founded the Ontological-Hysteric Theatre in New York in 1968. Since the late '60s, Foreman has written experimental texts such as *Rhoda in Potatoland, My Head is a Sledgehammer, Panic: How to be Happy*, and *Deep Trance Behavior in Potatoland* that seek to force the audience to shed their perceptual habits. He has developed his own vocabulary of stage techniques to facilitate this goal: he shines lights directly in the eyes of his audience, he is visible in the audience cueing his show, he uses strings to connect objects on the stage and direct the audience's vision, and he uses nonpsychological acting techniques. Mary Zimmerman also directs plays she writes—typically adaptations of classic texts—but although her aesthetic is imaginative and visual, she is known for a more collaborative staging process. Zimmerman works regularly with Chicago's Looking Glass Theatre Company and with the Goodman Theatre. Her well-known shows include *The Notebooks of Leonardo DaVinci, The Odyssey, The Arabian Nights, Metamorphoses* (for which she won the Tony for Best Director in 2002), and *Argonautika*.

Sometimes directors create texts with theatres companies. Rather than interpreting a preexisting text or creating a text independently, the director in this situation steers a group as they create a new work for performance together. An example of a director who works this way is Stephen Cosson, the artistic director of the Obie Award-winning The Civilians, a New York-based theatre company "that develops original projects based in the creative investigation of actual experience" (www.thecivilians.org). All the members of the acting company for a Civilians production help gather the interviews on which the company will base the show, which is usually a cross between documentary and musical theatre. For their work *Gone Missing*, the

A scene from Mary Zimmerman's Tony-winning production of, *Metamorphoses*

© Joan Marcus 2007

The Civilians *Gone Missing* at Barrow Street Theatre

Photo © Sheldon Noland and the Civilians

Photo © Craig Schwartz and the Civilians

The Civilians *This Beautiful City*

company interviewed New Yorkers about items they had lost. For *This Beautiful City*, the company traveled to Colorado Springs, Colorado, to interview members and leaders of evangelical churches as well as other residents of the city. Though the company collaborates in the gathering of interview material, Cosson, sometimes with the help of writer/dramaturg Jim Lewis, creates a final script, while composer Michael Friedman writes the music.

 ## DIRECTOR AND THE ACTOR

Casting

An essential part of the director's job is working with actors. This begins with casting, or choosing which artists will play which roles. Some professional directors work with casting directors to assist them in this important task. A casting director will gather head shots and resumes from actors before auditions begin. The casting director will help narrow the field of potential actors based on experience, appearance, and other factors particular

SPOTLIGHT
Directors on Directing

Bill Rauch, Oregon Shakespeare Festival: Whatever I start to perceive as an actor's limitations—I'm able to remind myself very quickly to not start mythologizing that actor based on their limitations, but to remember that that actor has incredible untapped reserves. Whether it's somebody who'd been acting for 45 years and is locked into crusty old habits, or whether it's somebody who's never set foot on stage before, they've got something in them that could move and dazzle audiences. Can I help them access it, within the limitations of time we have? That's the game, that's the joy.[2]

Daniel Sullivan: As an actor, I always was a little bit watching everybody else. The larger context was always more interesting to me than this sort of blinkered life of the actor and the role. I was just too curious about the way the whole thing worked.[3]

Bonnie Monte, Shakespeare Theatre of New Jersey: My scripts are completely color-coded. I have an amazingly detailed code and symbol system. I go into rehearsals with such a level of specificity—even though I am willing to throw it away the minute I find something better or an actor brings me something better. That is the collaborative part of the process.[4]

to given show (dancing or fight training, for example) before these actors read for the director. Sometimes directors will cast an actor immediately simply based on reputation and past experience. Casting for a repertory company is particularly challenging. In this situation, a group of actors will perform several plays over the course of a season. Actors need the versatility to perform different roles in several shows.

As directors cast a show, they are likely to look for several qualities in a performer. First, directors look for actors with an affinity for the given material. As actors read in auditions, directors look at the preliminary interpretation actors present. They also look at the performer's facility with the language in the script—if they can handle Shakespeare's verse or if they seem comfortable with frank dialogue in a contemporary script. Directors also look at the ways actors move through space—if they can shed their

Acclaimed American acting teacher and director, Lee Strasberg at a tablework rehearsal with the cast of *The Three Sisters*. Shown from left: Geraldine Page, James Olson, Barbara Baxley, Gerald Hiken, and Lee Strasberg.

own habits of behavior to inhabit a new physicality. It is also important to see how well actors take suggestion. A director may offer a new interpretation of a line or a new tactic for a character. If the actor can use the suggestion, changing a line reading or an apparent motivation in a scene, the director will suspect this performer will respond well to other kinds of direction during rehearsal. Finally, directors look at actors in relationship to each other. If a director is looking to cast three women as sisters, though a blonde woman may give a strong audition, s/he may cast a brunette instead if the other two performers are also dark-haired. The director will also look for chemistry between actors. This may be for a romantic pairing or for mortal enemies.

Character Development

Once the show has been cast, rehearsals can begin. During the early phases of rehearsal, many directors choose to work on character development. Some directors refer to this phase of rehearsal as "table work." During table work, actors read from the script that they will perform. As we noted in the chapter detailing the work of the actor, the initial reading of the script by the full cast is called a "read-through." Directors often ask the actors questions about their characters—what they want in a given scene, how the past has shaped them, and how they change over the course of the play. Actors need to understand every line they say, and why they say it, and directors pose questions with this goal in mind. They may also point out the images that give the play shape, calling the actors' attention to them so that they may think about ways they will use a prop or give emphasis to recurring words and sounds. At this point in a typical production process, the director has had far greater opportunity to spend time with the script. Table work gives the director an opportunity to share interpretive insights with the cast. Some directors choose to devote several rehearsals to table work, whereas others feel satisfied with what they can accomplish at a single read-through.

Outside rehearsal, the directors may schedule appointments—or character conferences—to discuss character issues with an actor individually. Directors may also assign actors "homework" of various kinds. Directors assume that actors will spend a great deal of time analyzing the script, but they may suggest that they look beyond the script as they start to shape their characters. They might ask actors to read about the period in which the show is set, or they might recommend that they collect images that could contribute to the physicalization of the character.

Some directors use improvisation to help actors flesh out their characters and make a transition from the reading phase of rehearsal to the blocking phase, where patterns of movement and spatial organization are set. The potential for improvisation is virtually endless. Some directors ask actors to move through the space, telling the story of the play without words. Others may begin to introduce props or set pieces with which actors can experiment. Still others may ask actors to respond to music, paint their characters, or use other nonverbal and nondiscursive forms of expression to get beyond the surface of the play text and to free their imaginations. Improvisation may continue throughout the rehearsal process. As actors become better acquainted with character, story, and image, improvisation can be an excellent problem-solving tool to fix issues with pacing, timing, and character relationships. For example, two characters in a romantic relationship might improvise a scene exploring when their characters first met. Or to better enhance the work of an ensemble in a domestic drama, the director might ask the performers playing members of the family to improvise a scene involving a typical family dinner.

Blocking and Stage Composition

A large portion of the typical rehearsal process is spent on blocking. At some point, actors need to physicalize the interpretive insights produced in the table work phase. Directors have two basic choices as they block the scenes of the play: They can preplan, or they can use organic blocking. As the name suggests, preplanning involves a director mapping out the movement patterns prior to rehearsal. They may use a model of the set, ground plans, storyboarding, or just their imagination to do so. The advantages to preplanning are several. First, it is extremely efficient. Directors know what they want and can simply convey that information to the actors. Second, it is very useful in crowd scenes or other scenes involving several actors. If many bodies require organization, it makes sense to have a vision of this prior to rehearsal. Third, if there are technical demands like moving scenery, complicated patterns involving dance or fight choreography, or textual demands that multiple things happen simultaneously, a firm directorial hand in blocking may be essential. Finally, if actors are inexperienced, they may be glad to have blocking chosen for them.

Other directors favor organic blocking primarily because it grants actors freedom and a collaborative voice. With organic blocking, actors have to

Photo © Michal Daniel, 2003

The blocking in this scene from *Caroline, or Change*, directed by George C. Wolfe, features expansion: there is considerable space between the multiple images (some of which represent reality and some fantasy), and the actors who help create them, on stage. In addition to giving visual form to the play's themes, the blocking also echoes the production's fragmented, postmodern score.

© Photostage

Director Katie Mitchell achieves a feeling of compression in this scene from *The Waves* thanks to close blocking of the actors and the doubling of their images on the video screen.

© Photostage

Though the actors in the background are crowded together, the actress in the foreground is isolated thanks to light and color.

Photo by Richard Feldman. Image courtesy of American Repertory Theatre.

Director Robert Woodruff plays with balance and rejects symmetry in this scene from *The Sound of a Voice*, with text by David Henry Hwang and music by Philip Glass: set pieces and actors are clustered stage right while stage left is nearly empty and the major set piece and the actor illuminated inside it are precariuosly balanced.

think on their feet. They move where choice and impulse takes them. As their understanding of the script and their character grows, their movement patterns evolve. This kind of blocking tends to be less formal and less "stagey." Actors and the director work together to give the script physical shape, which can be very satisfying for all involved. Organic blocking is also easier for many actors to remember because they helped to create it. They do not have to "memorize" a physical text written for them by a director.

Many directors use a combination of preplanning and organic blocking. A director who enjoys working collaboratively may still recognize a need for preplanning in complicated scenes. Or the director may have an image in mind for particularly important moments in the script—emotional climaxes or the introduction and conclusion of visual motifs. The director may preplan these moments while letting the other scenes flow organically around these high points.

As directors begin to set their blocking, finalizing the choices they envisioned before rehearsal or affirming the choices they made with their actors during rehearsal, they are likely to use several aspects of stage composition. First, directors play with compression and expansion. They may suggest that actors get closer to other actors or set pieces, thus compressing the stage picture. Crowded images convey different emotional impressions from those that feature expansion, or lots of space between bodies and objects. Isolation is a related and useful tool. If one character is isolated in one area of the stage while several others are jumbled together in another area of the stage, this begins to tell a story. Isolation may be enhanced with the use of light—creating a narrow pool around the single character—or with the use of color—dressing one character in white while all the rest are dressed in black. Balance and symmetry are also effective visual tools. When characters are organized proportionally in the stage space, when equal numbers of performers are positioned stage left and right or upstage and downstage, this is likely to create a sense of visual harmony. The dramatic world may seem to be a happy or a fair place. But if these proportions are unbalanced and asymmetrical, the stage picture is likely to seem less assuring. Arcs and angles are another aspect of visual composition. Sharp lines in the position of an actor's limbs, quick, hard turns, and straight, efficient movements all suggest formality, perhaps that associated with the military, a court, or a political context. Soft, loose gestures and slower, arced movements are less rigid and formal. These may convey private, familial, or romantic situations. Finally, directors like to use height. Stage designs often feature steps or risers, raked floors, or furniture. Any of these features allow some bodies on stage to be lower while others are higher. These levels create visual interest and are extremely useful in convey power relationships among characters.

Director Robert Wilson employs sharp angles in this scene from *The Temptation of St. Anthony*. Notice the way the actors' limbs repeat the sharp geometry of the set pieces.

Supporting a Director's Vision

Many artists work to support the vision of the director throughout the rehearsal process. The person whose work may first enhance the director's is the dramaturg. The dramaturg is one of the newest members of the American theatrical team. Dramaturgy began in Germany at the Hamburg National Theatre with Gotthold Ephraim Lessing in the eighteenth century, but did not emerge as a major theatrical specialization in this country until the second half of the twentieth century. There are almost as many definitions for this strange sounding German word as there are people who practice it, but a simple way to think of dramaturgy is as a link between the

Image courtesy of Marianne Combs/Minnesota Public Radio

Dramaturg Sarah Gioia listens to questions from director Peter Rothstein.

world of scholarship and the world of production and between the world of the theatre makers and the world of the audience. Production dramaturgs (as opposed to new play dramaturgs, who assist playwrights developing new scripts) often help directors by researching the play. They create casebooks, detailed documents outlining the history of the play in production, the biography of the playwright, major interpretive theories about the play, and the cultural context and other background ideas relevant to the play. With this information, the dramaturg helps the director get to know the play in a rich, intellectual manner. The dramaturg may also present this information to the cast during table work and write program notes and create lobby displays helping the audience come to terms with this information as well. Dramaturges also attend rehearsals. They watch the play develop, and they help to incorporate historical information into the production. They might help actors understand what kind of posture a character of a particular class might have had in the nineteenth century, what kind of telephone would have been common in a home in the mid-twentieth century, or the details of an eighteenth-century card game. They also advise the director on matters of play structure and interpretation throughout the rehearsal process. Once the show opens, they may help facilitate postshow discussions between the artistic team and the audience.

Dialect coaches and fight and dance choreographers also assist the director during the rehearsal process. Dialect coaches and choreographers

SPOTLIGHT
Society of American Fight Directors

In 1977, David Boushey returned to the United States from training in England with the Society of British Fight Directors. As he offered his services choreographing stage fights to professional theatres, he discovered there was little understanding of this valuable part of the theatrical process. So later that year, along with Erik Fredricksen, Joseph Martinez, Byron Jennings, and Rod Colbin, he founded the Society of American Fight Directors. In their Articles of Incorporation, the SAFD stated its goal: "to bring together into one organization those individuals who earn a living choreographing fight scenes for stage and film." By the next year, six full members (professional fight directors), twenty-three affiliates (fencing masters in drama schools), and three student members had joined.

Geoff Kent and Andrea Robertson work on their rapier technique.

Image courtesy of Geoff Kent

In the 1980s, the SAFD expanded its work, hosting a national fight school called the National Stage Combat Workshop; publishing a magazine, *The Fight Master*; and testing and certifying student combatants. By the end of the next decade, the SAFD's membership had grown to 700. Today, the group continues to be a vital presence, training teachers and performers for stage and film work, lobbying the Actor's Equity Association for safe fight conditions on stage, and generally elevating theatrical art by as, their logo proclaims, "fighting the good fight."

aid the director by helping the actor use the physical tools they have with more skill and precision. If the script is set in rural Ireland, for example, a dialect coach will help actors with pronunciation and the rhythms of line delivery. They also help actors project their voices in ways that won't damage their vocal chords and throats. If the script calls for a fight with rapiers, a fight choreographer will plan every move of the fight and teach it to the actors. They create an illusion of danger, but work very hard to keep performers safe. If a play includes a ballroom scene, a dance choreographer will teach the actors how to waltz. These specialists provide valuable detail for a production, sharpen actors' skills, and can enrich the overall effect of the performance tremendously.

DIRECTOR AND THE DESIGNERS

Another task of the director is coordinating the work of the design team. In some cases, the director is the first artist to arrive at a vision of the performance, or to formulate the production concept. The director then conveys these ideas and impressions to the set, costume, lighting, and sound designers. This may happen casually and individually, but often these discussions take place at a formal production conference. The first production conference brings the director and all the designers together, in some cases months before the first rehearsal. The director, sometimes with the help of a dramaturg, assembles a collection of images that can inspire thinking about the play. These images may have an obvious chronological connection to the play—nineteenth-century paintings for a nineteenth-century play—or they may not—contemporary advertising images for a seventeenth-century comedy. The images may show mood, a color palette, or an exact dress that the director wants a performer to wear. Directors may also bring songs, poems, film clips, fabric swatches, or evocative foods to inspire the thinking of the designers through the use of all their senses. After the designers have experienced what the director has offered and talked with the director about the play, they will go off on their own to create sketches. Once the director has approved the sketch, designers create models, renderings, cue sheets, and ground plans. At regular intervals the director and design team will reassemble to share their evolving work. After the director approves the designs, construction and assembly begins. Regular meetings of the director and designers will likely continue through the construction phase, concluding as technical rehearsals begin.

Just as some directors work collaboratively with actors to set blocking, some directors work collaboratively with designers to determine the team's approach to the look and feel of the show. Instead of determining a production concept independently, a director may find the approach to the show in concert with the designers. Over the course of a series of meetings, all the artists would gather images and share ideas.

© Mark Peterson/CORBIS

At technical and dress rehearsals, a director integrates the work of the designers and the actors. Here director James Lapine gives notes to the cast of *Amour*.

Regardless of how the production concept is reached, someone needs to be in charge of making sure that all of the design elements work well together. If the set emphasizes sharp angles and industrial materials, the lighting designer may want to reinforce these elements with tightly focused light, cool colors, and abstract gobos. Meanwhile the costume designer may choose to use sleek silhouettes and limited ornamentation. As the sound designer creates a soundscape for the play, that person may use a combination of computer-generated sounds and techno-pop dance tunes. It is up to the director to make sure that all members of the team are aware of each other's choices, are considering how another artist's choice affects their own, and that final choices are made in a timely fashion. The director also needs to remain mindful of how the designers' choices will eventually affect the actors.

Typically the director has limited contact with the designers at regular rehearsals. This is the director's time to concentrate on the actors. Some designers may attend rehearsals to check on blocking or other issues that will affect their work, but many designers attend few rehearsals until the cast and director are ready to run the show, just before the technical rehearsals begin. As we learned in Chapter 9, the technical rehearsals integrate the work of the designers into the rest of the production. Over the course of these last rehearsals before an audience witnesses the work—as the team moves from a dry tech to wet tech to dress rehearsals—the director sees the

Phillip Seymour Hoffman is a contemporary theatre director with a lively acting career on stage and in film. Here Hoffman appears in a scene from Sam Shepard's *True West*.

Photo by Joan Marcus/Photofest

designs fully realized and has the opportunity to make slight adjustments to the stage picture as needed. The director also helps the actors get used to working on a set, under light, with sound, and in costume. The director may adjust the timing of an actor's line delivery, suggest an increase in volume, or slightly adjust blocking. Radical reinterpretation should not, and really cannot, happen in this phase of the process. Instead, the director coordinates the transitions in the show that changes in set, light, sound, and costume mark. When the Angel enters at the end of *Angels in America, Part 1*, the director makes sure that the light and sound cues are precisely timed so that when the Angel crashes through the ceiling in her magnificent garb, the audience will be appropriately awed. The director makes sure that technical elements are functioning in such a way that they facilitate the telling of the story, the evocation of image, and the development of ideas, while supporting and enhancing the work of the actors.

A DIRECTOR'S TRAINING

Aspiring directors may take several paths in the contemporary theatre. Many seek academic training, first attaining an undergraduate degree in theatre and then pursuing a master's of fine arts in directing. Competition for places in graduate directing programs tends to be intense because whereas a production usually requires multiple actors, it only needs one director. Even large programs simply cannot train but a handful of directors at a time.

Other directors receive training on the job in other areas of theatre production. Because so much of a director's work is with actors, it only makes sense that actors sometimes trade hats and become directors. The Oscar-winning film actor and respected stage actor Phillip Seymour Hoffman provides a good example. Although Hoffman continues to act, he also regularly directs for the New York-based company he cofounded, the Labyrinth. Sometimes stage managers and dramaturgs also shift jobs. Both of these kinds of theatre professionals spend enormous time in rehearsal

Opportunities for Women Directors

Although women like Joanne Akalaitis and Mary Zimmerman have prominent directing careers, overall, it continues to remain difficult for women to find work in this important and powerful theatrical field. The last major survey of women in the theatre was released in January 2002. The New York State Council on the Arts funded the research of Susan Jonas and Suzanne Bennett, which they titled, *Report on the Status of Women: A Limited Engagement?* Giving some historical perspective to the issue, Jonas and Bennett cited "Action for Women in Theatre." That study found that between 1969 and 1975, 7 percent of regional and Off-Broadway plays were directed by women. The next survey came in the 1994–95 season and found women's representation had improved to 19 percent. The best year surveyed was 2000–01, in which 23 percent of productions were directed by women. When Jonas and Bennett looked at the then-current season of 2001–02, the number of women directors in the 1900 Theatre Communications Group member theatres was back down to 16 percent. And even when women are hired to direct, Jonas and Bennett found that they make 75.8 percent of what their male counterparts make. Jonas and Bennett eloquently summarized the challenges women in theatre face:

> Without historic precedent, without role models, mentors, consistent statistical data, and often not realizing they are operating at a disadvantage until late in their careers, women are constantly reintroducing themselves to the field. As perpetual newcomers, they are constantly elbowing for their place at the table and defending themselves against charges of inferiority. And they are caught in a paradox; they do not want to be counted as "women artists" but simply as "artists," yet when gender is not counted, it continues to count against women. What is not perceived cannot be challenged or altered.

To read Jonas and Bennett's full report, which is also concerned with the status of female playwrights, visit www.womensarts.org/advocacy/WomenCountNYSCAReport.htm.

observing directors as part of their jobs. Thus stage managers and dramaturgs have an excellent opportunity to watch the craft of directing even as they perform other important theatrical functions. Oskar Eustis, now the artistic director of the Public Theater, began his career as a dramaturg.

Once an artist is established as a director, it is not always easy to find work. Most professional directors are freelance. That is, they do not have a permanent home with a theatre, but are hired to direct a single show. Some seek financial and geographical stability by taking a position on a college or university theatre faculty. In addition to directing professionally, these artists also work with students. Among the contemporary directors based in the academic world are Daniel Sullivan, Anne Bogart, Lynne Meadow, Risa Brainin, Albert Innaurato, Frank Galati, and Mary Zimmerman. Many directors also choose to join the Society of Stage Directors and Choreographers. Though this organization may not be as well known as Actors Equity Association, the SSDC does provide its nearly 2,000 members and associates with union benefits.

CHAPTER SUMMARY

Actors dazzle audiences with their grace, charisma, and insight. Designers amaze audiences with the magic they create using material, wood, light, and sound. But without the director (and a team of collaborative assistants) to bring these kinds of theatrical creation together—interpreting, shaping, guiding, and managing at every phase of the production process—the play would not live in its most fully realized form. For many people, the director's name and face may be unfamiliar, but the director's holistic vision is vital to the way theatre is staged today.

 ACTIVITIES

Take a Seat

With a partner or a group, find five moveable chairs. Arrange these chairs in different configurations, making one chair more powerful or important than the others. Which techniques of visual composition did you find most useful? How well could your partner or the others in your group understand your ideas? Which configuration was most successful in showing a power relationship?

Names and Faces

Go to the *New York Times* Web site and find the title of a show currently playing on Broadway. Who is the director? Who are the actors? Did you recognize any of these names? Now Google the director to find out more about his/her previous work and training.

Postmodernism: Contemporary Playwriting, Solo Performance, and Mediated Art

Suzzy Roche, Kate Valk (upside down), Ari Fliakos in The Wooster Group's *House/Lights*.

© Morgan David de Lossy/CORBIS

Camera phones and other forms of technology mediate our lived experience and the ways we process art.

Two quintessential artifacts of the postmodern era might be found in your own book bag. The first is the iPod. With the aid of this small rectangular device, you can hold hundreds, even thousands, of songs in the palm of your hand. The songs may have been downloaded from the Internet, not as pieces of the artistically coherent and whole product formerly known as a studio album, but in pieces, according to your purchasing whim. Pink might precede Billie Holiday, who is followed by Madonna and Nina Simone. As you listen, you thumb a dial, moving effortlessly among artists, styles, and sounds, either intentionally or randomly remixing what was by its very nature an idiosyncratic collection to begin with.

A second common gadget among college-aged consumers is the text-messaging camera phone. The style of the moment dictates the size of the device—sometimes it should be tiny, other times it should call attention to itself and its capabilities—but regardless, you can surreptitiously "text" a friend across the lecture hall using an abbreviated system of letters and symbols that baffle older generations used to passing notes written in ballpoint, reacting instantaneously to any mundane (or significant) occurrence. Should the event be one requiring further broadcast, a quick photo could be taken, translating the moment into an image snipped from its context, now becoming consumable and reproducible for the ready list of global contacts maintained within the memory of the phone.

Clearly, you don't need to know the names of Jean Baudrillard and Fredric Jameson to understand the postmodern condition. You most likely own or at least have seen the products and commodities that shape this particular way of experiencing the world. This practical, lived experience leaves you well prepared to understand the theatrical art—and the ideas underpinning it—created in the last quarter century.

HISTORY AND DEFINITION OF POSTMODERNISM

The term *postmodern* was coined in the 1930s. Federico de Onis, a Spanish-American lyricist and literary scholar, first used the word in 1934, and Arnold Toynbee, a British historian, followed suit in 1938, but its ideas would not become prevalent for another couple of decades. Concepts associated with postmodernism became easily recognizable in architecture in the 1960s, and by the 1980s artists working in virtually every medium were variously playing with the possibilities of postmodernism, or struggling to maintain their artistic principles against it. We'll look at specific examples from the theatre and dramatic literature in a moment, but for now, let's set up a frame for examining those details and practice using them as we look at a famous photograph from the period.

However easy it may be to date postmodernism, it is much harder to define it. Some critics have argued that the postmodern is a break with the traditions of the modern—of its valuing of the internal, subjective individual experience and its experimentation with new forms aimed at revamping old value systems and ways of looking at the world—whereas others see the postmodern as continuation of the projects of modernity that we studied earlier in the book. For a while this debate even extended to the spelling of the word. Some people advocated the use of a hyphen to link "post" and "modern," thereby making the provisional nature of the terms' connection more obvious. Despite these multiple perspectives on postmodernism, most critics of contemporary art, literature, and theatre see some recurring preoccupations in the artistic practices and products from the late twentieth century on.

KEY IDEAS IN POSTMODERN THEORY

Postmodernism is frequently skeptical. It is suspicious of what the French literary critic and key theorist of the postmodern Jean-Francois Lyotard called the grand narratives of modernism, particularly about notions of human progress and liberation. It declines, if so polite a term is applicable in this context, to offer alternatives, but it is nevertheless linked to what it dismantles through that very act. Postmodern artists may use parody as way of establishing distance from formerly absolute theories and forms. They are often self-conscious as they do so, calling attention to the artifice of the work and the process of its creation. Consider the way you collect music on your iPod. You may see something humorous or odd, and certainly something very personal, in the way you can skip around from song to song and artist to artist. There is pleasure in the random disconnections, and you make no effort to conceal these strange, clever leaps to tell a smooth or lasting story meaningful to anyone other than yourself.

"Parading in Disneyland" Postmodern theorists critique what, if anything, lies below the surface of popular imagery.

As the totalizing, often comforting stories of the past are poked full of holes, a necessary consequence seems to be a devaluing, or in American political theorist and literary critic Fredric Jameson's words, an "effacement" of history. History can't provide stability and surety because it starts to seem like a collection of randomly collected images that artists and others can draw from capriciously, not unlike the way you use the iPod. As images become rootless, individual identity becomes less stable too. The human "subject" becomes decentered and looks like a series of strategic performances that have been pieced together rather than organically generated. There is no human core—just an ever-evolving playlist. People might start to see themselves, particularly if they occupy multiple positions that society has pushed to its margins—a Latina, a lesbian, and differently abled, for example—they might start to imagine themselves as what American theorist and scientist Donna Haraway has famously called a cyborg, a cybernetic organism, a blend of the human and the technological, that resists ideas of the "natural" and that can form complex networks of their own in an effort to circumvent or subvert the powers that might oppress them.

As people start to imagine themselves in relation to a complicated series of performances, it is not surprising that old notions of authenticity seem less certain. Jean Baudrillard, a French cultural theorist and philosopher, has analyzed simulations of reality, or simulacra—Main Street in Disneyland, for example—finding that below or beyond the created surface, a core of truth may no longer exist. The surface—the collection of images—is as real, if not more real, than truth we would like to make it represent. Think of the images you can capture with a camera phone. Sometimes it might seem almost as interesting to freeze this image of an event and then send it to an absent friend, as it is to be in the moment experiencing the occurrence. The still picture and its transmission seem to become more real than the memory, if not the experience, of the event.

Before looking at a variety of theatrical examples embracing these ideas, let's try applying these principles to the work of American photographer Cindy Sherman. Sherman's work, by virtue of the fact that it is apprehensible in an individual image instead of a series of images unfolding in time like conventional theatre, offers us an excellent place to hone our skills analyzing and interpreting postmodern art.

Charles Brown (as Lyons), James Earl Jones (as Troy Maxson), Mary Alice (as Rose), and Ray Aranha (as Bono) appear in a scene from Lloyd Richards's 1987 production of *Fences*, part of August Wilson's award-winning cycle of plays chronicling the African American experience in the United States.

perspectives. Although the point of view of the white male had long been dominant in dramatic literature, the stories of women and of people of various ethnicities came to occupy a more central position on world stages. August Wilson (1945–2005), for example, completed a cycle of ten plays chronicling the experience of African Americans in the twentieth century. His project aimed to begin to redress the injustice of erasing the history of African Americans and their particular social, political, and domestic experiences from the pages of history books and from the stage. Two of the plays from his Pittsburgh Cycle, *Fences* (1985), which treats the 1950s, and *The Piano Lesson* (1989), which explores the 1930s, won the Pulitzer Prize.

In some cases, the postmodern tendency to give voice to different perspectives extended to the rewriting of classic scripts that had marginalized the experiences of disempowered groups of people. Aimé Césaire's (1913–) *A Tempest* (1969) provides a prime example. Césaire, a writer and noted postcolonial theorist from Martinique, repoliticizes William Shakespeare's *The Tempest*. In Césaire's version, the audience usually sympathizes with the exiled Italian duke, Prospero. He's been on a largely uninhabited island for twelve years, living with his daughter Miranda, a helpful spirit named Ariel, and a creature who resisted his domesticating efforts, named Caliban. With the help of Ariel, Prospero magically shipwrecks a boatload

Caryl Churchill plays with time in the opening scene of *Top Girls*.

Photo © Michal Daniel, 2003

of his Italian acquaintances during a storm. Those shipwrecked have various adventures and intrigues traipsing about the island. Alonso's son, Ferdinand, has been presumed dead in the storm, but he has been safe, falling in love with Miranda. By play's end Miranda and Ferdinand are engaged, helping to heal the wounds of Prospero and Alonso. Prospero forswears his magical powers, frees Ariel, and prepares to return to Europe for the wedding of his daughter. Césaire retains much of this raw material, but he shifts the play's emphasis, foregrounding the tensions between Prospero as European colonizer and Ariel and Caliban as the colonized. In Césaire's telling of the story, Prospero has tried to conceal the island's potential for economic exploitation from his fellow Europeans, who are trying to find the island. As the self-consciously theatrical play unfolds, we see Prospero's harsh rule of the land and its native inhabitants, Ariel's work as a kind of overseer who helps Prospero exert his control, and Caliban's ardent desire for revolution. Until the last scene of the play, Césaire sticks close to Shakespeare's plot while giving voice to the subtext that Ariel, and especially Caliban, had never before been able to speak. But in the final scene, Césaire changes the story and summarizes his critique of the corruption of colonialism: Prospero refuses to go back to Italy because he has been so thoroughly seduced by his pleasure and power as a colonizer, and he will continue to torment Caliban, who never gives up the dream of freedom.

Playwrights translated postmodernism's critique of history into an adventurousness with dramatic time. In the opening scene of British play-

Tony Kushner blends the historical and the fictional in his characters Ethel Rosenberg (played by Kathleen Chalfant) and Roy Cohn (played by Ron Liebman) in his award-winning play, *Angels in America*.

wright Caryl Churchill's (1938–) *Top Girls* (1982), women from across the centuries gather for a dinner party to celebrate the promotion of Marlene, a contemporary woman, to head of the Top Girls Employment Agency. The scenes that follow to do not unfold in linear order as they reveal the choices Marlene made to get to the top, including giving her daughter to her sister to raise as her own. Instead all the following plot events actually precede the dinner party, and the last scene of the play was the first chronologically.

American playwright Tony Kushner (1956–) also works imaginatively with time. In his epic two-part play *Angels in America* (1991), Kushner, writing in the 1990s, returned to the 1980s to document the early years of the AIDS crisis. He juxtaposed an historical figure from the time, Roy Cohn, with the ghost of Ethel Rosenberg from the 1950s, fictionalized characters from the 1980s, and the ancestors of one of the main characters from centuries past. Within scenes, characters are not bound by normal working of space and time. In what Kushner labeled a split scene because the characters occupy different locations, Harper and Prior share a mutual hallucination in which they communicate with each other and can see into each other's futures.

Just as postmodern theorists called attention to the fragmented surface of imagery and experience, contemporary playwrights have experimented

Photo © Michal Daniel, 2001

Suzan-Lori Parks uses iconographical fragments of character in her award-winning play, *Topdog/Underdog*. Shown from left: Don Cheadle, Jeffrey Wright.

with fragmentation in a number of ways. German playwright Heiner Müller (1929–96) excised characters from *Hamlet*, recontextualizing them in the midst of fractured imagery drawn from twentieth-century social and political crises in his play *Hamletmachine* (1978). The term he coined to describe his particular style of dramatic construction was the "synthetic fragment." Audiences must sift through the accumulation of stark pictures and shards of poetic dialogue that Müller layers together to form his play.

In *Topdog/Underdog* (2002), American playwright Suzan-Lori Parks (1961–) also experimented with fragmentation. Though she employed a linear storyline featuring the struggle of two African-American brothers for dominance and self-determination, she used iconographic historical fragments of character to do so. The brothers are named Lincoln and Booth. Lincoln works in an arcade, where he is paid to dress up as Abraham Lincoln and where customers reenact his assassination. In middle of the play, Booth helps his brother rehearse for his job, advising him on how to stage a more compelling death. By play's end, Booth shoots and kills Lincoln. Parks has historical images collide with psychological characters. As she facilitated this layered kind of violence, she used her strategy of "Rep and Rev" to repeat and revise historical imagery and stereotypes of African-American men, shattering their surfaces, so that her audiences can interrogate the images they may not have questioned fully on their own.

SOLO PERFORMANCE: ANNA DEAVERE SMITH

Conventional plays and playwrights made substantial contributions to postmodern culture, interpreting and extending the fundamental ideas of the period as they put them to work on stage. But equally important are the artists in the realm of performance who somehow exceeded conventional bounds—testing theatrical and dramatic genres to their very limits. One such artist is American writer and solo performer Anna Deavere Smith (1950–).

Anna Deavere Smith began her series *On the Road: A Search for American Character* in 1982. For her series, Smith interviewed people, recording their experiences related to various controversial events. She then transcribed these interviews, using her interviewees' words verbatim in her solo performances. A show would contain a series of these interviews, with Smith playing all the speakers, regardless of their race or gender.

Though Smith had been developing her creative process for ten years, it was 1992's *Fires in the Mirror: Crown Heights, Brooklyn and Other Identities* that brought her national recognition and acclaim. Smith was inspired to create this piece because of events that took place in August of 1991 in the Crown Heights area of Brooklyn, New York. When a car transporting a Lubavitcher Hasidic rebbe ran a red light and swerved onto a sidewalk, two African American children from the neighborhood were struck. The seven-year-old boy, Gavin Cato, was killed. The accident escalated the tensions between the Jewish and African American communities living in close proximity in the neighborhood. Three hours after the automobile accident, a group of African American men stabbed an Hasidic scholar, Yankel Rosenbaum. Riots continued in the neighborhood for three days. Smith soon began interviewing residents of Crown Heights and others associated with the incident. In December of 1991 she performed an early version of the show at the Public Theatre in New York City; in 1993 her work found a much wider audience thanks to a PBS broadcast of her performance.

In many ways, Smith exemplifies the trends of postmodern theatre. First, she extends the ideas of one of the great theatrical artists of the modern era, Bertolt Brecht (1898–1956). Like Brecht, Smith rejects linear narrative construction. She works episodically, building the story through a process of accumulation. In another parallel with Brecht, she uses titles to announce sections of the show, in her case calling attention to thematic threads linking disparate speakers. The third section of *Fires in the Mirror*, for example, is titled, "Hair." In this section she weaves together the voices of an anonymous girl, The Reverend Al Sharpton, a Lubavitcher woman named Rivkah Siegal, and the scholar and activist Angela Davis.

Her acting style also demonstrates a debt to Brecht. He had the idea of creating a "gestus" or social gesture to delineate character instead of building a character psychologically as Constantin Stanislavski (1863–1938) and his followers suggested. Just as Helene Weigel (1900–71) so famously snapped the hungry jaws of the metal clasp on her purse while playing the lead role in Brecht's production of *Mother Courage*, Smith sums up her characters through the quirks of vocal delivery and gesture that make a person unique and that reveal key aspects of their social background. Smith has said, "I can learn who somebody is, not from what they tell me, but from how they tell me. This will make an impression on my body, and eventually on my psyche."

SPOTLIGHT

George C. Wolfe

Writer, director, producer George C. Wolfe embodies the postmodern trend of bringing new and diverse voices to the theatre.

Wolfe (1954–) grew up in Kentucky. After high school he enrolled at Kentucky State University, but later transferred to Pomona College in California. In 1979 he moved to New York City. He earned a master's degree in playwriting and musical theatre from New York University. His first major New York success as a writer came in 1986 with his play, *The Colored Museum*. He gained the attention of legendary producer Joseph Papp, the founder of the New York Shakespeare Festival, who produced the play at the Public Theatre. In 1989 he received an Obie Award for best director of his play *Spunk*, which he adapted from three stories by Zora Neale Hurston.

In the 1990s, Wolfe became increasingly well known for his work as a director. Papp made him a resident director at the Public in 1990. In 1992, his musical about the life of jazz great Jelly Roll Morton, *Jelly's Last Jam*, moved to Broadway and earned him his first Tony nominations for best book of a musical and best director. In 1993, Tony Kushner asked him to direct the Broadway production of his play, *Angels in America*. When Wolfe won the Tony for best director, it was the first time a black director had won for a show not primarily about black people.

Shortly before Papp died in 1991, he had appointed Joanne Akalaitis artistic director of the Public Theatre. Akalaitis lasted a brief

Photofest

Wolfe's direction of *Jelly's Last Jam* earned him his first Tony Award Nomination.

twenty months in that esteemed role before the board of the theatre asked her to step down. Their choice to replace her was Wolfe. Wolfe survived, and in fact thrived, in that much-scrutinized position for more than ten years. During his tenure as artistic director he helped to cultivate some of the most outstanding and diverse voices in the contemporary American theatre, giving them a stage and sometimes directing their work himself. Among the artists whose work he fostered are Anna Deavere Smith, Suzan-Lori Parks, Nilo Cruz, Diana Son, Jose Rivera, and Jessica Hagedorn.

When both Wolfe and the Public were about to turn fifty, Wolfe decided to step down to pursue opportunities directing film. His first effort, *Lackawanna Blues*, by Ruben Santiago-Hudson, was well received at the Sundance Film Festival and went on to further acclaim when it was broadcast by HBO. In an interview with the *New York Times* shortly before he left the Public, Wolfe said, "The thing I love about this job more than anything is creating structures so that other artists can play." Whether these structures are on the stage or on film, Wolfe has created ones that free the best writers to play in adventurous ways and broaden the scope of familiar voices in postmodern performance.

Wolfe's first film project was *Lackwanna Blues*. Shown from left: Macy Gray (as Pauline), S. Epatha Merkerson (as Rachel "Nanny" Crosby), Rosie Perez (as Bertha).

Anna Deveare Smith performs two of the characters from her play, *Twilight: Los Angeles.*

When Smith creates character through language and the way stories are told, she makes an eloquent statement about the number of voices that need to be heard in contemporary culture and embodies the plurality of perspectives that postmodern theorists have tried to describe and promote. Smith gives characters of different races, genders, classes, and religions equal time in her show, allowing multiple perspectives to coexist in her work.

While she coordinates this multivocal story, she asks her audience to re-think their ideas about history. When multiple speakers—the famous and the anonymous, the powerful and the unempowered—each get to articulate their angle on an issue, it becomes clear that there is not one truth about the event under discussion. As audiences realize this is true about a riot in New York in the 1990s and the racial tensions that fueled it, they may reconsider the other stories from the past that they have accepted as truth as well. Instead of effacing history, Smith gives history several new faces as she gives it multiple voices.

Smith's multiplication of character, voice, and perspective provides yet another link to postmodern trends. Her work is emblematic of the post-modern fascination with fragmented surfaces. Though *Fires in the Mirror* does proceed chronologically, setting the scene and contextualizing the vi-olence in Crown Heights, then moving from the death of Gavin Cato and the death of Yankel Rosenbaum to the aftermath of the violence, the stories she uses are short and sometimes contradictory. The effect is not an idealized blend, but a messy confrontation about a messy subject. She does not lull the audience into thinking there is a simple solution to the problems of race in America. She resists resolution and uses the fractured surface of the play to mirror the fractured national psyche.

Perhaps the revolutionary nature of Smith's work can best be seen in the controversy surrounding her play following *Fires in the Mirror*, *Twilight: Los Angeles, 1992*, which documented the riots in Los Angeles following the acquittal of Rodney King's assailants. Though *Twilight* was at one time considered a favorite to win the Pulitzer Prize for drama, the award committee removed it from consideration in the spring of 1994, claiming that it did not qualify for the award because "the language of the play was not invented" and because, they claimed, "the play is not reproducible by other performers because it relies for authenticity on the performer's having done the interviews." Smith's postmodern working method raised questions about genre and authorship—what exactly is the job of the playwright and what defines the limits of the creative act—that some of the nation's most sophisticated critics and arbiters of taste were not prepared to answer.

MEDIATED PERFORMANCE: THE WOOSTER GROUP

Innovative experimentation with trends in postmodern theatre is not the exclusive domain of playwrights or even solo performers. The Wooster Group, an alternative collective of artists led by director Elizabeth LeCompte (1944–), has created a body of work that has expanded definitions of how the postmodern and the theatre can intersect.

In 1980 Elizabeth LeCompte and Spalding Gray (1941–2004) left another alternative theatre group, the Performance Group, where LeCompte had worked as an assistant director to Richard Schechner (1934–), to pursue the ideas about theatre they had been experimenting with for five years outside the Performance Group. When the Performance Group later dissolved, several company members—Willem Dafoe, Ron Vawter, Libby Howes, and Jim Clayburgh—joined LeCompte and Gray to become the Wooster Group. The Wooster Group took over the Performance Group's Performing Garage, a theatre that we cited as an example of a found space in Chapter 6.

The Wooster Group's early work revolved around autobiographical material from Gray's life. Although this might sound like the company had a conventional interest in story and psychology, exactly the opposite was the

case. LeCompte and Gray's early work together (now anachronistically referred to as the first productions of the Wooster Group), such as *Sakonnet
Point* (1975) and *Rumstick Road* (1977), involved improvisation, dream-
like movement, loosely connected images designed to evoke memories in
the audience, and experimentation with language and sound. In their tastes
and emphases, postmodernism's tangled relationship to modernism again
becomes apparent.

The Wooster Group's aesthetic has striking similarities to the artistic philosophy of one of the giants of modernism—Gertrude Stein
(1874–1946). In her lecture "Plays," Stein declared that she was tired of
the telling of stories. Everyone knew so many of them, she said, that there
really wasn't much point in telling another one. She thought it would be
better if artists imagined theatre as a landscape. When she had her first ride
in an airplane in the 1930s, she marveled at seeing so much ground all at
once, unlike her many rides on trains, where landmarks went by sequen-
tially and in a straight line. She imagined ways to apply this new spatial perspective to dramatic literature. She advocated a sensory experience in which
images were knowable simultaneously and subjectively and where linear
story telling that relied on moment-by-moment discovery was abandoned.
Likewise in *Rumstick Road*, the Wooster Group created a theatrical landscape that rejected linear narrative in favor of an accumulation of subjectively derived and resonant images that could be processed differently by
each viewer. Over the next thirty years, the Wooster Group would continue
to refine their particular version of the theatrical landscape, integrating fragments of well-known texts, popular imagery, and cutting-edge technology,
creating a stage picture and theatrical experience unlike any that Gertrude
Stein could ever have imagined as she gazed down from an airplane in the
1930s.

In the 1980s, the Wooster Group became increasingly interested in using famous or canonical dramatic works in their performances, whereas
Gray became increasingly interested in creating solo performances on his
own. When the Wooster Group approached famous plays, however, they
did not stage them in conventional ways. Just as Gray's memories and personal artifacts became tools for experimentation in performance, so too
were well-known works like Arthur Miller's (1915–2005) *The Crucible*
(1953). In 1981 the Wooster Group used Thornton Wilder's (1897–1975)
Our Town (1938) and blackface to construct *Routes 1 and 9*. Though
LeCompte claimed she was using the historically loaded image of blackface
performance ironically and as a comment on masks, character, and race in
America, many audience members were deeply offended by her choices.
Complaints came pouring in, and eventually the New York State Council
on the Arts withdrew their financial support from the company. In 1984

the Wooster Group began work on *L.S.D. (. . . Just the High Points . . .).* The controversy over *Routes 1 and 9* gave them intimate experience with censorship and persecution, so it is not surprising that they were attracted by Miller's play on the Salem witch trials that is widely regarded as a meditation on the repressions of McCarthyism.

The Wooster Group's approach to Miller's *Crucible* (or to Wilder's *Our Town*) is a case study in the postmodern artistic strategy of deconstruction. Rather than affirming the stories of the past and the philosophies they conceal, postmodernists like the Wooster Group question readings and interpretations that have been taken for granted. They revisit texts, putting new pressures on their structure and ideas, to see how what appeared to be a central concern can be pushed to the margins, and how what seemed to be at a text's fringes might be resituated in the center. In their production of *L.S.D.*, they revisited the black face controversy of *Routes 1 and 9* by having the white actress Kate Valk play Tituba, a black character from *The Crucible*. They also blended music, dance, beat poetry, the vaudeville-esque debates of Timothy Leary and G. Gordon Liddy from the 1970s, and edited versions of Miller's text, including a videotape of the company rehearsing *The Crucible* while affected by the hallucinogenic drug L.S.D.

Just as Smith's work provoked questions about the role and nature of playwriting in the postmodern era, so too did *L.S.D.* Arthur Miller threatened to sue the Wooster Group over what he considered unfair use of the play he authored. The company tried various strategies to circumvent his objection—having Michael Kirby write a similar scene that they could substitute for Miller's words, trading Miller's words for nonsense sounds, and finally a written appeal from LeCompte to Miller explaining their ironic techniques—but ultimately the company had to pull the production to avoid legal action.

The Wooster Group's deconstruction of play texts also connects them to postmodern attitudes regarding history. As they worked with *The Crucible*, they sampled a piece of it, taking that fragment from its original context, repositioning it to fit the ideas they wished to explore. In their hands, *the Crucible* was not about, or was not just about, the 1950s and the Red Scare, it was about the 1980s and their own battles to express their artistic ideas in whatever form they wanted. The original historical substance of *The Crucible* had been effaced—or refaced—with Kate Valk's painted image.

Voracious borrowing and creative juxtaposition continue to be trademarks of the Wooster Group's artistic style. In their more recent work, *House/Lights*, first staged in 1998, they appropriated imagery and/or chunks of dialogue from Gertrude Stein's 1938 libretto *Doctor Faustus Lights the Lights* (itself a reworking of the Faust legend), a 1960s B-film *Olga's House*

SPOTLIGHT

Santo Loquasto and Jennifer Tipton

Jennifer Tipton and Santo Loquasto are two of the most respected designers working in the contemporary American theatre, and they often work together. These artists exemplify the postmodern trend of working across performance genres.

Jennifer Tipton designed the lights for the Public Theatre's 2001 production of Anton Chekhov's *The Seagull*. Shown: Meryl Streep, Kevin Kline.

Photo © Michal Daniel, 2001

After graduating from Cornell University with an English major, Jennifer Tipton (1937–), an Ohio native, went to New York City in the early 1960s to study dance. She got her start with lighting design as an apprentice to Thomas Skelton and soon began working for the newly formed Paul Taylor Dance Troupe. Her first internationally acclaimed lighting design was for Jerome Robbins's 1973 *Celebrations: The Art of the Pas de Deux*. Throughout her career she has designed for major choreographers, including Twyla Tharp, Mikhail Baryshnikov, Jiri Kylian, and Dana Reitz. By the mid-1970s she was working in the major New York theatres and regularly earning awards, including the Drama Desk (for Ntozake Shange's *For Colored Girls Who Have Considered Suicide/ When the Rainbow is Enuf*), the Obie (for sustained excellence at the New York Shakespeare Festival), and the Tony (for *The Cherry Orchard*).

Tipton's success has not been limited to dance and to commercial theatrical productions. In fact, she is equally well known for her frequent collaborations with avant-garde directors of theatre and opera like Robert Wilson, Peter Sellar, Joanne Akalaitis, and Elizabeth LeCompte. Her influence also extends to the university setting. She teaches at the Yale University School of Drama and regularly designs at the Yale Repertory Theater. She says, "Ninety-nine and nine-tenths of the audience is not aware of the lighting, though 100 percent is affected by it." For more than thirty years, whether audiences across the performance genres have realized it or not, they have been affected by her beautiful work.

Photofest

For Colored Girls Who Have Considered Suicide/When the Rainbow is Enuf. Lights designed by Jennifer Tipton. Tipton won the Drama Desk Award for this design.

Santo Loquasto (1944–) went to King's College in his hometown of Wilkes-Barre, Pennsylvania. He went on to study theatre at Yale, and after spending a few summers at the Williamstown Theatre Festival in Massachusetts, he became resident designer at the Public Theatre in New York. His first design at the Public was for *Sticks and Bones* by David Rabe in 1974. In 1977, on two successive nights, his costume design for *The Cherry Orchard* opened at the Public (for which he would win his first Tony), and his set design for *American Buffalo* (for which he was nominated for another Tony) opened on Broadway. Over the course of the next thirty years, Loquasto would establish himself as one of America's most sought-after set and costume designers, working in theatre, dance, and film. In a 1988 *New York Times* interview he said, "It can feel like you're always working because you never stop looking. Even walking to the subway, you begin to register shapes and designs that have possibilities." In 2007 it also seemed that Loquasto never stopped working. Within a span of eight weeks in the spring, Broadway

Lincoln Center Theatre/Photofest

Lights designed by Jennifer Tipton, costumes designed by Santo Loquasto. Both Tipton and Loquasto won Tony Awards for their work on *Cherry Orchard*.

© Gary Hershorn/Reuters/CORBIS

Audra McDonald and John Cullum wear costumes designed by Santo Loquasto in the 2007 revival of *110 in the Shade*.

Santo Loquasto was production designer for Woody Allen's 1994 film *Bullets Over Broadway*. Pictured: Dianne Wiest and John Cusack.

audiences saw his set design for the revival of *Prelude to a Kiss*, his set and costume designs for *Inherit the Wind*, and his set and costume designs for the revival of the musical *110 in the Shade*. Highlights from his illustrious career include eleven Tony Award nominations and three wins as well as Academy Award nominations for his production designs of Woody Allen's *Bullets Over Broadway* and *Radio Days*.

Photo © Mary Gearhart. Courtesy of the Wooster Group.

House/Lights pictured (l-r): Kate Valk, Suzzy Roche directed by: Elizabeth LeCompte

of Shame, Busby Berkeley's 1930s filmic water ballet, *Under the Waterfall*, *The I Love Lucy Show*, *Young Frankenstein*, and Johnny Cash's "Burning Ring of Fire," to name but some of the items in their theatrical pastiche. The combination of materials—old and new, high art and popular—occurred at breakneck speed, and the performers seemed frequently to be winking conspiratorially at the audience across the fractured surface of the performance.

In *House/Lights* the Wooster Group played with postmodern fragmentation in yet another way. The company is well known for the ways they use high-tech video and other technological mediation of live performance in their work. In *House/Lights*, the set was dotted with video monitors displaying movie clips and "copies" of the live actors in the performance. Kate Valk was again a principal performer in the show, and she often interacted with a video image of herself. In addition to giving the spectator a feast of images to devour, the company was making several complex statements. First, the audience had the opportunity to consider the postmodern idea of simulations and their connection to reality. Audiences had to choose where to look—at the live, present Valk or at her equally compelling images (sometimes further refracted four or more times) on the monitors around the stage. The authority of the technologically mediated image, the one provided by television screens, was pitted against the presence of a charismatic actress. The audience had to decide if there was a real Valk in this devious onslaught of beguiling images. Second, the audience could contemplate the power of the postmodern cyborg. When Valk and her image were multiplied, she was no longer only human or organic, she was also cybernetic—digitized, colorized, with shockingly red lips, for example, and often with a voice that was distorted through the use of a microphone and a sound feed that was further altered by a computer. Character, image, and identity were mingled in such a way that the power and possibilities of each term were radically reconfigured through this quintessentially postmodern performance.

A final piece of the Wooster Group's relationship to postmodernism is revealed through their attitude toward the development of a performance. Although postmodernism is easy to date as a movement, the Wooster Group's works are not. They begin a piece as a workshop to which they invite a paying public, then they stage the piece again over intervals separated by a number of years. Each time they return to a show, they rework parts of it, adding and subtracting performers, episodes, images, and cultural fragments. They create, through these renegotiations with their own creative products and process, a postmodern theatrical scrapbook unlike anything imagined and realized by centuries of artists before them. Their work is never finished, a performance is never complete, and through this adventurous play with fragmentation, history, and a broken surface of technologically mediated imagery, postmodernism is at once summarized and continually redefined.

 ## CHAPTER SUMMARY

Recent trends in playwriting, solo performance, and the work of a theatre collective that uses technologically sophisticated media all play with some of the most important ideas animating postmodernism. As they reconsider or overturn the grand narratives of the past, as they broaden the range of voices represented on stage, as they borrow historical iconography for characters, as they make surprising combinations of images, as they question the relationship between fractured surface and interior, and as they probe the limits of the human, they show how postmodernism can enliven the theatre and how the theatre can enrich postmodern lives.

 ## ACTIVITIES

Do-It-Yourself Pastiche

Find a partner. One person collects three images that they find striking. Use different sources (including a camera phone if you wish). Don't try to pick them based on theme or idea. The other person collects three sentences from songs, books, advertisements, or television. Together use the sentences as captions for the images. Discuss how the random connection of text and image changes the meaning of the words and the pictures. How could your collage be a foundation for or used in a theatrical production? Does it tell a story? Would you want it to?

Can You Hear Me Now?

Find a partner. Read a story in your campus or local newspaper covering a controversial event. Call your partner's cell phone and leave a two-minute voice mail retelling what happened or describing your own reaction to it. Your partner should do the same. When you're each done, transcribe the message you received on your phone, being sure to record for yourself the words and pauses exactly as they were spoken by your partner. Read your transcripts to each other. Discuss how your words sound coming out of someone else's mouth. Discuss any differences you and your partner had in describing and processing the event. How did the use of the technology—of your phones—affect storytelling and memory? Would the event you described benefit from further exploration on a stage?

The Theatre Profession in the Postmodern Age

Postmodernism rejects the "master narrative" and is therefore, as we discovered in the previous chapter, skeptical of "universal truths" and the myths used to support them. Take, for example, the traditional master narrative of the life of the theatre artist: pretty, misunderstood farm girl heads for the big city, is discovered stepping off the bus from Des Moines, instantly stars on Broadway tap dancing and singing, and lives happily ever after (until she heads off for the Betty Ford clinic and/or moves to California to make movies). This is the myth of the theatre worker, and it masquerades as "the" universal story. Postmodernism, however, facilitates multiple voices telling multiple stories: There is no single story for how one lives as a theatre artist. There are many different stories featuring different kinds of people doing much more interesting things than the fictional farm girl turned Broadway star in the preceding scenario.

Through a series of personal interviews, this chapter will focus on eight contemporary lives in theatre. The individuals chosen for inclusion are not likely to be names previously known to you. They represent countless others leading fruitful and rewarding artistic lives while working actively in and making meaningful contributions to the profession—but not necessarily becoming "household names." Our goal is to provide a representative sample of theatre workers in the field today: careers represented range from playwriting, directing, performance, and tech, to theatre management, dramaturgy, and design. To further heighten the sense of multivocality, we've let these individuals speak for themselves: each section is largely comprised of verbatim quotes. You'll find that some of the featured individuals work in more than one area (such as a solo performer who writes her own plays and a dramaturg who is also a college instructor). You'll find educational backgrounds ranging from numerous graduate degrees to no college degree. Individuals with degrees include those with advanced studies in their discipline (a playwright with an MFA in playwriting) as well as degrees in theatre but not in the area of theatre in which they are now employed (an arts manager with a degree in acting). Some individuals are in the early stages of a career, whereas others are more established.

These people are leading "theatre lives," and you can, too. By questioning the master narrative and experiencing a sampling of "real" voices in theatre, you can begin to imagine where your own unique "theatre life" might take you. If you think you might be interested in a career in theatre, this chapter will give you a greater sense of available careers and help generate guidelines for your own career path. Each featured individual was asked to pass along tips or advice for college students interested in careers in their particular field. The responses are included at the end of each section. Or perhaps you want theatre to be part of your life as a recreational pursuit or source of entertainment but not as an occupation or profession. These profiles can bring you greater awareness of the everyday lives of individuals working in theatre today and, by extension, growing understanding of theatre as an art form—and perhaps a mounting suspicion that many other fields, including perhaps one you are considering for your own future, have similar depth in terms of career possibilities.

TECH: ZACH STINNETT

Zach Stinnett is a technician experienced in carpentry, sound, lighting, and "deck." The latter, short for deckhand or stagehand, entails "setting up the stage for the show, running the backstage during the show, completing changeovers during the show, and helping to strike the show." He lives in New York City and freelances around Manhattan. Currently, he works for a company that does lighting for events such as corporate parties and weddings as well as doing work for the Lincoln Center Out of Doors series and other performing arts events in the New York area.

A typical workday for Stinnett begins with "unloading the truck." After that, he says, "It depends on what I'm doing. If I'm a carpenter I help build the deck, which is putting platforming together then putting up flats or drape. It's setting up the physical space. If things need to be built, the carpenters build it. If I'm lighting, we run power, then we look at the light plot and hang, patch, focus, and gel all the lights. If I'm sound, we run power then we set up mix positions, hang speakers, patch amps, patch speakers, test sound system, and set up, patch, and test microphones. Deck is doing all the backstage stuff during the show. Then at the end of the day, we strike everything and put it back in the truck."

Of his experience as a college student, Stinnett says: "I built a good base of skills in college. I took a lot of classes. I worked in the scene shop and worked on a lot of the productions. I also did a lot of work on student productions and student showcases. . . . I think college is where most of my training has come from."

Early in his career, Stinnett completed a technical internship with The Wooster Group, a performance ensemble discussed at length in a previous chapter. His description of that experience conveys the balance of practical and creative value it provided: "What I did was help them on load ins, setting up the stage and load outs. I was really there to help whatever

Zach Stinnett

department needed a hand that day. During the run of the show I would set up the tech table for rehearsals, retape the floor, clean the stage, and help fix props sometimes. The real treat was I got to watch the Group's process: how they create a show, work on a show daily, how they work as a group and a theatre company. . . . I got to see how they work, and that was amazing. I got to live a dream every day." As is the case with many internships, the position did not provide monetary compensation, but Stinnett, knowing the experience would be valuable, saved up for two years to be able to accept the position. "Internships are important to get your foot in the door but also to let you know what you are in for working for a company. It's also a great way to make new contacts, which lead to other jobs." He continues to do occasional freelance work for The Wooster Group.

Stinnett is drawn to theatre that, as opposed to focusing on escapism, facilitates a meaningful exploration of life. "I think that is the point of theater! If a play does not have a message, then why do it? It's all about holding a mirror up to our society and ourselves." He enjoys both classical and traditional theatre forms: "A good script is a good script. I don't care if it is new or classical. If it's exploring an interesting thing, I'm going to want to work on it or see it."

To future techies, Stinnett offers this advice: "Take every theatre class possible and work in the scene shop. . . . The most important advice I can give someone is show up early, be ready to work, and be honest about what you know. It's okay to say, " I've never done that." Ask questions don't guess. Remember that every gig is an audition, and they don't have to call you for the next gig. Learn one word and that word is "next." I finish one task, and I ask what the next one is, and that's why people call me to work for them and why they pass my info to other people."

PLAYWRITING: DANO MADDEN

Theatre experiences in high school and college greatly affected Dano Madden's choice of occupation: "I had a variety of career dreams growing up, including but not limited to: Baseball Player, Cartoonist, Basketball Player, Sports Broadcaster, Sports Journalist. I fell in love with theatre at Borah High School in Boise, Idaho. While at Borah, I was primarily an actor, and I continued on at Boise State University as at Theatre Arts Major. During my third year at BSU, I began to explore directing and playwriting. This is when the light really went on for me. I loved acting, but something about being in control of the larger picture appealed to me more. When an eight-minute play of mine called *The Soft Sand* was well received in a BSU Theatre showcase, I was sold. I fell in love with writing plays, and I've never really looked back." Madden completed an MFA in playwriting at Rutgers University in 2007. In the same year, he was named "One of 50 to Watch" in *The Dramatist,* the magazine of the Dramatist Guild of America. His plays have been produced by Actors Theatre of Louisville, The Source Festival, Mile Square Theatre, Northwest Playwrights Alliance, Idaho Theatre for Youth, Kitchen Theatre Company, Rutgers University, The University of Tulsa, and Sand and Glass Productions, among others.

Dano Madden

"Part of what I love about being a playwright is the chance to travel and see different places and meet new people. I am presently based on the East Coast, but I travel throughout the year for readings and productions of my work. I love working with all kinds of theatres, small and large. My goal at the moment is to begin to have my work produced more frequently by larger regional and New York area theatres. The reason for this goal is because more established theatres will bring higher visibility to my work and more financial compensation. But in the large scheme I'd love to work in as many theatres as possible."

"I think to be a writer you must take in everything around you. Your upbringing, education, travels, reading—everything that makes you who you are also prepares you to be a writer," says Madden. "I love theatre that tells a good story and surprises me. This is what I want my plays to do. I am very open to various genres and styles and mixing them if a great story is being told." Madden also wants his plays to make audience members think: "My goal as a playwright is to tell great entertaining stories while also challenging the beliefs of the audience. I don't think each play has to have a specific message, but I do hope that each play will provoke each audience member to reevaluate their own beliefs when they walk out of the theatre."

So, how does a playwright spend his days? "My best workday is one in which I can do three to five hours of productive writing. The life of a playwright is very busy, especially because various means of income are often required to pay the rent. A great workday is one in which I can focus primarily on my work as a playwright. If on that day I make significant, positive progress on the play, so much the better." Since moving to the East Coast, Madden reports taking on a variety of jobs to pay the bills, including "Off-Broadway sound board operator, caterer, Writing 101 teacher at Rutgers University, and presently, protean office employee in midtown Manhattan." Taking on such jobs is not uncommon for theatre artists, particularly in the early phases of a career. "My dream job is to be a full-time, financially secure writer. I have so much writing to do, and life seems to go by so fast. My goal is to reach a place where most of my time is spent writing and revising plays. I would also like to mix in some teaching. To be a part-time college professor and a full-time playwright would be my dream job. Also, it is a dream of mine to continue working with all of my dearest friends and theatre collaborators for my whole life."

He cautions individuals thinking about a career in theatre to be motivated by passion and not the allure of so-called glamour: "The career of the playwright, in my experience, is about hard work. The work of writing plays, the work of trying to get those plays into the world, the challenge of always believing in yourself. . . . I think this is true of most theatre artists: actors and directors and designers—it is hard work to do it well. And the time in the trenches busting your rear significantly outweighs the moments of so-called glory. And this is fine, as long as you love the work."

Madden's advice for would-be playwrights: "Fill up the well as much as you can: Travel, take courses in history and art, read newspapers, learn about your family, go to museums, read as much as you can, pay attention to the world around you as much as possible. Discover what you are interested in writing plays about. Find your voice. But most importantly, write as much as you can whenever you can. A great playwright and mentor of mine, Lee Blessing, once told me that there are only two things that a playwright truly has in his or her control: persistence and resilience. I live by this advice every day."

 ## DRAMATURGY: MARTINE KEI GREEN

Martine Kei Green had never heard of dramaturgy until her academic advisor suggested it as a natural synthesis of her theatre major and history minor. Green dramaturged her first show, *Medea*, in 2002 as an undergraduate at Virginia Wesleyan College. Now a PhD candidate and college instructor, Green's dramaturgy credits include productions at Oregon Shakespeare Festival, Madison Repertory Theatre's New Play Festival, 2008 WI Wrights New Play Festival, and the Classical Theatre Company in Houston.

This is how Green describes dramaturgical duties: "I research whatever play I'm working on. I sit in rehearsals and point out any inconsistencies between the text and the way it is being performed in rehearsal. I consult with designers and directors in order to work on historical accuracy as well as just 'telling the story.' I guess the best way to describe really what I do on a regular basis is to make sure that the story is being told. That also takes the form of working with new playwrights and helping them develop their stories."

A typical workday for Green is built around attending rehearsals. "I'm usually reading and rereading scenes from the play that I'm working on. Depending on what theatre company I'm working for, I could be putting together an actor packet or articles for the education department. I've also done lectures. All kinds of things." While the uninformed might categorize dramaturgy as a "bookish" vocation, Green counters: "It's not as much library time as you would think. I spend much more time in rehearsal. I think that's the key to being a good dramaturg: Investing the time in the rehearsal room. Always being that objective eye." One of the things that Green likes best about dramaturgy is the balance of working with people and working alone: "Being a dramaturg really forces me—in a good way—to stretch my imagination. To really pay attention to the detail but then also pay attention to the big picture at the same time. I really appreciate the fact that it creates this bit of mental workout every time I sit in rehearsal or sit in a meeting—just trying to keep big picture and little picture in mind at the same time."

Image by Sarah J. Heidt, courtesy of Martine Kei Green

Martine Kei Green

Where does Green find inspiration?: "Theatre inspires me. Especially new takes on the classics. The inventiveness and imagination of some of the directors and actors I've worked with. They inspire me. Beautiful plays from both the classics as well as contemporary works. The artistry itself inspires me. I couldn't imagine doing anything else with my life! Theatre inspires me on a daily basis."

Green is drawn to both traditional classic forms and new plays. "To be honest, I love all of it. That's why dramaturgy was a good choice for me." Green's specialties include plays by William Shakespeare and contemporary works by African-American women. She strongly believes in the unique power of theatre to affect the way people see the world around them: "There are some forms of entertainment that don't require much of people—that don't require people to feel anything or have a visceral reaction. It's so rare that a form of entertainment can do that. I think that, as a result, more people need to go to the theatre. I think that people need to feel more, in general, on a regular basis." Green's commitment to theatre with a message led her as a graduate student to get involved with a cultural and social awareness theatre group. "Seeing how people react and come to

This 2008 production of *Fences* at Oregon Shakespeare Festival was directed by Leah C. Gardiner with dramaturgy by Martine Kei Green.

Image © by David Cooper, courtesy of the Oregon Shakespeare Festival. Used by permission of the photographer.

terms with the world around them through theatre is a huge learning experience. I've learned a lot about myself and who I am and how I see the world through working with them." Now, as a college instructor, she is teaching courses in social justice theatre.

Advice to college students interested in a dramaturgy career: "Keep up with what's going on in the field currently. Read all the time. . . . I'm always reading to see what new plays are out and what trends in theatre are going on at the moment. Not just American theatre, but internationally: What is going on in the theatre? That is what determines whether or not my job is valid on any given day. Talk to working dramaturgs and literary managers. Take a vested interest in finding out what people are doing in theatre. A dramaturg's job is influenced by what's going on in the here and the now as well as 100 years ago."

DESIGN: ALAN YEONG

Alan Yeong always knew he wanted to entertain people but, like many others, he is indebted to an undergraduate mentor for helping him select a more specific career path: " I was in awe of my undergraduate mentor, Bob Scriba—his tremendous intelligence, passion and dedication as a theatre artist. He guided me to the design world. He showed me how exciting it can be to transform an empty space into any given fictional world as provided by the playwright's words. The reward is to be able to watch audiences willingly suspend their disbelief with my designs." After earning an MFA in scenography and another in costume design, Yeong is now mentoring undergraduates himself as a faculty member at the University of West Georgia. He teaches courses in design and theatre appreciation in addition to serving as resident costume designer and costume shop supervisor. He also freelances regularly for theatres in the metropolitan Atlanta area.

"A typical day is divided into two sections: The morning section is solely dedicated to departmental and teaching activities—office hours, classes, and faculty meetings. Afternoons are strictly dedicated to the costume shop—supervising the costume shop staff and mentoring all costume and properties designers." Such a schedule necessitates strong skills in time management and organization: "A 'best' workday is signified by successfully achieving 80% of tasks listed in the daily 'To-Do List.'" Despite the hectic schedule, Yeong pulls it all off with grace, humor, and a strong sense of a designer's unique role within the production team. "All costume designers will work overtime and lose sleep to ensure the costume design will enhance the actor's performance—contrary to popular belief that all costume designers purposely choose unflattering clothing to ruin your appearance," he says with a smile. Yeong believes that it is particularly important for a theatre artist to live a balanced life: "Always set aside personal 'me' time no matter how hectic your work schedule. You need to find a positive activity that has no relationship with your nature of work as a relaxation tool. A rested mind and body help rejuvenate your creativity."

Alan Yeong

Image by Steven Broome, copyright © University of West Georgia

Yeong sees theatre as part of the very fabric of which our lives are constructed: "All cultural events that you experience with your friends and family are "theatre." Sporting events, rock concerts, wedding ceremonies, and so forth are all forms of theatre. Theatre is life, life is theatre. We all live on a big stage as Jacques puts in succinctly in Shakespeare's *As You Like It*: 'All the world's a stage. And all the men and women merely players.'"

To future theatre practitioners, Yeong says, "All aspiring theatre artists should first of all be an avid observer. Good observation skills are key to becoming a good verbal or visual artist. We are all living reporters hence we should cultivate skills to effectively utilize all sources available to us." In terms of getting started with your career, Yeong continues, "Always have a plan of attack—Do you have a five-year plan? How about a ten-year plan? Good planning ensures good results. . . . Always build a strong foundation first. Don't try to run before you know how to walk! Stay humble and push yourself to learn new skills constantly. Never settle for less, strive for the best you can offer. Always walk in other's shoes—for example, a costume designer should take movement classes. Actors should learn the functions of theatre designers. A good designer is a good director and vice-versa. . . . Always say 'YES!'"

Costume renderings by Alan Yeong for a 2007 production of Pirandello's *Six Characters in Search of An Author* at LaGrange College.

PERFORMANCE: LAUREN WEEDMAN

If Lauren Weedman's face looks familiar, you may have seen her on Comedy Central's *Reno 911* or *The Daily Show* with Jon Stewart. In addition to her television work, Weedman is a solo performer and writer. Her solo work has been performed Off-Broadway, toured with the Seattle Repertory Theatre, and received accolades ranging from publication in *Women Playwrights: The Best Plays of 2002* to awards for Best New Play and Best Solo Performance by the Seattle Times' Footlight Awards. She is the author of *A Woman Trapped in a Woman's Body: Tales from the Cringe*. Weedman attended college for several semesters, taking courses in theatre, women's studies, and film. Because her response to our questions reads like a monologue she might perform in one of her plays, we have printed it as one:

> *I spend most of my days writing—performing. For theatre, film, TV, and now the Web. My main work is the work I do with solo theatre. Writing-developing and touring my shows.*
>
> *Here's an example of what my day was like today—and it's actually a good example—*
>
> *I got up and responded to e-mails. Sent out some packets with DVDs of my show BUST to a theatre in Berkeley that I'd like to perform in—they don't know my stuff so I had friends who know the theatre call and give me an intro and then I put together a packet to send to them. No matter how BUSY and/or SUCCESSFUL I ever feel, the need to constantly promote and get the next job has never gone away. . .*
>
> *So . . . today, I sent e-mails . . . put together mailings . . . worked on an audition for an independent film. Wrote a first draft of a short story that I was asked to write for a festival in Seattle.*
>
> *I do a lot of TALKING and PLANNING. Like talking to the artistic director of the theatre that commissioned my new play about what sort of scenic designer we should try and find that would fit the play the best.*
>
> *The best work day is when I remember how amazing it is that I get to work full time as an artist—that my days are spent exactly how I'd hoped they'd be spent when I was a kid. I have friends in the corporate world who say to me, "You're so lucky . . . you never had to grow up." And though I'd disagree a bit with that—it's sort of true. I still work in make-believe and play.*

Lauren Weedman

Image by Dana Patrick, courtesy of Lauren Weedman

Lauren Weedman in her solo performance piece BUST.

Image © Jeff Swensen, courtesy of Lauren Weedman. Used by permission of the photographer.

A best workday for me is when I'm working on a new show and I find a scene . . . when I find a moment that rings TRUE . . . that surprises me . . . and entertains me. . . .

What I like best about what I do is that EVERYTHING IS INSPIRATION. Life and living and people. Good days, bad days. Also I love that all I need is to be aware—. I can go out into the world with a notebook and those are my tools.

And that really—all of life—when I'm looking for it—is art. Just exploring what it means to be a human being. And entertaining people. . . .

And it's never boring—and if it is—it's my fault. I . . . I get to be, crave to be, shook up—challenged and brought out of the idea of who I thought I was. Again and again and again.

And I love that I am still doing exactly what it was I wanted to do when I was in third grade.

Everything I've done has prepared me for what I do. Outside of theatre school and classes—working in restaurants helped me work on my skills as an actor—learn how to "read people." Even when I worked in offices as a temp—I would think about how much people needed to be shook up from their trapped ideas of living and how things are done.

What might it surprise people to learn about me? That I'm still poor sometimes. Because I do theatre and then TV—my money goes up and down and up and down. And I am still basically living the apartment-dwelling artist life that I did when I was in my 20s. My friends will see me one time for 3 seconds on TV and think that I must be doing really well in Hollywood—and it's true that I choose to live in LA for higher-paying jobs to fill in the gaps when I take time to do theatre—but I'm still very much living like an artist.

The solo theatre life is lonely. Obviously. But I like that.

And if you want to continue to create—to always push and find new collaborators and new inspiration . . . it takes a lot of work. That moment of "okay, now I GET IT . . . now it will be easy" never comes. Some things get easier. But I guess like childbirth—it's always an intense process—and you forget how hard it was until the next time you try to do it again.

I'd like to see more theatre and more different kinds of theatre brought to kids in high school and earlier. Open those TV minds up. . . . It's happened when I've performed that I've been told that "I've never seen live theatre before . . . besides Wicked*." The age of sitting back and watching TV—impassive and so distant from what you're watching . . . that kills me. I want people to know that what is happening is happening live in front of them. A group catharsis—that is what live theatre is. But folks are getting more and more shut down—and don't even know how to watch live theatre. But theatre is how we learn about ourselves—together—connection—in a room. Live.*

Advice for college students seeking a similar career? Be sure to find an environment where you feel allowed to fully explore who you are—and be interested in all that is life. Everything. Open to the things that you don't understand—and as corny as it may sound—you must get out of your comfort zone. That is how you get away from the ideas of who you think you are—and into taking in life.

Take in and do as much as you can. That's what I've always been grateful I've done—I don't turn down invitations to travel—to visit somebody's ashram or to go line dancing. Get outside what is comfortable. Living abroad was a great experience for me. Completely intense and overwhelming at times—but it took me out of the expectations of my parents and other people.

Seeing as much dance-experimental theatre and live music as well.

Being open to all.

ARTS MANAGEMENT—BROADWAY: AMY STEINHAUS

Raised in Los Angeles, Amy Steinhaus left California to study theatre and film at the University of Kansas and moved to New York after graduating in 1995 to pursue a career in acting. She inadvertently began a career in ticketing as a membership associate at Circle in the Square Theatre, where she was also an acting student. Since then she has had made her way up the ticketing and managerial ladder, managing the box offices at Forbidden Broadway and The New Victory Theatre, then moving on to assist in the opening of the then-new Off-Broadway three-theatre complex, 59E59 Theatres, and working there as the director of sales. Steinhaus joined the

Amy Steinhaus

Courtesy of Amy Steinhaus

Broadway League in 2006 and is currently the manager of ticketing and hospitality. The Broadway League is the national trade association for the Broadway industry, made up of Broadway theatre owners, producers, general managers, and road presenters and Broadway touring venues. Steinhaus oversees the operations of the Broadway Concierge and Ticket Center, a one-stop shopping full-price ticket center for all Broadway and many Off-Broadway shows, as well as full concierge service. She also handles all ticketing and hospitality needs for Broadway League sponsors and VIP for Broadway and the Tony Awards and assists in new Broadway marketing and branding initiatives.

"I had no intention of having a career like this. I had planned on pursuing a career in acting. . . . Though it wasn't planned, I am very pleased with where I've gotten in my career and where I am now," says Steinhaus. " It can be just as gratifying working behind the scenes in theatre as up onstage. As much as I miss performing, I am very happy to be an influential part of the theatrical process. . . . As far as having a career in theatre, working for Broadway in New York is about as good as it gets."

In a typical workday, Steinhaus receives and confirms house seat requests for VIP and sponsors, works on maintaining and creating existing and future events at the ticket center, fields calls from special VIPs/sponsors for hospitality and ticketing needs, and attends numerous meetings. She also gets to work on special projects—some of which utilize her wit and sense of humor: "One thing I'm doing is creating supplemental handout materials for customers to help them choose the best show for them. I came up with 'personality' guides for men, women, boys, and girls that are a little 'tongue in cheek' to make it more fun. I have listed various personality types and have a suggested show to go with that type as well as a corresponding restaurant to dine at, and maybe some sort of attraction to visit. All of it ties into the personality of that person and the theme of the show they are seeing. Something else we've done is to create a 'Family Guide,' which includes theatre terminology, the 'do's' of going to the theatre, and a crossword puzzle. So in my job I also have the opportunity to show my creative side!"

Following is a sample of one of the personality guides developed by Steinhaus:

AL'S GUIDE TO BROADWAY			
	Dinner	*Theatre*	*After Dinner*
The Party Gal	*Bourbon Street Bar & Grill*	**XANADU**	*karaoke & cocktails at Spotlight Live*
The Girlie Gal	*Blue Fin*	**THE LITTLE MERMAID**	*rooftop cocktails at Highbar*
The Independent Gal	*Café Un Deux Trois*	**GYPSY**	*take the A train to Dizzy's Club*
The Rebellious Gal	*Hard Rock Cafe*	**CHICAGO**	*lethal concoctions at Tonic*
The NYC Gal	*John's Pizza*	**IN THE HEIGHTS**	*mojitos with the locals at Hell's Kitchen*
The International Gal	*Chop Suey*	**BOEING-BOEING**	*infused vodka at the Russian Vodka Room*
The Career Gal	*Insieme*	**LEGALLY BLONDE**	*private drinks at conversation at Bar Centrale*
The Family Gal	*Ruby Foo's*	**MAMMA MIA!**	*healthy late-night snack at Red Mango Frozen Yogurt*
The Hopelessly Romantic Gal	*Wine and fondue at Swizz*	**GREASE**	*cuddle in a cozy corner at Kemia Bar*

Before your big night out at the theatre . . .

Freshen up at Sephora in Times Square by sampling their wide variety of cosmetics and perfumes

For Steinhaus, one of the benefits of working in arts management at this level is attendance at a wide variety of events: "I like that there are many perks working for Broadway, like seeing all the shows, going to special events like the Tony Awards and other Broadway events, and working with high-level sponsors. . . . Seeing really great theatre and amazing performances inspires me. It makes me realize that I have a very unique job and live in the best place for what I do and love."

Though Steinhaus works in the Broadway realm, she appreciates and attends a wide range of theatre: "I'm lucky that I get to see all the Broadway shows, but I worked Off-Broadway for many years and really love seeing something truly daring and progressive. I was able to spend some time at the Edinburgh Fringe Festival a few summers, and saw some of the most amazing theatre I've ever encountered there. . . . I'm a fan of any theatre that strays from the norm."

When asked if theatre can or should strive to be a form of mainstream entertainment today, Steinhaus replies, "Working for Broadway, I can say that professional theatre has already become part of mainstream entertainment. I wish less commercial work could reach more audiences, but that is a challenge. The biggest challenge with theatre being mainstream is often the price is too high for the general public. For theatre to be completely mainstream, there needs to be more consideration of the lower-income population when pricing."

As to the balance between theatre as entertainment and theatre "with a message," Steinhaus says, "I like to be a part of something that makes people think when they leave the theatre. Whether it's a 'message' or some form of catharsis or even just a feeling of satisfaction, I don't really mind. As long as you go away feeling something more than you felt going in, then I'm happy (unless it's a feeling of time having been wasted!)."

Advice to students wanting a similar career?: "I've worked up the ladder to get where I am, not having studied ticketing or anything management related. With a job like this, it is best to get on-the-job experience, but if there is anything I would suggest studying to be useful in many areas, it would be marketing. I would also definitely suggest an internship in the field that interests you, as that is invaluable."

DIRECTING: LEAH C. GARDINER

Although time spent in rehearsal might be the most obvious activity undertaken by the director, and a very important one, according to Leah C. Gardiner, it is just a drop in the bucket of what a director actually does on any given day: "When we are not in rehearsal, we are normally working at our desks mapping out a plan for how we want to attack any given play we are working on. We normally work on a minimum of five projects at a time, so it can get overwhelming at times. We are also fielding phone calls from producers, planning meetings with designers, working with casting directors in search of appropriate actors we wish to see for auditions. When we are not at our desks, we are usually casting shows, in design studios with designers planning the overall look of the show, meeting with playwrights if we are directing new plays, and meeting with other theater artists to plan for other shows we will direct. When we are in rehearsals for the play, we usually work for five weeks, six days a week from 10 am to 6 pm with the actors. After rehearsals we are inevitably in meetings with various departments planning the execution of the play. The sixth week of rehearsal is spent in technical rehearsals in the theatre in which we will perform. Here we put together the technical elements with the acting and directing work. We work closely with the designers, production manager, and technical director to make sure our vision is being made clear to the audience." In addition to directing, Gardiner is coauthoring a book and tries to spend some of each day working on that project as well.

Leah C. Gardiner

Courtesy of Leah C. Gardiner

Though working with mentors such as George C. Wolfe, a director discussed at length in the previous chapter, has helped Gardiner hone her art, even as a child she had what could be called a strong sense of "direction": "I directed my first play when I was in the first grade. It was a play using flashlights that were operated by my classmates. There was a stage with a balcony. Live music accompanied the movements of the flashlights and then periodically a person would speak. I directed my classmates to move up and down the stairs creating pictures, as it were, with the lights. It was very avant-garde for a six-year-old." Though she has advanced considerably from flashlights, Gardiner remains interested in finding nontraditional or experimental approaches to traditional theater: "I love to make theatre that mixes genres and styles. I am interested in modern technology and how that plays itself out onstage; as well as incorporating other theatre art forms like Noh theatre into my practice as a director. I believe the more versatile we can be as theatre artists, the more exciting and liberating we will find the art form. It's important to keep it fresh and new."

So, what kind of projects does Gardiner undertake? "As a freelance director, I get to choose my projects and am also asked to interview for projects. I usually get asked to direct large, epic traditional plays/musicals or new plays that are epic in scope. I get very excited on those rare occasions when I am asked to direct plays with two or three characters. I agree to take on a project if I find something in the piece that excites me artistically," she says. For example, Gardiner directed the world premiere of Pulitzer finalist *Bulrusher*, by Eisa Davis, August Wilson's *Fences* at Oregon Shakespeare Festival, and the national tour of *Wit*, starring Judith Light. Though based in New York, Gardiner works throughout the country. She has also directed in Japan and is in the process of doing more international work. "At the moment, I dream of creating an epic drama à la Robert Wilson. This will be a story sung in many languages which embraces Americans past in order to incorporate the goodness that is America and all its worth. It's a piece that will use images, Indonesian shadow puppetry, music, and movement from various cultures with very little speaking to tell the history of the transformation of race in America. I see large pieces of fabric that transform the world of the stage. It will incorporate images of slavery; the Japanese interment camps; the Chinese Coolies; the Mexican migrant workers, etc; to modern-day people of color in the United States working on Wall Street, owning bodegas, farming land, and becoming an integral part of the American landscape. This is a piece about landscape. It is estimated that within our lifetime, half of the population in this country will be nonwhite. What does that look like on stage? How does the evolution of race in America play itself out in the here and now? And how do we motivate an audience to think about its ramifications without getting mired in its politics?"

This project could help illuminate an underlying issue in American theatre, which Gardiner feels keeps it from becoming a more mainstream form of entertainment: "The American theatre is normally ten years behind mainstream entertainment in my opinion. If you look at their hiring practices of women and people of color, you will see the percentages are much lower than other forms of entertainment in this country. Until the professional American theatre can tackle this as a larger issue, I am not sure it will be ready for the prime time." Gardiner links her dedication to social change to the inspiration she receives from her family. "I was adopted into a family of five generations of women and men who have given their lives to social change. They were/are successful doctors, businesspeople, professors, homemakers, politicians, dentists, firefighters, bishops, police officers, nurses, artists, athletes, etc., and their legacy has given me and my child much to continue to work towards."

To would-be directors, Gardiner cautions: "Directing is HARD work. You put in a lot of hours for very little pay at the beginning of your career. But, if you hang in there, it can be one of the most rewarding collaborative art forms out there." More advice from Gardiner: "When I knew I wanted to become a professional director, . . . I studied every possible book I could on directors and directing. I searched until I found the directors I felt had similar styles, thoughts, and beliefs in directing as I did. It's important to read as much as possible—not just the intellectual books on directing and playwriting, but books which encourage you to look at managing your directing career, how to find an agent, etc. since the business aspect of directing will ultimately guide your career. . . . I am a firm believer that the theatre finds a place for you, and you do not choose that place. So trust when you look within and ask and your questions on what direction you should take will be answered."

ARTS MANAGEMENT—NONPROFIT: TERRENCE D. JONES

As president and CEO of Wolf Trap Foundation for the Performing Arts, Terrence D. Jones oversees all aspects of the operating and programming arm of Wolf Trap National Park for the Performing Arts and related foundation programs and properties, with an annual budget in excess of $30 million, endowments of $18 million, 80 full-time staff, a part-time staff of approximately 300, and more than 1,200 volunteers. Jones arrived at Wolf Trap in 1996 after running the vast Krannert Center for the Performing Arts at University of Illinois at Urbana-Champaign for ten years. At that time, Wolf Trap had no strategic plan, and its performance venues—the Filene Center (which hosts nearly 100 shows between late May and the first week of September) and The Barns at Wolf Trap (an indoor performance venue that operates year-round) were known primarily for housing touring performances by nationally known musicians and artists. Though the presentation of touring acts continues to be a much-loved Wolf Trap staple, the operation has evolved under Jones's guidance to include the Center for Education at Wolf Trap, home to nationally acclaimed programs like the Wolf Trap Institute for Early Learning Through the Arts, scholarships, master classes, and internship programs. Perhaps most important to Jones, Wolf Trap has also become known for commissioning new works: "The people and the ability to create new work are what I like best and enjoy most about my job. Examples would include opera commissioning, such as the creation of the comic opera, *Volpone*, as well as *Face of America.*"

Volpone, based on the classic Ben Jonson play of the same name, was created for the Wolf Trap Opera Company, one of the nation's outstanding resident ensemble programs for young opera singers. The world premiere took place at the Barns at Wolf Trap in 2004. You might have seen the *Face of America* performance series featured on PBS's *Great Performances*. Each commissioned performance, a unique combination of live performance and high-definition imagery on giant screens, has its world premiere at Wolf Trap National Park for the Performing Arts. The inaugural *Face of America* debuted in 2000 with a groundbreaking performance by aerial dance troupe Project Bandaloop at Yosemite National Park. The artistic adventure

Terrence D. Jones

Image courtesy of Chris Guerre

began when the dancers took flight, suspended over the sheer granite cliffs of Yosemite Falls. American Indian Dance Theatre and Native American flutist Robert Mirabel commemorated the Native American heritage of the High Sierra. The series of multimedia performances, celebrating both the creativity of artists and the grandeur of America's national parks, subsequently featured Virgin Islands National Park and Coral Reef National Monument in 2001; Mammoth Cave National Park in 2002; Dayton Aviation Heritage National Historical Park, Tuskegee Airmen National Historic Site, and Wright Brothers National Memorial at Kitty Hawk (with "A Celebration of Flight") in 2003; and Hawai'i Volcanoes National Park, Pu'uhonua o Honaunau National Historical Park, and Haleakala National Park in 2006. The journey continues with *Face of America* 2009: Glacier National Park, a performance that, Jones says, "will address issues of 'loss' as it is related to the environment and biosystems within the park as well as the cultural loss within the native populations." Jones sees this series as a tremendously fitting project for Wolf Trap, America's only national park for the performing arts, to undertake in support of "a deep commitment to the preservation of natural and cultural resources that is a basic tenet of our National Park community. . . . *Face of America* showcases the natural and cultural diversity of these national treasures while expanding the boundaries of the American performing arts repertoire."

Under Jones's leadership, Wolf Trap has made a commitment to environmental sustainability: In 2007, "Go Green with Wolf Trap" was launched to take Wolf Trap to a zero-waste, carbon-neutral operation. Jones explains, "From enhancing recycling efforts and switching to biodegradable cups for concessions to optimizing energy use in the foundation offices and onstage, Wolf Trap is taking many steps to help the environment. We have found the performing arts to be a very effective means by which we can communicate this issue to a broad public audience." In pursuit of this goal, Wolf Trap recently hosted a National Summit on Arts and the Environment.

The holder of three graduate degrees in theatre, Jones has worked as an actor and a designer. He feels that his training in design and production has served him quite well in management: "My training taught me how to manage people, control budgets, develop schedules and meet deadlines—all of which are important in and transferred well to managing performing arts programs and venues."

Jones's tips for students seeking a career in arts management: "Take advantage of every opportunity to network—opportunities arise through interpersonal relationships and conversations. Internships, if they are good ones, are one of the best ways to gain practical experience and to build your

Image courtesy of Scott Suchman

Part of Wolf Trap's *Face of America* series, this performance was inspired by Mammoth Cave National Park.

Image courtesy of Scott Suchman

The Filene Center at Wolf Trap National Park for the Performing Arts seats 6,800 people.

professional network. Attend appropriate professional development conferences and/or workshops. There are several good arts management/ theatre administration programs, which can be undertaken at the undergraduate or graduate level. I would recommend studying an arts discipline at the undergraduate level, and then studying arts administration at the graduate level. A strong foundation in the arts is needed to be a successful arts administrator." He continues, "This job is not all fun and games. From the outside, it looks like it is all about performances, dinners, and parties— which are all good. The reality is that these activities follow a full workday and even when you are at performances or events—you are still responsible. You are the 'host,' not the guest. Sixty to eighty hour workweeks are not unusual—this is not the job for you if you are not willing to put in the hours."

CHAPTER SUMMARY

Rejecting the traditional master narrative of the theatre artist provides the opportunity to discover and listen to the many unique voices working in contemporary theatre. Individuals working in theatre today have myriad options. Artists can freelance or work exclusively for a particular theatre or organization. Careers can evolve: a person training for a career in acting can find themselves having a rewarding but surprising career in theatre management; a working designer can wind up CEO of one of the nation's largest nonprofit arts venues. Connection to the world in terms of reading, travel, and "people-watching" are important. Hard work and long hours are common. Few people get rich, yet many—if not most—find their work immensely rewarding. These profiles suggest that there are as many different ways to have a "theatre life" as there are lives in the theatre. Consider your own future: Where do you see theatre fitting in? Imagine your own life in theatre. . . .

ACTIVITIES

Interview Your Future Self

It's 2029, and you've been asked to answer some interview questions for a textbook chapter focusing on contemporary lives in theatre. Create a fictitious future persona and answer the following questions accordingly. When you are finished, find a partner, share your responses with each other, and discuss. Do you believe this persona to be an accurate prediction of where/who you could be in twenty years? If so, what might be some intermediate steps to get you there? If not, why not? Is it too far removed from your current career goals? Does it just seem too "unlike" you? How would you need to be different to arrive at your "imagined future" in 20 years?

- Your job title/occupation:
- What duties or tasks might be included in a typical workday for you?
- What do you like best about your work?
- What job, class, person, or experience most prepared you for your current work?
- Who/what inspires you?
- What kind of theatre/art do you take the time to see?
- Describe your dream job/project:
- What recent project has been particularly meaningful for you?
- Do you get to choose your projects? If so, what makes you decide to take a particular job?
- Where do you most like to work? (City, type of theatre.) Are you based in a single place or do you travel?
- Do you like to make/view theatre that mixes genres or styles?
- Can/should theatre strive to be a form of mainstream entertainment today?
- Do you like (to create) theatre that has a message?
- Do classic/traditional forms of theatre draw you as an artist and/or spectator, or do you most enjoy new work?

Small-Group Career Research

Form a small group with three to four students in your class. Choose an area of theatre to investigate (such as performance, tech, management, or directing). Identify three to four individuals working in that area of theatre. Try looking at the program from the last play you attended, reading your local paper, and searching online to locate suitable candidates. Consider balancing your selections in terms of area of the country in which they work, gender, size of theatre, nonprofessional or professional.

Each member of the group is to take on researching one of the chosen individuals. (For a shorter version of this exercise, the group as a whole can investigate one individual and then summarize this information for presentation to the class.) Find out all you can about the individual's particular job situation and training. Do they freelance or are they on staff? Do they hold a college degree (or more than one)? If so, is it in the field in which they are employed? If not, what kind of on-the-job training did they undertake to gain the experience necessary to work in that area? After doing a fair amount of preliminary research on the individual, try to exchange e-mails or speak with them. Ask them questions about their work. What is a typical workday for them? What do they find most challenging about the work? What do they find most rewarding? It would be great if you could actually observe them at work. Take notes on what you see and hear.

Once you have completed your individual research, come back to the small group and share your findings. Identify similarities and differences between the individuals researched. What trends do you see in terms of individuals working in this area of theatre? What findings seem most significant? What seems most surprising? Create a short "report" encapsulating your group's work. Share your report with the class and, in turn, learn the findings of other small groups in the class. If more that one small group chose the same area, how were the findings similar? Discuss differences in findings. What might account for those differences? Do the group findings strengthen or shatter any preconceived ideas or stereotypes you previously held about individuals working in theatre? Are your views of theatre artists different today than when you began this exercise? Since you began this course? How so?

But There's More! . . .

This chapter presents a variety of "theatre lives," but is by no means exhaustive in its coverage. Spend a few minutes in small-group discussion generating additional career possibilities that could have been covered in this chapter. Try to include both theatre-centered occupations such as high school drama teacher or wardrobe mistress as well as occupations in which theatre is addressed more tangentially such as a psychologist who utilizes drama therapy in their practice or an education director at a local history museum who writes and performs plays at area schools.

Notes

CHAPTER 1

1. Suggestions for further reading on this topic include: Erving Goffman's *The Presentation of Self in Everyday Life,* Richard Schechner's *Between Theatre and Anthropology,* Victor Turner's *From Ritual to Theatre,* and Stephanie Arnold's *The Creative Spirit.*

CHAPTER 2

1. David Wiles's analysis of Greek theatre is foundational to the commentary provided in this chapter. See his books *Tragedy in Athens: Performance Space and Theatrical Meaning* (Cambridge: Cambridge University Press, 1997) and *Greek Theatre Performance: An Introduction* (Cambridge: Cambridge University Press, 2000).
2. See *Theatre Histories: An Introduction.* Phillip Zarilli, Bruce McConachie, Gary Jay Williams and Carol Fisher Sorgenfrei (London: Routledge, 2006) for further thought on this topic and for the Greeks' interest in what happens inside and outside the skene. Oliver Taplin provides a related analysis of entrances and exits in *Greek Tragedy in Action* (Berkeley, University of California Press, 1978).
3. See David Wiles, *Greek Theatre Performance: An Introduction,* pp. 171–73.

CHAPTER 3

1. For a related analysis see Oscar Brockett's section on characterization in *The Essential Theatre.*
2. See Adam Rapp's interview in *American Theatre,* October 2007.
3. See writermag.com, "How I write."
4. See Harold Pinter's Nobel Prize speech at www.nobelprize.org

5. See interview with Maria Irene Fornes in the *New York Times*, 9/24/2000.
6. See interview with Edward Albee in *American Theatre*, January 2008.
7. See Naomi Wallace's essay in *American Theatre*, January 2008.

CHAPTER 10

1. Summary provided by Oscar Brockett in *The History of Theatre*.

CHAPTER 12

1. Marvin Carlson has identified four similar directorial strategies that he calls illustration, translation, fulfillment, and supplement. For further discussion see Geoffrey Proehl's "The Images Before Us: Metaphors for the Role of Dramaturg in the American Theatre" in *Dramaturgy in American Theatre: A Sourcebook*.
2. Interview with Bill Rauch in *American Theatre*, October 2006.
3. Interview with Daniel Sullivan in *American Theatre*, March 2007.
4. Interview with Bonnie Monte in *American Theatre*, April 2008.

Glossary

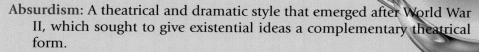

Absurdism: A theatrical and dramatic style that emerged after World War II, which sought to give existential ideas a complementary theatrical form.

Action: What happens in a play. Action in the theatre can be psychological as well as physical.

Aesthetic: Artistic or aiming toward a standard of beauty.

Amateur: From *amare* meaning to love. One who undertakes a task for love of doing it. Usually used in opposition to the word "professional."

Antagonist: The character who opposes the central figure in the main action.

Arena: (Also called theatre-in-the-round) places the stage in the middle of the space with the audience completely surrounding the action.

Arts Management/Theatre Management: Term encompassing the "business side" of the creative endeavor. Jobs in arts management and theatre management range from box office staff to public relations to chief officer in charge of operations.

Auditions: The process in which actors compete for roles in a play or membership in a company.

Beat: The small sections into which an actor divides his part. Each beat has an objective.

Black box theatre: Usually a one-level square-shaped room with a black floor, black walls, black ceiling, black drapes, etc. Has no permanent architectural features.

Blocking: The onstage movement of actors. This word is also used to describe the process of giving actors directions for that movement. Can be organic or pre-planned.

Book musical: A musical organized around a linear narrative or story. Plot and character development are given heavy focus.

Box set: Type of stage setting that give the illusion of three walls (and sometimes a ceiling) surrounding an open living space.

"Break a leg": Phrase used by and to actors instead of "Good luck."

Casting: A part of pre-production work when actors are selected for a show.

Catharsis: The purgation or purification of pity and fear in the audience thanks to what they witness on stage.

Character: A fictive being inhabiting a story who does something. In a play, they are the agents of the dramatic action.

Character conferences: Meetings between a director and actor to discuss character objectives, throughlines, and other matters of character development.

Chorus: A group of 12–50 performers who brought spectacle, music, and dance to Greek tragedy while also commenting on a play's action.

Circular structure: A method of play construction in which dramatic action is repeated or in which characters seem to end up where they started.

City Dionysia: The annual civic and religious festival where tragedies were first performed in Athens, Greece.

Climax: The point of highest intensity in the play.

Collaboration: Involves multiple artists working together. It is a key feature of theatre.

Comedy: Type of dramatic literature.

Complications: Also called rising action. Events in the play often based upon discoveries of new information or arrivals of new characters that keep dramatic action moving forward.

Concept: An overarching idea or interpretation of a script, most often articulated by the director, that informs the work of all the theatre artists working to produce a play.

Concept musical: A musical organized around a central concept or idea (as opposed to a story).

Confidant(e): A secondary character who listens to the main character, allowing him/her to reveal inner thoughts and desires.

Conventions: A readily understood practice that communicates ideas.

Costume designer: Member of the production team in charge of the visual appearance of actors onstage—including not only clothing but also hair and make-up.

Costume shop manager: Oversees the pulling of costumes from stock and/or the construction of costumes as per the costume designer's vision.

Crisis: The point at which the outcome of the play's main action is set.

Cyborg: A cybernetic organism blended from the human and technological.

Denouement: Also called falling action or resolution; the unraveling of the play's complications.

Dialect coach: A member of the production who helps actors with projection, pronunciation, dialects, and vocal characterization.

Dialogue: The key form of dramatic exchange in which one character replies to another.

Diction: The verbal language in a play; the specific ways a character speaks in a play.

Dionysus: The Greek god of wine and patron of theatre.

Drama: A type of literature usually involving action, characters and dialogue.

Dramatic literature: Another phrase for "scripts" or "plays."

Dramaturg: Assists in the production process by conducting research as needed and facilitating the use of that knowledge by the director, actors, designers and audience. Also works with playwrights in the development of new plays.

Elements of stage composition: Compression, expansion, balance, symmetry, proportion, arcs, angles, and height are things directors use when creating a stage picture.

Epic Theatre: Bertolt Brecht's style of theatre, which sought to awaken the audience's critical thinking.

Episodic structure: An associative, cumulative method of play construction often involving large casts and variety in terms of chronological and geographical setting.

Exposition: The background information in a dramatic story.

Farce: An extreme form of comedy often involving visual and physical humor.

Fight choreographer: A member of the production team who stages fight scenes and onstage violence safely.

Foil: A character who acts as a point of comparison to the main character.

Found space: Performance space originally constructed to serve another function. Based upon the premise that theatre can be performed almost anywhere.

Free plantation scenery: Set pieces that can be placed wherever theatre artists desired.

Genre: A type of dramatic literature evoking similar expectations and, therefore, grouped into a category together.

Gesamtkunstwerk: The total artwork in which all component parts are smoothly integrated into a coherent whole.

Gestus: An aspect of Bertolt Brecht's performance theory that suggests that character might well be created through the social gestures that define and distinguish individuals.

Group rituals: A larger scale playing of roles, typically with repeated elements that help to cement a community's ideals.

Improvisation: An important rehearsal tool used to free the imagination of the director and actors.

Inciting incident: Dramatic event that puts the main action into motion.

Independent Theatre Movement: Nineteenth-century European theatres that were generally organized on a subscription basis and that were committed to staging the new realistic dramas.

Individual rituals: Playing roles in everyday life in order to shape the presentation of ourselves in the world and to get the things we want and need.

Lighting designer: Member of the production team responsible for creating a plan for basic illumination of the stage as well as the creation of mood and atmosphere through the use of light.

Linear structure: Also called causal or climactic. Plots move in straight lines, with one event leading logically to the next, as the events in the play progress toward a climax.

Little Theatre Movement: The American version of the European Independent Theatre Movement.

Liveness: A feature of theatre and some other performing arts where artists and spectators share the same space and time.

Mansions: Small scenic structures representing particular places in the medieval theatre.

Master electrician: Supervises the electricians in the implementation of the lighting design.

Mediated performance: Live theatrical performance that incorporates video, film, or computer-generated imagery.

Melodrama: A popular nineteenth-century form of theatre with clear distinctions between good and evil, sensational stories, and a heavy dependence on spectacle.

Music: In plays, music may include songs, instrumental pieces, incidental songs and noise, sound effects, and the ways characters converse with each other.

Musical: Type of dramatic literature.

Myth: Stories used by a people to provide answers for the mysteries in their world.

Narrative: A story.

New Comedy: Comedy treating the domestic affairs of the middle class. It often involved cases of mistaken identity, meddling fathers, and wily servants.

Objective: What the character is trying to do in that particular beat. "I want to _____." The blank is filled in with a verb.

Old Comedy: A satirical form that engaged current political and social problems.

Organic blocking: A method of finding patterns of movement and stage positions in rehearsal as a result of collaboration between the director and actors.

Outdoor amphitheatre: Outdoor performance spaces typically featuring a hillside (or man-made equivalent) to "rake" the audience seating.

Paraesthetics or paratheatricals: Elements beyond those of the artistic or aesthetic that nonetheless impact out interactions with a theatre event. Examples: the volume level of the lobby music, the attitude of the box office staff, etc.

Performance text: Differs from production to production. It is the script as staged through theatre languages.

Periaktoi: Three-sided painting used in the ancient Greek theatre.

Pinakes: Flat paintings used in the ancient Greek theatre.

Platea: Generalized playing space in the medieval theatre.

Plot: The ordering of the incidents in a play.

Point of attack: The place in the play where the story is taken up.

Postmodernism: A variously defined term and delineated movement in arts in ideas associated with the late twentieth century. Some regard postmodernism as breaking with modernism while others see it as a logical next step in the same artistic project.

Pre-planned blocking: A pattern of movements and stage positions for actors planned by the director in advance of rehearsal.

Proscenium arch: An architectural device that frames the opening to the stage and the audience's view.

Proscenium theatre: The most prevalent form of theatre architecture today. Gets its name from the proscenium arch, a "picture frame" effect around the stage.

Protagonist: The central figure in the main action.

Raisonneur: The character who most clearly expresses the playwright's opinion and who helps to reveal the play's thought.

Realism: A theatrical and dramatic style that emerged in the nineteenth century, which sought to emulate real life.

Rehearsal: Meeting of actors with the director to work on the play.

Repertory company: A group of actors coming together for a length of time and staging a number of plays on a rotating basis.

Ritual: An action or set of actions executed in particular, usually repeated ways to gain control that involves participation.

Romanticism: A form of artistic expression that developed in Germany in the nineteenth century. Romantic works tend to celebrate nature, emphasize the spiritual over the rational, valorize rebellion, and idealize the artist-genius.

Running crew: The various technicians necessary to run the show. Running crew members are often assigned to one of four specific areas: scenery, costumes, lighting and sound.

Satyr play: A satirical play following and commenting on a trilogy of ancient Greek tragedies.

Scene shop foreman: Responsible for overseeing the construction of the set by a crew of stage carpenters and the painting of the set by scenic painters.

Scenic designer (sometimes called a set designer): Member of the production team responsible for the visual appearance of scenery and stage properties such as furniture and decorative elements.

Script: The written text of a play; a blueprint for a performance.

Simulacra: A simulation of a reality that may no longer or may never have existed.

Single-point perspective: A drawing or painting technique that conveys depth and a sense of dimensionality by featuring objects that appear to get smaller as they recede into the distance.

Skene: The scene house.

Slapstick: A play that features over-the-top, even violent, physical comedy.

Solo performance: A form of theatrical presentation most often involving a single artist performing and writing the show.

Sound designer: Member of the production team responsible for selecting (and sometimes creating) internal sound cues within the play, any background music used during the show, and music played before or after the show. Also handles the amplification of actors' voices when necessary.

Spectacle: The images on stage.

Stage manager: Assists the director with administrative tasks during the rehearsal process and, once tech rehearsals begin, "calls" the show.

Stock scenery: Generalized set pieces owned by a company that could be reused for many plays.

Synthetic fragment: A term coined by Heiner Muller to describe his particular form of dramatic construction involving fractured imagery drawn from many sources.

Table work: An early phase of rehearsal when the directors and actors read from and discuss the script they are preparing to produce.

Tech rehearsals: Rehearsals dedicated to the incorporation of technical elements—such as costume and scenic changes, lighting and sound cues—into the production.

"Techie": Slang term for theatre technician.

Theatre languages: The elements utilized to bring to life a unique interpretation of the script: costumes, lighting, sound effects, scene design, properties, acting choices.

Theatre of Cruelty: Antonin Artaud's vision for theatre involving a rejection of classical and western habits of creation and viewing.

The Syndicate: A theatre management organization that controlled the American professional theatre in the early years of the twentieth century.

Thought: Theme, meaning, or argument in a play.

Thrust stage: Gets its name from the positioning of the acting space in relation to the audience space: the former juts out into the latter. Because the playing space projects into the viewing space in this way, spectators surround the action on three sides.

Tragedy: Type of dramatic literature.

Tragicomedy: A form that mixes elements of the comic and tragic. Often contains small or archetypal characters caught in situations that while darkly humorous, are lonely and alienating.

Trilogy: A series of three related plays.

Trope: A liturgical passage sung or spoken alternately.

Bibliography

GENERAL THEATRE HISTORIES

Brockett, Oscar, with Franklin J. Hildy. *History of the Theatre*, 8th edition. Boston: Allyn and Bacon, 1999.

Brown, John Russell, ed. *The Oxford Illustrated History of the Theatre*. Oxford: Oxford University Press, 2001.

Wilson, Edwin and Alvin Goldfarb. *Living Theatre: A History*, 5th edition. Boston: McGraw-Hill, 2008.

Zarilli, Phillip, et al. *Theatre Histories: An Introduction*. New York: Routledge, 2006.

RITUAL

Brook, Peter. *The Empty Space*. New York: Avon Books, 1968.

Goffman, Erving. *The Presentation of Self in Everyday Life*. New York: Doubleday, 1959.

Kirby, E.T. *Ur-Drama: The Origins of Theatre*. New York: New York University Press, 1975.

Rozik, Eli. *The Roots of Theatre: Rethinking Ritual and Other Theories of Origin*. Iowa City: University of Iowa Press, 2002.

Schechner, Richard. *Between Theatre and Anthropology*. Philadelphia: University of Pennsylvania Press, 1985.

Turner, Victor. *From Ritual to Theatre*. New York: PAJ, 1982.

THE GREEKS

Arnott, Peter. *Public and Performance in Greek Theatre*. London: Routledge, 1991.

Case, Sue-Ellen. *Performing Feminisms*. Baltimore: Johns Hopkins University Press, 1990.

Taplin, Oliver. *Greek Tragedy in Action*. Berkeley: University of California Press, 1978.

Walton, J. Michael. *Living Greek Theatre: A Handbook of Classical Performance and Modern Production*. Westport, CT: Greenwood, 1987.

Wiles, David. *Greek Theater Performance: An Introduction*. Cambridge: Cambridge University Press, 2000.

—. *Tragedy in Athens: Performance Space and Theatrical Meaning*. Cambridge: Cambridge University Press, 1997.

DRAMATIC STRUCTURE

Aristotle. *The Poetics*. Trans. S.H. Butcher. In Critical Theory Since Plato. New York: Harcourt, Brace, and Jovanovich, 1971.

Artaud, Antonin. *The Theatre and Its Double*. Trans. Mary Caroline Richards. New York: Grove, 1958.

Brecht, Bertolt. *Brecht on Theatre*. Trans. London: John Willett, 1978.

Carlson, Marvin. *Theories of the Theatre: A Historical and Critical Survey from the Greeks to the Present*, expanded ed. Ithaca: Cornell University Press, 1993.

Dukore, Bernard. *Dramatic Theory and Criticism: Greeks to Grotowski*. New York: Holt, 1974.

Esslin, Martin. *The Theatre of the Absurd*. Garden City, NY: Double Day, 1969.

Savran, David. *In Their Own Words: Contemporary American Playwrights*. New York: Theatre Communications Group, 1998.

GENRE

Block, Geoffrey. *Enchanted Evenings: The Broadway Musical from* Show Boat *to Sondheim*. New York: Oxford University Press, 1997.

Bloom, Ken and Frank Vlastnik. *Broadway Musicals: The 101 Greatest Shows of All Time*. New York: Black Dog and Leventhal Publishers, 2008.

Grout, Donald Jay, with Claude V. Palisca. *A History of Western Music*, 3rd edition. New York: W.W. Norton and Company, 1980.

Jones, John Bush. *Our Musicals, Ourselves: A Social History of the American Musical Theatre*. Brandeis University Press, published by University Press of New England, Lebanon, NH, 2003.

Kislan, Richard. *The Musical: A Look at the American Musical Theater*. New York: Applause Books, 1995.

Krutch, Joseph Wood. *The Modern Temper*. Harvest Books, 1956.

Mates, Julian. *America's Musical Stage*. Westport, CT: Greenwood Press, 1985.

PERFORMANCE SPACE

Berkowitz, Gerald M. *New Broadways: Theatres Across America 1950–1980*. NJ: Rowman and Littlefield, Totowa, 1982.

Fischer, Lisa E. "Douglass-Hallam Theater: Excavation of an 18th-Century Playhouse," The Colonial Williamsburg Foundation Web site, 2008, <http://research.history.org/Archaeological_Research/Research _Articles/ThemeVirginia/Hallam.cfm>.

Flanagan, Hallie. *Arena*. New York: Noble Offset Printers, Inc., 1940.

Jones, Margo. *Theatre-in-the-Round*. New York: Rinehart and Company, Inc., 1951.

Langley, Stephen. *Theatre Management in America*. New York: Drama Book Publishers, 1980.

Magnus, Dorothy. "Matriarchs of the Regional Theatre." *Women in American Theatre*. Helen Krich Chinoy and Linda Walsh Jenkins, editors. New York: Theatre Communications Group, Inc., 1987.

Sheehy, Helen. *Margo—The Life and Theatre of Margo Jones*. Dallas: Southern Methodist University Press, 1989.

Stone, Edward Durell. Sketches. National Cultural Center, Washington, D.C. Edward Durell Stone Papers, D4. Special Collections Division, University of Arkansas Libraries, Fayetteville.

"University Art Center—Architect Stone's sure hand with countless details creates a harmonious home for seven arts under one Arkansas roof." *The Magazine of Building*, September 1951.

Waley, Arthur. *The Nō Plays of Japan*. Mineola, NY: Dover Publications, Inc., 1998.

Williams, Simon. *Richard Wagner and Festival Theatre*. Westport, CT: Praeger Publishers, 1994.

Zeigler, Joseph Wesley. *Regional Theatre: The Revolutionary Stage*. Minneapolis: University of Minnesota Press, 1973.

ACTING (HISTORY AND CRAFT)

Barba, Eugenio. *The Dictionary of Theatre Anthropology: The Secret Art of the Performer*. London: Routledge, 2005.

Bogart, Anne and Tina Landau. *The Viewpoints Book: A Practical Guide to Viewpoints and Composition*. New York: Theatre Communications Group, 2005.

Bradbrook, M.C. *The Rise of the Common Player: A Study of Actor and Society in Shakeapeare's England*. Cambridge, MA: Harvard University Press, 1964.

Cliff, Nigel. *The Shakespeare Riots*. New York: Random House, 2007.

Cole, Toby and Helen Krich Chinoy. *Actors on Acting*. New York: Crown Publishers, 1949.

Easty, Edward Dwight. *On Method Acting*. New York: Allograph Press, 1966.

Grote, David. *The Best Actors in the World: Shakespeare and His Acting Company*. Greenwood Press, Westport, CT: London, 2002.

Hagen, Uta with Haskel Frankel. *Respect for Acting*. New York: Macmillan Publishing Company, 1973.

Hay, Peter. *Theatrical Anecdotes*. New York: Oxford University Press, 1987.

Stanislavski, Constantin. *An Actor's Handbook*. New York: Theatre Arts Books, 1985.

Stanislavski, Constantin. *An Actor Prepares*. New York: Theatre Arts Books, 1984.

Stanislavski, Constantin. *My Life in Art*. New York: The World Publishing Company, 1966.

DESIGN (HISTORY AND CRAFT)

Cairns, Christopher. *The Renaissance Theatre: Texts, Performance, and Design*. Brookfield, VT: Ashgate, 1999.

Crich, Helen Krich and Linda Walsh Jenkins. *Women in American Theatre.* 3rd edition New York: Theatre Communications Group, 2001.

Gillette, J. Michael. *Theatrical Design and Production.* 5th edition. New York: McGraw-Hill, 2005.

Mulryne, J.R. and Margaret Shewring. *Theatre of the English and Italian Renaissance.* New York: St. Martins, 1991.

Taymor, Julie. *The Lion King: Pride Rock on Broadway.* New York: Hyperion, 1997.

Vince, Ronald. *Renaissance Theatre: An Historiographical Handbook.* Westport, CT: Greenwood, 1984.

Wilmeth, Don and Christopher Bigsby. *The Cambridge History of American Theatre.* Vol. 2. Cambridge: Cambridge University Press, 1999.

DIRECTING (HISTORY AND CRAFT)

Ball, William. *A Sense of Direction.* New York: Drama Book Publishers, 1984.

Bogart, Anne. *A Director Prepares: Seven Essays on Art in the Theatre.* New York: Routledge, 2001.

Booth, Michael. *Theatre in the Victorian Age.* Cambridge: Cambridge University Press, 1991.

Carlson, Marvin. *The French Stage in the Nineteenth Century.* Metuchen, NJ, 1972.

—. *The German Stage in the Nineteenth Century.* Metuchen, NJ, 1972.

Cole, Toby and Helen Crich Chinoy. *Directors on Directing.* New York: Allyn and Bacon, 1963.

Clurman, Harold. *On Directing.* New York: Touchstone, 1997.

Innes, Christopher. *Avant Garde Theatre: 1892–1992.* London: Routledge, 1993.

McConachie, Bruce. *Melodramatic Formations: American Theatre and Society 1820–1870.* Iowa City: University of Iowa Press, 1992.

Osborne, John. *The Meiningen Court Theatre.* Cambridge: Cambridge University Press, 1988.

Wilmeth, Don and Christopher Bigsby. *The Cambridge History of American Theatre,* Vols. 1–2. Cambridge: Cambridge University Press, 1998, 1999.

POSTMODERNISM

Aronson, Arnold. *American Avant-Garde Theatre: A History*. New York: Routledge, 2000.

Carlson, Marvin. *Performance*. New York: Routledge, 1996.

Reinelt, Janelle and Joseph Roach. *Critical Theory in Performance*. Ann Arbor: University of Michigan Press, 1992.

Savran, David. *The Wooster Group, 1975–1985: Breaking the Rules*. Ann Arbor: UMI Research Press, 1986.

Shank, Theodore. *American Alternative Theatre*. Ann Arbor: University of Michigan Press, 2001.

Index